North Korea Demystified

North Korea Demystified

EDITED BY

Han S. Park

with Regan Damron and Jonathan Polk

CAMBRIA PRESS

Amherst, New York

Requests for permission should be directed to:
permissions@cambriapress.com, or mailed to:
Cambria Press
University Corporate Centre, 100 Corporate Parkway, Suite 128
Amherst, NY 14226

Library of Congress Cataloging-in-Publication Data

Park Han S.
North Korea demystified / edited by Han S.
Park with Regan Damron, and Jonathan Polk.
p. cm.
Includes bibliographical references and index
ISBN 978-1-60497-814-8 (alk. paper)
1. Political culture--Korea (North) 2. Korea (North)--
Politics and government. 3. Korea (North)--Economic
conditions. 4. Korea (North)--Foreign relations. I. Park, Han S.

JQ1729.5.A91N67 2012
951.9305--dc23

2012046855

Table of Contents

List of Tables

List of Figures

North Korea Demystified

Introduction

Establishing a Theoretical Lens

Han S. Park with Regan Damron and Jonathan Polk

North Korea as a state is not a typical case study. In order to understand the manner in which the North Korean system has been formulated and has evolved, it is important to establish a theoretical basis that will assist in developing such an understanding. In this regard, certain theories can help not only contextualize but also identify why North Korean foreign policy behavior is not an aberration in the global political arena. This chapter establishes the theoretical lens through which one can effectively understand and explain the dynamics of political and social life that account for policy patterns in both the domestic and foreign arenas in North Korea.

The Theoretical Basis

A theory is meant to be useful in addressing empirical and historical problems by helping the social engineering efforts of governments, nongovernmental organizations, civic societies, and individuals. The social engineering process is one of problem solving. In fact, the concept of social engineering was initially designed to solve problems. There are two grand strategies for solving problems. The first one is the incremental approach—that is, if one has a problem, one removes the problem. The other approach is the synaptic approach, in which one tries to strengthen the organism so that the organism is a part of the solution itself. We are of the opinion that both approaches are needed, for they are and should be mutually complementary. Unfortunately, the synaptic approach has been almost completely eliminated in the name of science. Instead of taking a holistic approach, scholars and practitioners look only at specific problem areas in order to surgically treat them.

Though it appears that different political systems experience different current social and political problems, there is a remarkable similarity in the nature and causes of these problems. In this respect, a theory that is widely applicable is more powerful than one that is not. Based on this principle, one might say that a theory that is "macro" as well as "micro" is more viable and superior. At the same time, a theory should offer an explanation that ascertains the causes of a problem. To construct a complete explanation, one needs to know all the factors and forces that can account for the outcome, which is the problem to be addressed.

This study requires such a theory. One concept that has consistently been accepted as universally applicable is that of development, for all societies and political systems experience changes that are often called development. Karl Marx attempted to build a universally applicable theory in his theory of history, but it was a description of the historical evolution of the world that he used as his laboratory—namely, the industrialization of Europe. The Marxist spectrum of historical evolution included both micro and macro perspectives: a micro perspective in terms of human psychology and a macro perspective in terms of the causes of revolution. This was done in an attempt to make the theory more universally applicable than other ideological constructs, such as classical democracy or non-Marxist variations of socialism. An admissible theory of development should also capture the mechanism of change—that is, how things change—as well as where a change came from and where it is headed. In this way, a theory should be able to explain and predict change. Finally, a theory should also address relevant and significant problem areas in the real world. If a theory is not relevant and cannot resolve empirical and historical problems, it loses its raison d'être.

Development has common objectives at any level of social complexity: individual, group, state, and that of the global community itself. The common objectives suggested here are survival for the individual, continuity (maintenance of patterned structures and functions) for the group, security of the state, and peaceful coexistence within the global community. One universal and important objective of development is need satisfaction. This concept is applicable universally; thus, development can be defined as the process in which members of the political system (country) pursue and obtain need satisfaction. This conception of development is so universal that it defies ideological and cultural barriers. We would submit that this is virtually an axiom in development studies; it is true even of the Democratic People's Republic of Korea (DPRK).

The question, then, is whether one can identify a set of specific human needs that are truly universal. Based on an earlier theory of development introduced by this book's lead editor (Park, 1984), we contend that there is indeed a hierarchically structured set of needs common to all human beings: survival, belonging, leisure, and control (relative gratification). On the premise that a state's political power is legitimized by the support (consent) of the people, the goal of any government is to generate the people's support, an aim that requires the provision of need satisfaction for the public. This premise is not a democratic creed but a universal one.

North Korea is not an anomaly in this sense. In order for the government to achieve the objective of satisfying people's needs, it establishes its own policy goals for the political system. The systemic policy goals are (1) national security, (2) political integration, (3) resource expansion, and (4) conflict management. The expectation is that these goals will be pursued in this very order of preference, in which national security precedes all other policy goals and is followed by political integration and resource expansion. In the case of North Korea, the regime has constantly felt that its national security is precarious owing to the presence of the United States, which has maintained strategic alliances with South Korea and Japan.

This sense of a security threat can explain Pyongyang's foreign policy behavior, especially controversies surrounding the nuclear conundrum, placing that behavior in the geopolitical context in which the two Korean regimes have had to compete for political legitimacy vis-à-vis the entire peninsula. Thus, the ideology of *juche* ("self-reliance") emerged, initially as an instrument to consolidate the leadership and integrate the regime. But this ideology has also been instrumental in claiming that the state of the DPRK is consistent with nationalism and thus more legitimate than the South's regime. In this way, the ideology of *juche* has been employed as a means of attaining national security.

One must realize that the threat to regime security arises not only from external sources but also, and just as important, from domestic sources.[1] Because of the powerful political ideology of *juche*, the nontraditional sources of national insecurity have been largely negligible, but continuous and sustained shortfalls in meeting people's basic needs, especially the need for food, could turn out to be a vital source of political and civil unrest even in North Korea. This would be the case especially if the next generation of leadership surrounding Kim Jong Un is unable to alleviate the acute food-shortage problem. When people's basic needs are consistently denied, no ideology can guarantee regime stability, and the North Korean leadership is keenly aware of this. This means that even for the sake of regime security, the government must shift its policy priority to meeting people's basic needs through economic growth. Does this mean that the political system might collapse under a rebellious mass public?

Following the successive uprisings in Egypt, Libya, and elsewhere, a renewed interest has arisen regarding the issue of regime stability in the DPRK. In order to conduct any credible analysis, one must know the nature of the relationship between the leadership and its people, especially in the context of a particular culture. When one appreciates the peculiar paternalist culture deeply rooted in the mass belief system of the DPRK, as well as the institutional and structured life of its people, one may come to the conclusion that the occurrence of mass rebellion is most unlikely.

The Framework of the Book

The authors of this volume are uniquely qualified to assess the situation in the DPRK because all of them have had personal experience with North Korea, as either foreign residents or frequent visitors. Their knowledge and information are neither merely speculative nor skewed by ideological or normative biases. The volume contributes uniquely to study of the DPRK in its interdisciplinary nature; it examines a range of life situations including history and collective memory, ideology and culture, economic conditions and policies, domestic politics, and foreign policy orientation and behavior. The contention of this volume is that the political dynamics and policy patterns of the DPRK are hardly inexplicable or mysterious. The usual claim that North Korea is an anomaly and cannot be understood because its policy behaviors are mysterious, at best, or entirely irrational is a product of either ignorance of the system or a predetermined refusal to examine the system the way it is. The chapters of this volume can help readers see North Korea as it actually exists.

Following this introductory chapter, a series of domestic issues are dealt with. Examining the nature and role of the ideology of *juche*, chapter 1 advances the theme that in order to understand a government's policy behavior, it is necessary to understand the way the people in the society see themselves and their role in the world. To illuminate the North Korean case, Han S. Park explains the development, content, and implications of *juche* ideology for North Korean society, government, and foreign relations. The author argues that *songun* ("military-first" politics), rather than an independent ideology or a mere policy stance, is an extension of *juche* and as such supplements it by performing similar functions. The chapter concludes with a set of concrete policy recommendations for other states derived directly from this understanding of the sociocultural context in which the government of the DPRK operates. The chapter demystifies North Korea by illuminating its ideological foundations and by demonstrating ways these affect daily life in a place few have witnessed firsthand.

Chapters 2 and 3 argue that the economy of the DPRK is not extraordinary in itself; rather, its current shape is the result of the usual forces' operating in an unusual environment. Therefore, it can be understood using the principles of new institutional economics. In making his case, Rudiger Frank first evaluates North Korea's natural resources and climate, various sectors of its economy, and foreign trade as economic endowments, then turns his attention to economic and fiscal policy and the doctrine of self-reliance. Frank describes the possibility of economic reform and evaluates contemporary evidence of it, ending with a series of policy recommendations aimed at countries other than North Korea that are designed to support reform within it. Frank's second chapter advances an in-depth analysis of the economy by stripping away layers of complexity to expose the basic economic principles that underlie even such an apparently abnormal society.

Chapter 4 illuminates an intriguing development in which the socialist economy has gradually, and in small steps, incorporated incentive-based market practice. Hazel Smith observes that a process of "marketization without liberalization" has been taking place in the DPRK since the mid-1990s; the transformation of the North Korean political economy from state to market was a bottom-up process and was not accompanied by political liberalization from the government downward. Outsiders have little understanding, however, of how that economic transformation has been sustained domestically since the mid-1990s—for over a decade now. Smith focuses on provincial differences in order to illustrate the differential way in which marketization became embedded in North Korean society, as well as the consequences of postfamine marketization. This approach takes issue with the common-knowledge approach to studying North Korea, which assumes that the state and society are homogeneous and unchanging. Provincial differences in, for instance, the areas of agricultural productivity and of the population's nutritional status are quantified and demonstrated, as are their changes over time. The chapter sheds light on North Korea's processes of marketization—a process itself not commonly identified with the country—and does so at the subnational level, a perspective not often examined.

Shifting from economics to politics, chapter 5 discusses the issues surrounding the army's role in the political processes of North Korea. In particular, Alexander Zhebin details the importance of the army with regard to the political behavior of the DPRK and then explains the constraints under which senior military officials operate. The chapter highlights the increased role of the armed forces in North Korea as an extension of the traditional, centuries-old rivalry of the two main branches of the ruling elites in Korea—civil and military.

Chapter 6 covers the concept of good governance as a precondition for international aid to developing countries and argues that this notion of a prerequisite is a barrier to the sort of change the international community would like to see in the DPRK. Geir Helgesen chronicles the development of the concept of good governance as a politically neutral, nonideological basis for development assistance and concludes that it was largely a consequence of and reaction to the collapse of Soviet-style communism. A cultural sociologist, Helgesen discusses the content of the phrase *good governance* and how this affects judgments based upon its use. He suggests that an ability to see reality through the eyes of the North Koreans—even though one may strongly disagree with their views—is necessary in order to render their policy behavior intelligible. Helgesen concludes that ethnocentrism is the primary obstacle one must overcome in order to achieve empathy and that good governance may best be interpreted with cultural sensitivity. The chapter is akin to a policy position paper, the argument of which parallels that of the broader text: one can understand North Korea only after seeing the world through its lens.

Shifting the focus to the international arena, the next set of chapters deals with North Korea's diplomatic history, the evolution of foreign policy, and Pyongyang's policy pattern toward the West. Chapter 7 provides an overview of recent US foreign policy toward North Korea, arguing that it has been fundamentally flawed and that another approach is needed. Bruce Cumings chronicles the failed predictions of Washington pundits regarding regime collapse in the DPRK and examines the threat of war as a tool for effecting regime change. He writes of Seoul's achievements engaging the North, then assesses the likelihood of the DPRK's returning to the negotiating table given the contemporary situation. Cumings concludes by recommending that the world shed its polarized Cold War mindset and move in the direction of a calm, steady, nuanced, and persistent policy process with respect to Pyongyang.

Chapter 8 illuminates the process of foreign policy decision making. Alexander Zhebin focuses on the institutions and officials responsible for the decisions; he describes the mechanics (both formal and informal) of their interplay, illustrating his points with historical examples. Zhebin then discusses the role of personality in foreign policy, detailing the Kim dynasty. Changing focus from domestic determinants, he then proceeds to examine the DPRK's nuclear ambitions and how the North Koreans exploited the US–China dimension of the crisis. Looking forward, the author ascertains the North Korean position regarding a multilateral security regime in northeast Asia and examines the issue of reunification. Finally, Zhebin suggests lessons that may be drawn from the preceding discussion, as well as possible policy responses from other nations toward the DPRK.

Chapter 9 explores the character of both Western public opinion regarding North Korea and the North Koreans' perceptions of the West. Helgesen argues that these perceptions matter for the possibility of rapprochement between the two and that because culture changes slowly, the way to achieve the necessary change in perceptions is to include emotions in the cultural perspective. Helgesen ends with a discussion of the physiological roots of emotion, as illuminated by neuroscience, and calls the discipline of political science to bring emotion into its analyses as a way to achieve the empathy necessary for true dialogue. This contribution demystifies North Korea by shedding light on the barriers to communication between it and the West and by suggesting how these might be overcome.

Chapter 10 discusses the issues surrounding the transfer of power to the next Kim and argues that domestic policy considerations should not be downplayed when assessing the decision making of North Korea's leaders, even with regard to something as apparently insulated as succession within a family dynasty. Alexander Zhebin outlines four factors that explain Kim Jong Il's reluctance to publicly name an heir and then discusses the unity of the ruling elite when facing external forces, as well as the schisms within the elite with regard to domestic reforms. This chapter elucidates North Korea's internal politics and goes far beyond considering merely the cult of personality surrounding the Kim family.

The analyses in this volume comprise a rich body of information and knowledge leading to the concluding remarks, in which Park places these chapters in the context of the current leadership transition to the third Kim, Kim Jong Un. Tracing the evolution of the DPRK's leadership across three generations, the book's final chapter highlights the importance of continuity for North Korea's leadership and reinforces the importance of understanding the preexisting culture, ideology, and policies of the

DPRK for accurately grasping North Korean society in the contemporary era of the "Great Successor."

This project represents the culmination of two successive seminars that took place at the University of Georgia, organized by its Center for the Study of Global Issues. We express our sincere appreciation to the Korea Foundation for providing a generous grant that funded the project. We also wish to thank the authors of this volume, as well as the staff of Cambria Press, for their painstaking efforts to revise their manuscripts multiple times in order to make them as current as possible in light of the rapidly changing political climate in both North Korea and the geopolitics of the region.

Endnotes

1. Kyung-Ae Park, ed., *New Challenges of North Korean Foreign Policy* (New York: Palgrave Macmillan, 2010).

Chapter 1

The Culture and Ideology of the DPRK

Han S. Park

The concepts of culture and ideology have been used often without definitional clarification. In order to examine the nature and role of *juche* in North Korea in a systematic way, one must begin with such an explanation.

Conceptual Clarifications

A culture is largely seen as a system of norms, values, and beliefs that characterizes the symbolic identity of a people. It is the affect system, as opposed to the cognition system, that is deeply imbedded in the people's psychological predisposition and that determines their "personality," or basic collective traits. A culture, then, is much like a civilization. It is formed through a long process of common experience shared by a people within the salient context of geopolitical conditions and historical legacies. Therefore, it cannot be effectively created or discarded by a political system. In contrast, political culture is closer to ideology in that "it refers to all aspects of meaning, subjective or inter-subjective, related to politics."[1] An ideology is also a system of norms, values, beliefs held by the people. Typically, it is related to the relationship between the government and the governed, and it often works as the basis of legitimacy. An ideology is created, not given, for political needs of the system. Accordingly, an ideology is created, altered, and can even be discarded by a regime or a political leader. Culture, as a salient force, precedes ideology in time. However, ideology does not develop in a cultural vacuum. The ideology of liberal democracy, on the one hand, evolved in the cultural context of Christianity. On the other hand, the ideology of Maoism emerged from cultural underpinnings of Confucianism. An important theorem in this regard is that when an ideology deviates from the cultural attributes of salient norms, values, and beliefs, it is destined to fail. Thus, when examining the viability of an ideology such as *juche*, one must begin by evaluating its compatibility or consistency with the underlying culture.

THE CULTURE OF THE DPRK: CONFUCIAN CIVILIZATION AND NATIONAL CHARACTER

Economic disparity, social and political contrasts, and the ideological manifestations of North Korea's *juche* and South Korea's autocratic democracy have shown their affinity to Confucian ethics and norms, despite ideological divides between the two countries. In both North and South Korea, ordinary people's lifestyle in managing social relationships has not shown much deviation from the cultural legacy of Confucianism. The five cardinal rules of the cultural system that guide human and social interactions and relationships are evident in the common life of the people in both systems. Underneath the colorful display of *juche* ideology, the cardinal rules of Confucianism remain intact and revered in the Democratic People's Republic of North Korea (DPRK): the idea that the relationship between the ruler and the ruled ought to be based on righteousness is largely intact. Despite the seemingly autocratic and brutally dictatorial governance, the notion that the ruler should be benevolent and should pursue the well-being of the people is deeply imbedded in the ruling philosophy. The norm that guides the relationship between senior and junior must be proper order. The relationship between parents and children ought to be maintained by intimacy. Trust must govern the relationship between friends. And separate roles should be mutually respected by people of different genders.

As a rule, one might observe that in an ordinary revolutionary setting where new programs and ideologies are to replace traditional and conventional ways of life, the existence of any age-old cultural legacy is counterproductive in the revolutionary cause. This was evidenced in China, where Confucianism was considered an obstacle to the socialist consolidation. This in part prompted the Great Proletarian Cultural Revolution in the mid-1960s. But North Korea did not encounter much resistance from Confucianism. On the contrary, Confucianism in North Korea facilitated the development of charismatic leadership and paternalist socialism; indeed, without the Confucian cultural influences inherent in its historical heritage, the system itself would not have been made in the way it has been.

The focus of Confucianism is the human, and the principle of social and economic change is human or spiritual determinism, as opposed to material determinism. Although the human is the epicenter of society and history, Confucian ethics never endorses individualism. Individuals are not credited with intrinsic value in isolation from collectivity. The objective, or goal, of Confucianism is to condition individuals and teach them how they should fit into a greater social network and to ensure that they are fulfilling their roles in family and society. Confucian political culture emphasizes, above all else, group loyalty and obedience and a consensual style that avoids direct confrontation. Thus, the nature of Korean Confucianism gives little value to individuals' acting out of self-interest. The individual is given worth and value only in the context of his or her relationship with and contribution to the family. Families are assigned worth and value based on their lineages or on the successes of their family members. Thus, individual orientation and individual action are discredited as anathema to the development of a strong, learned, virtuous individual, anathema to the betterment of the family and society as a whole.

Confucianism led to the development of a particular social order in Korea. In addition, it is clear that the Confucian familial and social structure contributed to the development of a distinct political culture and to the observable configuration of values, symbols, orientations, and behavioral patterns. Although the North Korean regime made efforts to eliminate Confucian beliefs and behavior from North Korean society and political culture, it can be argued that strong vestiges of Confucianism exist in the current North Korean political and social structure.

In short, several salient and characteristic elements of Korean Confucianism have clearly reinforced the formation and maturation of the political ideology of *juche*. Elements such as a family-centered outlook, the human (rather than matter) as the center of the universe, and the notion of life after death have all exerted profound influence on the philosophical structure of *juche* ideology.

The Ideology of the DPRK: *Juche*

Briefly, the doctrine of *juche* may be comprehensively understood in terms of two fundamental principles. The first is human centeredness (human centrism)—that is, the idea that humanity is the master of the universe. It is hard to avoid this notion in publications that promote the ideology. This human centeredness is further translated into human determinism, which states that if humanity wants, there is nothing that it cannot do. In this respect alone, it is wrong to understand *juche* as a variation of the Marxist perspective, which is predicated upon material determinism. As already observed, *juche* is thoroughly consistent with the age-old Confucian beliefs. The second fundamental doctrine of *juche* is collectivism in which the boundary of the collectivity is the nation. What is good for the nation is also good for its members—not the converse. In contrast to Confucianism, however, here loyalty to the head of the household is only secondary to loyalty to the head of state. Yet the state in the political beliefs of North Koreans is an extended version of the family. Thus, *juche* avoids any conflict with Confucian familism.[2] In fact, in North Korea the head of state is referred to as the father.

In order to realize these two principles, *juche* advanced three policy goals: (1) military self-defense, (2) economic self-subsistence, (3) political self-rule (sovereignty). Since the advent of the *juche* doctrine during the pre-1945 era, the concept has evolved continuously, the ideology being adapted to the changing environment in domestic and foreign domains alike. In order to capture the full spectrum of the ideology, one must examine the way it has evolved in response to the changing domestic and external political context. The following paragraphs describe a series of phases in the evolution, along with the conditions that might have prompted a particular path of change.

The North Korean foreign policy orientation has also evolved in such a way that its national objectives are to be pursued appropriately. One must realize that North Korea, as odd as it often seems to critical observers around the world, has been exceedingly consistent in pursuing its systematic objectives of national security, ideological identity, and economic prosperity. In this regard, North Korea is hardly a deviant political system.

Juche as Anti-Japanese (Mid-1920s to early 1950s)

Kim Il Sung, credited with having created *juche*, employed this ideology in his deeply felt anti-Japanese colonial politics and used it against those

Korean leaders who were incapable of preserving national independence and political sovereignty. He argued, as did many others, that Koreans must fight to win back their nation through promoting combat capability and spiritual solidarity against the militarily stronger Japanese soldiers. In fact, the formation of Kim Il Sung's charisma began with the theme that he sacrificed his personal well-being for the noble cause of saving the country from Japanese colonialism. Even as a boy at the age of twelve, it was said, he had been preoccupied with the aspiration of national independence.[3] Because the liberation of the country from Japanese control was the most important policy goal, the country naturally advanced the popular theme of anticolonialism. At this stage, the term *juche* meant little more than antagonist sentiment against a specific target. In this sense, *juche* was not yet established as even a rudimentary form of ideology.

In this initial stage of the ideological evolution, North Korea could not afford to look beyond its immediate and comfortable ideological allies: the Soviet Union, the Eastern European states, the People's Republic of China, Vietnam, and Cuba.

Juche as Antihegemonistic (Mid-1950s to mid-1960s)

Following the Korean War (1950–1953), North Korea found a new enemy that helped South Korea and destroyed much of the northern half of the country with massive air strikes: the United States of America. During the war the city of Pyongyang was practically leveled, leaving no physical structures and millions of people dead or wounded.[4] Since the war there has been genuine fear among North Korean residents that American forces might renew hostilities.[5] That US forces have been stationed continuously in the South, routinely performing military exercises, often jointly with South Korean armed forces, has always made North Korea uneasy and apprehensive. Since the adoption of the armistice agreement in 1953, Pyongyang has persistently demanded the withdrawal of US troops from the Korean Peninsula. North Koreans were particularly resentful of the hegemonic expansion of US military influence.

Coupled with the presence of the United States in Korea, the growing Sino–Soviet dispute in 1960, which drove the two communist giants to the brink of war, and Soviet involvement in Eastern Europe and Vietnam were instrumental in the growth of antihegemonistic feeling in the North Korean political and diplomatic spheres. Pyongyang was put in a precarious position between the two super powers of the communist bloc, for it did not wish to antagonize either of them by maintaining intimate relations with one at the expense of the other. This forced the Pyongyang government to declare a path of equidistance—and thus self-reliance. But it was the Soviet Union that became a more convenient target of North Korean criticism because of Moscow's expansionist policy. By contrast, China provided a role model of sorts by indulging in the massive indigenization of Marxism and Leninism during the fanatic phase of the Great Proletariat Cultural Revolution in the late 1960s. Though North Korea did not express great enthusiasm for the Cultural Revolution, it refrained from publicly denouncing the Chinese campaign to create a personality cult around Mao Zedong. In fact, North Korea followed the footsteps of Mao, instigating concerted efforts to develop an indigenous ideology and creating charismatic leadership for Kim Il Sung himself. Just as Mao criticized Moscow for its hegemonic policies, Kim too expressed displeasure with the Soviet Union's interventionist policies. As just pointed out, this doctrine of antihegemonism was further reinforced by Pyongyang's interest in denouncing the American influence in South Korea. In short, the ideological insistence on political sovereignty under *juche* was reinforced by the political reality on the peninsula.

Pyongyang was forced to strengthen its self-reliance posture, but it was quickly arrested by its own ideology in terms of expanding its economic activities beyond the handful of socialist allies. This was the period in which South Korea broke away from a stagnant economy and embraced ambitious programs for economic development. This was done mostly under the leadership of Park Chung Hee, who installed a series of economic growth plans.

Juche as Nationalist Ideology (1960s to 1970s)

By the end of the 1960s, North Korea had become a stable regime, devoid of any immediate source of opposition against Kim's authority. His leadership could not be challenged because it was steadily gaining a charismatic quality. By this time almost all political enemies had been eliminated from leadership circles. Furthermore, the economy had fully recovered from the aftermath of the Korean War. It may sound unbelievable, but the North Korean economy in this period was superior to that of South Korea.

What Pyongyang needed at that time was a persuasive ideology with which to legitimize Kim's charismatic leadership and to demonstrate ideological superiority to the South. It may be generalized that once a regime is established and stability is secured, the next step that the regime must take is to expand its legitimacy through political education. This stage of development may be termed *political integration*, during which the ruling elite attempts to further the basis of regime legitimacy by introducing an official political ideology. In many newly independent countries, the flowering of nationalism grows into this official ideology; North Korea is not an exception.

It is this transition of circumstances that prompted the accentuation of nationalism as the cornerstone of *juche*. That South Korea was led by Syngman Rhee, who was educated in and had been a long-term resident of the United States, indicated a strong American influence on the Rhee regime. This provided Kim Il Sung with the necessary ammunition to condemn the South for being shamelessly antinationalistic and pathetically subject to foreign domination. In contrast, the North was in a position to declare a policy of equidistance vis-à-vis its communist allies and to join the nonalignment movement. Pyongyang managed to establish *juche* institutes in several nonaligned countries, including India. This political climate proved ideal for Pyongyang's adopting ultranationalism as the foundation of *juche* ideology.

Nationalism in the mid-1960s was still primarily "antiforeignism" and lacked a coherent philosophical structure. But as the ideology was refined in the late 1960s and much of the 1970s, a set of goals and strategies for implementing nationalism was articulated. Specifically, *juche* was defined in terms of three analytically distinct objectives: political sovereignty, economic subsistence, and military self-defense. The aim of political sovereignty forced the regime to limit political and diplomatic ties, maintaining relations only with countries that Pyongyang found ideologically compatible and thus restricting foreign relations to a handful of socialist countries. It was in this period that North Korea campaigned against the South for superiority in legitimacy. Overwhelmed by nationalist sentiment, authorities in Pyongyang believed that the Seoul regime could be overthrown by its own masses on the grounds that the South lacked nationalist solidarity and thus political legitimacy. The North Korean government held that the people in the South would be induced to participate in an antiregime mass movement only if the trigger were pulled to disrupt the precarious stability. The infiltration of the Blue House (the presidential residence in Seoul) by a North Korean commando unit in 1968 could be interpreted as an expression of Pyongyang's determination to disturb political stability in hopes of inciting mass uprisings against the Park Chung Hee regime.[6]

The policies of economic self-reliance have deterred economic growth, causing North Korea to fall further behind its neighboring countries, especially South Korea. This period happened to coincide with the high growth years of the newly industrializing countries (NICs) and the "Asian tigers," which included South Korea. All these countries employed the export-led strategy for economic growth. Instead of promoting balanced growth, as North Korea did, the NICs concentrated their efforts on producing export goods that would be competitive in the international market. But North Korea alienated itself from the world's economic activities in order to establish a *juche* economy. One should not forget that at this time there was growing support in Third World countries for the *dependencia* movement, whereby economic and cultural independence was proclaimed the only way of avoiding certain subjugation to the industrial hegemonic countries.[7]

What has been most economically detrimental is the principle of military self-reliance. Kim Il Sung's opinion on the importance of military power was unambiguously demonstrated in his early years in power when he was campaigning for national independence. In his Manchuria days, his group was known for employing militant means in order to secure weapons at all costs. He criticized Kim Koo, Yo Woon Yong, and Ahn Chang Ho, who had a broad base of support for their patriotism and reliance on the nonmilitary or nonviolence principle. According to Kim, a nonviolent revolution would not work in the fight against colonialism and expansionism. In fact, military self-reliance was viewed as a necessary condition for political sovereignty. In this case, no amount of resources devoted to building military strength was considered too large; North Korea has consistently and disproportionately invested its national wealth in the weapons industry. Kim had also witnessed the dramatic turn of events when Japanese imperial forces boldly invaded East and Southeast Asia, Russia, and eventually the Hawaiian Islands and then had to unconditionally surrender to the power of American atomic bombs. Given this, it is not surprising that Kim was engulfed in his own obsessive desire for weapons—specifically, atomic bombs.

Although the military principle may have deterred economic growth in general, one should not discount the fact that North Korea's primary source of foreign-currency earnings has been the export of weapons, a wide variety ranging from conventional ones to sophisticated missiles. There seems to be no shortage of demand for North Korean weapons on the international market, especially in the Arab world. The controversy surrounding North Korea's nuclear weapons production must be seen in the greater context of North Korea's ideological doctrine of military self-reliance.

In short, the policies designed to uphold the principles of political, economic, and military self-reliance may not be designed to attain maximum material payoff. In fact, they have been largely counterproductive for the development of industry and often detrimental to the welfare of the society as a whole. Nevertheless, the principles were intended to promote nationalism among the masses and to demonstrate the northern regime's position of superiority vis-à-vis its southern counterpart. As already suggested, it is believed that during this period North Korea increased its sales of weapons, including short-range missiles to selected Middle Eastern states.[8]

Juche as Paternalist Socialism (1980s)

As the ideology became intimately tied to the regime as an instrument of legitimating its power, the leadership articulated a new theoretical dimension in which the leadership itself was sanctified as the generator and embodiment of the ideology. This process coincided not only with a quantum leap in the charisma of the Great Leader but also with the regime's need to officially promote Kim Jong Il's leadership, which began in conjunction with the Sixth Party Congress in 1980. Kim Il Sung saw a great flaw in the socialist systems of the Soviet Union, Vietnam, and China in the almost universal inability of the ruling elite to resolve the succession issue. It was not accidental in North Korea that the hereditary approach became the succession mechanism. The North Korean people had never seen a popularly elected leader in their entire history; the dynastic systems of early modern Korea had been replaced abruptly by Japanese colonial power. Kim Il Sung was quickly and naturally seen as a royal leader of sorts. Thus, deification of the leader's family did not deviate from the age-old Oriental despotic cultural perspective.[9]

A significant implication of paternalism is that not only the father himself but indeed the whole family is destined to rule. This naturally sanctifies the hereditary succession of power. Thus, it was no coincidence that Kim Jong Il was officially designated the heir apparent at the same party convention in 1980. It is intriguing to note that the young Kim's ascension to power was initially promoted on the premise of his qualifications and ability rather than on grounds of the family tie. In fact, one scholar at Kim Il Sung University unequivocally told me in summer 1981 that the legitimation of Kim Jong Il's leadership would have been easier if he had not been Kim Il Sung's son; he explained that the junior's ability and achievements tended to be discredited because of his relationship to the Great Leader. However, as the process of building his charisma advanced more quickly, the young Kim benefited from the family relationship. Just as the father had gained charisma as the paternal leader, the son was naturally expected to display the charisma of the family. At Mankyongdae, the birthplace of Kim Il Sung, a family museum was erected in the early 1980s in which the Kim clan is heralded as the center of the independence movement. The historical documentation ends with the young Kim having demonstrated unusual leadership qualities and unparalleled patriotism.

Given that during this period the North Korean leadership needed the effective political orientation of the masses, it was desirable for the system to keep the people shielded from the external world, especially South Korea and the West. This ensured that the country's economy was even further isolated from the world market, necessitating a self-reliant economy contained within the system.

Juche as Weltanschauung (Late 1980s to 1990s)

Unlike the earlier stages of ideological evolution, *juche* soon evolved into a legitimate Weltanschauung with a philosophical structure. As discussed earlier, the articulation of the structure of human nature and the theory of political-social life are relatively recent developments. This is not to suggest that *juche* represents a unique and complete worldview but that it is a worldview nonetheless with some coherent structure as opposed to a mere political slogan.

The idea that humankind is the center of the universe is by no means a new perspective; neither is the doctrine of political sovereignty or self-determination. Furthermore, nothing is new about *juche*'s emphasis on human consciousness as the determinant of human behavior. What is original, however, is the theory that coherently integrated yet distinctly different components of human faculty perform unique and diverse functions.

As discussed more fully later in this chapter human nature inherently longs to be the center of the universe, whereby the individual's relationship with nature and society is clearly prescribed. Nature exists solely for the sake of human beings; therefore, humanity is fully entitled to explore natural resources. Yet humanity is also obliged to manage and "control" the global physical environment. According to *juche*, science is a tool designed to utilize as well as rehabilitate nature for the advancement of human well-being in both the present and the future. According to this perspective, no person should be subject to another person's capricious control, nor should one be submitted to institutional manipulation. Institutions, science among them, are designed to serve human beings rather than be served by them. Even ideologies themselves are regarded as institutional means to human well-being. Another component of human nature is the faculty that makes value judgment possible; human beings are endowed with the natural rights and capabilities to make behavioral choices through free consciousness. Yet another component of human nature allows a person to avoid enslavement to instruments of life, such as material resources and social institutions.

These elements of human nature, however, are to be cultivated and developed through socialization and political education. It is for this reason that ideological education becomes an integral part of human development, and such an education should be continuous throughout one's life. The practice of "education through work," manifest in the factory college, should be seen in this vein. In a factory college, college-level classes are offered at factory locations as part of degree and certification programs in a variety of specialized fields. College professors from regular institutions of higher education, such as Kim Il Sung University and Kim Chaek University, are mobilized as instructors. Classes routinely begin with rituals intended to glorify the two Kims' work and legacy.

North Korea introduced an eleven-year public education system in conjunction with the expansion of *juche*, for the regime felt it necessary to provide ideological education. Eleven years of compulsory education are followed by education through work for individuals of every background and occupation. Practically all workplaces and schools in North Korea are required to set aside at least one full day for "study-learning" (*haksop*), in which every citizen participates. A typical *haksop* day begins with the announcement of directives and instructions from the party, followed by "self-criticism." In this session, members confess wrongdoings committed during the preceding week and vow to redeem themselves through deepened loyalty to the party and the country. After this, discussion centers on *juche*.

Juche as Weltanschauung becomes more obvious in its exposition of the human mind. The human faculty is viewed as having a series of concomitant properties. They are consciousness (*uisiksong*), creativity (*changuisong*), and self-determination (*jajusong*). According to this view, human dignity is attained when life is conducted in congruence with these three elements. It is further claimed that *juche* is an ideology designed to facilitate these qualities and that human dignity is guaranteed when one's life is consistent with the principles of *juche*.

As human *uisiksong* becomes the force engineering human behavior, one must create specific means and programs to realize what *uisiksong* dictates—hence, the arrival of *changuisong*. This concept refers to creativeness that seeks to find ways of implementing desirable ideas in concrete historical situations. This aspect of human nature might be perceived as a cognitive attribute. Here rational and scientific assessment takes place in terms of the validity and effectiveness of specific approaches and concrete programs. Furthermore, *jajusong* (self-determination) prescribes a proper relationship among the world's nation-states. According to this theory, the international division of labor is counterproductive and perpetuates the dependence of nations with raw materials and labor upon nations with capital and technology. The ideology basically adheres to the claims of the *dependencia* school of thought, which views the world essentially as an exploitative system as long as nations are unable to sustain the self-sufficiency of providing their own basic needs and military self-defense. Here, *juche* faces the formidable task of discrediting the achievements of the NICs, especially South Korea, because these countries have shown that international division of labor and export-led economies can be prosperous. This challenges the very premise of the *dependencia* school. For this reason, North Korea was always sympathetic with the nonalignment movement and maintained close ties with the Group of Seventy-seven (G-77).

Furthermore, the epidemic breakdown of socialist systems in Eastern Europe and the Soviet Union itself, as well as reform-oriented Chinese development, forced North Korea to dissociate itself from this global trend. The very need for dissociation from other socialist countries has been instrumental in the rapid transition of *juche* as a unique ideological system under the banner "socialism in our style" (*urisik sahoejuii*). This ideological position may sound similar to other forms of nationalized socialism as evidenced by China under Deng Xiaoping and by Yugoslavia under Tito. But what is radically unique about North Korea is that *juche*, in its advanced version, is a completely different breed of ideology, not simply a variation of socialism.

As observed previously, in an effort to address the issue of political consolidation, to wage the "war" for legitimacy vis-à-vis the South, and to shield the population from unwanted influences from the West, North Korea has opted to develop and continuously refine the ideology of *juche*. In the process, its foreign and diplomatic activities have been severely restricted, especially in the economic arena. One should remember that it was in this period that North Korea lost the support system of the communist bloc. Further exacerbating the situation, the DPRK has faced a successive string of economic and political sanctions from the West for its nuclear programs.

Juche and Military-First Politics (Late 1990s to the present)

In its long process of evolution, *juche* ultimately incorporated a premise that the military is the heart, the brain, and the body of the political system. This accentuation of the military as an institution occurred after the adoption of the 1998 constitution. What was conceived in the constitution was the seed of the military-first (*songun*) doctrine, but it grew into a fully comprehensive ideological and philosophical system in the ten years that followed. The most recent constitution, adopted in April 2009, clearly documents this. This new constitution elevated the Military Commission to the level of supreme leadership and named its chair, Kim Jong Il, the "supreme leader" with virtually omnipotent power in the system.

Without a proper understanding of *juche*, one cannot comprehend Kim Il Sung's North Korea. One might also say that a proper understanding of Kim Jong Il's North Korea is possible only with a proper comprehension of *songun*. *Songun* theoreticians claim that *songun* has advanced *juche* to a higher plane by providing it with a realistic perspective of history and world politics. Like *juche*, *songun* is allegedly a constant process of evolving toward perfection. At present, there are limited written sources regarding *songun* from which a researcher might discern its definitive picture. Yet after consulting available publications from North Korea and a series of personal interviews with scholars who are the leading advancers and theoreticians of this system of ideas, one might portray the essence of its philosophical and theoretical attributes. It is hoped that the following pages may be of some help to North Korea observers who seek to explain the system characteristics and policy behaviors of the DPRK under Kim Jong Il. For this important reason, it is necessary to investigate further the conceptual and philosophical underpinnings of *songun*.

Songun: An Anatomy

It would be problematic to understand *songun* politics as simply a doctrine that provides the military absolute power, rendering the rest of the political system secondary and subservient to that institution. Using limited sources of documents and publications from Pyongyang, combined with my own personal contacts, I have ascertained the following functions of the military, which are consistent with the *songun* principle.[10]

The military is the center of the political system.

Since the death of Kim Il Sung in 1994, the concept of the center of the Workers' Party of Korea (WPK)—*Dang Jungang*—has been used in North Korea to refer specifically to Kim Jong Il. *Center* in this context means more than the focus of power; it means the central nervous system of the political, economic, and social body. The military is the guardian of the brain, which must be protected and never be made vulnerable. When the military is theorized as the center, it carries the same connotation. In this sense, the military is not only an institution designed to defend the country from external hostility, but it also provides all other institutions of the government with legitimacy. All policy goals are articulated by the military, and they are disseminated to other organizations with specific strategic and tactical recommendations for implementation. Once policies are implemented, their effectiveness is evaluated by the military. In this way, the military serves as the brain of the nervous system of the body politic.

The military is the deliverer and provider.

To North Koreans, the military is not an abstract authority but a practical performer. It responds directly and effectively to the wants and needs of the people. It delivers in a way that no other institution or individual can; it provides services and goods to the people, and it protects their security. When I asked a farmer about his understanding of the *songun* doctrine, he responded, "It is the military that makes farming possible, as the soldiers come into the village to work on a whole range of farming from toiling soil, seeding, irrigating, and harvesting. The military," he continued, "not only protects the people's lives from foreign hostility, but it also delivers food and services."[11]

It is common to notice in the streets of North Korea that soldiers carry bags of grain to civilian homes. In fact, the concern commonly expressed by the foreign providers of food is that the military may snatch the food aid away from the civilians. This is rather speculative. The reality is that the military has food and other necessities in relatively ample supply owing to the independent accounting system, whereby the military retains the revenues it generates from exporting military equipment, including missiles and conventional weapons. Thus, the military is in a position to share resources with the public. It may also be possible for the military to perform the service of delivering foreign-aid food to civilians in remote villages. But the military's delivery and provision functions are not limited to services and food; they extend to virtually all kinds of commodities.

The military is the problem solver.

Not only is the military regarded as the embodiment of legitimate power and authority, but it is also considered the most able problem solver in practically every sphere of everyday life. Each unit of dwellers, defined as a *ban*, is assigned to a military post that is responsible for looking after all types of people's needs. This ranges from providing technical assistance and repairing household electrical appliances to fixing faucets and maintaining sewage systems. In the *songun* society, the people are supposed to trust that the military is equipped with the resources, knowledge, and skills to solve problems in the daily lives of the people. In this way, the doctrine calls for the people's complete dependence on the military. The popular belief under the banner of *songun* is that "no problem is too big or too small for the military to solve." In this way, the idea is promoted that without the military, people cannot sustain their existence.

The military is the engine of social engineering.
The military is also the prime opinion leader. People trust that soldiers are extremely well educated when it comes to ideological preparedness. In fact, military education always places ideology and politics among its top priorities. The soldiers are the ones who teach the villagers. When they are on leave from military barracks, soldiers are assigned to their hometowns and to the villagers in such a way that the commoners will be prepared to carry on "revolution" just as effectively as the soldiers. In my numerous trips to North Korea, I have consistently been amazed by soldiers' ability to spell out their mission as soldiers and as leaders of the "revolutionary struggle." It might be appropriate to characterize the mission of the military in North Korea today as one of social engineering, a concept of future orientation. Social engineering requires structuring society for the future and driving the course of social change toward desired goals. People are expected to look up to the military for its visionary leadership, and they only need to follow the guidance of the military. The norms and values that are socially desirable will be created by the military, which is also designated to disseminate them to the people. In this sense, the military is the greatest educator. At the heart of military education is the Military University, the institution central to developing the ideology of *songun*, to training military officers, and to disseminating *songun* philosophy to other educational institutions throughout the country.

The military is the creator and advancer of a new culture.
Cultural change occurs in every society, and North Korea is no exception. Despite the common expectation that as any society becomes modernized, the youthful population becomes disillusioned with the establishment and is attracted to a consumerist lifestyle, there seems to be no

appreciable generation gap in North Korea. In this regard, there is little apparent discrepancy between rural and urban areas in the DPRK; the country has maintained a remarkable degree of uniform cultural orientation. This uniformity has been created largely through the institution of the military. Although North Korea does not have a draft system, military populism has enabled the regime to maintain a huge military (over one million strong), ensuring that virtually every family has at least one soldier in uniform. As pointed out previously, the military performs an extensive role in civilian villages, and in addition, practically all physically able citizens in the country are mobilized in the People's Militia. In fact, there is hardly separation between the military and civilian sectors. In this context, it is no surprise that military culture is North Korean culture. Cultural traits include uniformity and the clear definition of a common enemy; resolve or determination is upheld as the highest virtue. The *songun* doctrine has created a belief system in which the public must follow the military because the latter is always right. It is no longer the party that leads the way, nor is it the government that assumes the role of leadership.

One intriguing feature of North Korean culture is the pervasive sense of equality: the participation of rank-and-file people in decision-making processes provides them with a significant sense of self-worth and boosts morale. Everyone is supposed to be equal in the sense that all are involved in making decisions that affect everyone. Therefore, life in North Korea is one of successive meetings and deliberations at every level of society, including within the military itself. These meetings typically begin with self-criticism (confessions) by every participant, as already mentioned, and conclude with remedial recommendations for any wrongdoing by any member, regardless of his or her standing in the social and political strata. The principle of "one for all, and all for one" is no longer merely a slogan. It works and is felt in the country. This doctrine epitomizes the military way. Thus, the same practice is emulated in civilian life. Every administrative unit, or *ban*, convenes a weekly meeting for the purpose of disseminating information from the center (the supreme leadership) and in order to stage the process of self-criticism.

The military is the synthesizer of body, mind, and spirit.
Unlike the *juche* idea of self-defense, *songun*'s is a more comprehensive doctrine by which its task is not limited to physical and material aspects but treats as equally important the psychological and spiritual domains. In this way, *songun* has become a source of political and social philosophy, just as *juche* was in the Kim Il Sung era. One should remember that the doctrine of *juche* reached its height as it advanced the philosophical outlook of the political-social body in the late 1980s. This perspective attempted to articulate the theory of human development (maturation) through a progressive theory of personal development according to which one becomes a social body—transforming from an essentially biological being to a social being. The biological being is one full of instinctive desires for physical comfort; the social being, however, is charged with social and political consciousness (*eusiksong*). The concept of human development thus became an important feature of *juche* philosophy. The philosophy of *songun* attempts to integrate the three components of human existence, mind, body, and spirit. Here, the notion of ideal personhood is created, in that one matures through the attainment of a physical skill, such as martial arts (body), through education and training in arts and sciences of one form or another (mind), and through devotion to a sense of mission for life (spirit). The curriculum in education, in both the military and the civilian sectors, is designed to promote all three.

The military is the exemplar.
During my frequent travels in North Korea, my favorite question to ask a single woman or girl is what kind of man she would wish to marry. Of late, I have noticed that the most common answer is a soldier. One must appreciate this in the context that the military institution represents the best manifestations of excellence in body, mind, and spirit. For

instance, military artists are revered because they are among the most accomplished artists in the country; the military boasts the best scientists, as demonstrated by the advancement of nuclear physics and the engineering of the atomic bomb; and of course, the military demonstrates the resolve and unwavering loyalty to the cause of fighting the "most powerful enemy" in the world, the United States.

Even the cursory view of *songun* presented here clearly suggests that it is a peculiar system of ideas not commonly found in world politics. The birth and evolution of *songun* reflect closely the international political environment led by the American administrations, especially that of George W. Bush, which North Korea regarded as particularly hostile and threatening.

CONCLUDING REMARKS

This chapter has examined the nature of belief systems embedded in the ideology of *Juche*. The ideology is consistent with the salient cultural conditions of Confucianism, and *juche* has exhibited a series of evolutions that culminated in current military-first politics (*songun*). This process of evolution shows that the ideology has adapted to changing international, inter-Korea, and domestic conditions. Despite the continuity and consistency in the ideology of *juche*, one distinct impact of this self-reliance doctrine is its detrimental effect on the promotion of economic growth. However, *juche* politics has been the conscientious choice of the leadership, which also sees the merits of this ideology in vying with the South for legitimacy and in boosting the morale of its people in the face of economic difficulties. *Juche* ideology and *songun* politics may have been instrumental in equipping the state with nuclear capabilities, which clearly has provided the system with elevated status in the international arena and with bargaining leverage. The timely question today is this: Will the North Korean state "bargain the nuke away" for security and development advances? The question is beyond the scope of this chapter, but a simple answer has to be affirmative; such a development will lead to a complex dynamics of negotiations through multiple channels and forums in the years ahead.

Endnotes

1. *International Encyclopedia of the Social and Behavioral Science*, ed. Neil J. Smelser and Paul B. Baltes (Oxford: Elsevier, 2001).
2. The evolution of *juche* is explicitly discussed in my book, Han S. Park, *North Korea: The Politics of Unconventional Wisdom* (Boulder, CO: Lynne Rienner, 2002). Portions of this section are reiterated from that source.
3. The National Museum of History and Mankyong Dae, the birthplace of Kim Il Sung, are among the places where Kim's activities for national independence are richly documented.
4. Over 250,000 South Koreans, some 54,000 US troops, and 132,000 Chinese soldiers were killed in the conflict. An accurate number of North Korean casualties has not been officially documented, but the war left devastating effects in human and structural losses.
5. This fear led North Korea to construct the Pyongyang Subway System, the average depth of which is one hundred meters; the system can be used as a bomb shelter for the capital city's entire citizenry. It is known that every community has also built deep bomb shelters in order to avoid suffering devastating consequences in the event of another conflict.
6. In 1968 a specially selected thirty-one-man North Korean commando team crossed the demilitarized zone (DMZ) to conduct a raid on the Blue House, the South Korean equivalent of the White House, in an unsuccessful attempt to assassinate president Park Chung Hee by cutting off his head.
7. The *dependencia* school, which emerged in the 1950s, is a school of economic theory that explains the lack of development in Latin America. The theory attributes the backward nature of the economy in the Third World to the structural exploitation of the peripheral economy by the central economy of the West.
8. Unfortunately, there is no credible way to show the volume of arms sales.
9. One might consider the current emergence of Kim Jong Il's son, Kim Jong Un, in this cultural context. On this particular theme, see Han S. Park, "Succession in North Korea," *Global Asia* 4, no. 2 (Summer 2009).
10. These features of *songun* were introduced initially in Han S. Park, "Military-First Politics (*Songun*): Understanding Kim Jong Il's North Korea," KEI Academic Paper Series 2, no. 7 (September 2007): 1–9.
11. Interview with farmers near Pyongyang on August 24, 2009.

Chapter 2

Fundamental Characteristics of the North Korean Economy

Foundations and Reform Trajectories

Rudiger Frank

At least since the mid-1990s, the Democratic People's Republic of Korea (DPRK), or North Korea, has occupied a prominent space in Western media as well as in public and political discourse in Europe and the United States. This is remarkable given the geographical distance, the country's relatively small size in terms of area and population, and its low level of economic development. The reasons for such oversize interest include geopolitics and the nuclear issue, to a lesser degree also the humanitarian dimension around a chronic undersupply of food, concerns about human rights, and the perception of the North Korean leadership as bizarre. The West is flabbergasted by the stubborn resilience of a system that was, according to conventional wisdom, supposed to have either collapsed or started a transformation almost two decades ago. North Korea's post–9/11 inclusion in the "axis of evil" provided a dubious ennoblement.

Generally speaking, North Korea is seen as an anomaly and hence attracts the West's interest. The latter is amplified by an information problem. In this chapter, I am reluctant to speak of a *lack* of information, for this is simply not accurate; however, the *type* of information available on North Korea in many regards indeed differs from what would be standard for other countries. Reliable statistics and opportunities for regular fieldwork are in short supply. Information, including quantitative data, must be gathered by incorporating historical and cultural factors and through tedious qualitative research. Languages, access, and knowledge of sources and of context are crucial. This makes North Korea an economist's nightmare—and an area specialist's (last) paradise.

This chapter explores some basic information on the North Korean economy, including natural conditions. (The question of reform is covered in chapter 3.) I begin with agriculture, the importance of which cannot be overstated, given the chronic food shortage and its many consequences. I then turn to industry—the part of the economy that has suffered most from international isolation but that at the same time seems to be the key to resolving many of North Korea's pressing economic problems. After laying this factual foundation, I explore the DPRK's economic policy to see how the country's resources are used.

My intention is to show a certain consistency in North Korea's economic development, to highlight the sources of the emergence of the North Korean economic system, and to provide some regional and systematic context for its understanding. The underlying theoretical hypothesis of this chapter is that the North Korean economy is not an extraordinary case as such.[1] Rather, its current shape is the result of the usual forces operating in an unusual environment. This analysis is informed by a rationalist understanding of an economy. I assume that people, regardless of their nationality or circumstances of life, maximize utility, although there are significant differences as to what constitutes utility, how it is measured, which options for its pursuit exist, and how these are ranked.

To appropriately combine this economic view with the perspective of area studies, I implicitly rely on new institutional economics (NIE), which regards institutions as the "rules of the game" in a society.[2] These rules of the game strongly narrow and restrict the options of behavior available to individuals and firms. They also shape the evaluation of the costs and the value associated with various outcomes and behavioral options.[3] Neoclassical economics describes how people behave in principle; institutions explain how people act in a specific context. NIE can thus be seen as an interface between the theoretical understanding of economics and the practical knowledge of area studies. Even if it is not mentioned more than once in the text, it forms the study's metatheoretical foundation.

Basic Facts: Resources and Industries

Climate, arable land, mineral and other natural resources, population, and geographical location can help an inefficient system survive or make even the smartest economic policy bear little fruit. North Korea is both blessed and undersupplied from this point of view, with an advantage in minerals and a disadvantage in agriculture. This resource endowment defines the operating environment for economic policy and can make success harder to achieve and failure harder to prevent.

Minerals

The DPRK is a country with a territory of around 123,000 square kilometers and an estimated population of 24 million.[4] Unlike South Korea, it has an outstandingly rich supply of various natural resources. These are well documented in studies undertaken before 1945, when access was unrestricted. One of the most authoritative and detailed studies of this kind was conducted by the German geographer Hermann Lautensach, who contended that "of the leading mineral products of the earth only petroleum and tin are missing [in Korea]."[5]

Owing to nature's caprices, most of these riches are found in what today is the territory of the DPRK. There are substantial reserves of gold, iron ore, copper, nickel, graphite, anthracite, silver, zinc, lead, bismuth, tungsten, molybdenum, lignite, kaolin, alunite, fluorite, barite, mica, quicksilver, manganese, antimony, nickel, and asbestos. In 1936 there were 5,518 mines in Korea. In 1937 some 18,662 kilograms of gold were produced in Korea, a remarkable 1.7 percent of that year's world production. Silver production was 46,655 kilograms in 1937 (0.5 percent of world production). In 1934 Korea's production of coal reached about 982,000 tons. Lignite production in 1934 was about 706,000 tons. In 1936 Korean tungsten production amounted to 7.5 percent of world production. In 1935 Korea produced 22 percent of the world's graphite and was the second-largest producer in the world. Furthermore, Lautensach contended that Korea was "one of the largest mica producers on earth."[6]

The situation as described by Lautensach has changed little over the past decades; North Korea is still enormously rich in minerals. Recently, the problem of extracting these resources seems to have been solved with the help of foreign investors. In the first decade of the twenty-first century, the attractiveness of North Korea as a source of minerals has been particularly illustrated by growing Chinese interest (and South Korean nervousness about it). As Thompson noted in his study on Chinese–North Korean joint ventures, of the 138 established joint ventures between 1997 and August 2010, 41 percent were in extractive industries.[7] According to the Institute of Far Eastern Studies (IFES), by early 2011 a total of two hundred Chinese companies were active in North Korea.[8]

A recent report on mineral resources in North Korea estimates the 2007 annual production of gold at 2,000 kilograms; copper, 12,000 tons; iron ore, 5,130 tons; lead, 13,000 tons; silver, 20 tons; tungsten, 600 tons; zinc, 70,000 tons; magnetite, 1,000 tons; and coal, 24,100 tons.[9] Yoon noted that the DPRK's reserves of tungsten, molybdenite, black lead, barite, and fluorite place it among the world's top ten countries in terms of reserves.[10] The same author provided some newer estimates (as of 2004) on the DPRK's mineral resources, the total value of which is thought to be over USD 2 trillion (see table 1).

Table 1. Major natural resources in the DPRK.

Classification	Unit	Deposit	Value (USD, millions)
Gold	1,000 tons	1.5	19,171
Silver	1,000 tons	4	745
Copper	1,000 tons	2155	2,044.9
Lead	1,000 tons	6,000	1,178.4
Zinc	10 million tons	1.5	6,709.1
Iron	100 million tons	30	71,866.3
Tungsten	1,000 tons	250	219.4
Molybdenite	1,000 tons	2	8.2
Manganese	1,000 tons	200	6.5
Nickel	1,000 tons	15	3.6
Black lead	1,000 tons	6,000	3,316.5
Limestone	100 million tons	1,000	996,230.7
Kaolin	1,000 tons	2,000	30.2
Talc	1,000 tons	600	75
Asbestos	1,000 tons	13	0.9
Fluorspar	1,000 tons	500	12.5
Barite	1,000 tons	2,100	163.6
Magnetite	100 million tons	35	126,000
Anthracitic coal	100 million tons	117	767,138.9
Bituminous coal	100 million tons	30	168,000
			2,162,927

Source. Yoon, *Status and Future*, 6.

The numbers in table 1 are estimates and naturally not highly accurate. Nevertheless, they illustrate the enormous potential of North Korea in terms of mineral production. A notable fact is the high level of activity among Chinese mining companies in North Korea. There is also a major difference compared to the German case, in which the formerly socialist East had little to contribute to a unified economy. The North's economic role in a possible Korean unification would definitely be much larger.

Table 2. Output of major metallic ores in the DPRK.

	Gold (tons)	Silver (tons)	Copper (1,000 tons)	Tungsten (tons)	Lead (1,000 tons)	Zinc (1,000 tons)	Iron ore (1,000 tons)
1990	5	50	15	1000	80	230	8,430
1992	5	50	16	1000	75	200	5,747
1994	5	50	16	900	80	210	4,586
1996	4.5	50	16	900	80	210	3,440
1998	4.5	50	14	500	70	100	2,890
2000	2	40	13	500	60	100	3,793
2001	2	40	13	500	60	100	4,208
2002	2	40	12	600	60	100	4,078
2003	2	20	12	600	60	100	4,579
2004	2	20	12	600	12	100	4,580
2005	2	20	12	600	13	100	5,000
2006	2	20	12	600	13	100	5,000

Source. Yoon, *Status and Future*, 6.

This potential is, however, far from being realized. Table 2 shows that the actual output of key minerals as of 2006 was lagging behind the production of 1990, pointing at the largely untapped potential of minerals for the development of the North Korean national economy.

Climate

The Korean Peninsula is not very large, extending only about 890 kilometers from Mt. Paektu in the North to the Southern part of Chŏlla Province (990 km, if one includes Cheju Island). The distance between the Chinese border and the sea south of Korea is merely 700 kilometers. The distance from Korea's east coast to its west coast rarely exceeds 300 kilometers. However, climatic conditions differ significantly between North and South. This is particularly true for the winter season. A distance of just 600 kilometers accounts for a difference in the average January temperature of 10°C (0°C in South Chŏlla, −10° in South Pyongyang). If one includes the two extreme points—that is, Cheju to the south and the Chinese border to the north—the difference increases to 24°C (5°C vs. −19°C) over a distance of just 900 kilometers. In one station in the North (Chunggangjin), a low of −43.6°C stood opposed to a high of 38°C, resulting in the enormous temperature range of 81.6°C. In 2009 the average annual temperature in the South Korean capital of Seoul (12.9°C), about 60 kilometers south of the demarcation line, was as much as three degrees higher than that in Sinŭju (9.9°C), North Korea's northwestern border town.[11] As Lautensach observed, with regard to its climate, Korea is in a transition zone between the continental and maritime spheres.[12] The North is much colder than the South, with the exception of the east coast, where the climate is milder. However, arable land there is limited to a narrow strip between the T'aebaek Mountains and the Eastern Sea. The overall climatic conditions—in particular, the low winter temperatures—prevent autumn planting in the North, where most cultivated plants are spring crops.

For precipitation, the same is true; that is, the difference between northern and southern parts of the peninsula is significant. In addition, variations in precipitation are extreme over the year. Most of the rain falls during the monsoon season and is associated with typhoons and cyclones. In overly wet years the amount of precipitation can exceed the mean by 90 percent; in overly dry years it can be 57 percent below average. A deficit of more than 40 percent "has a devastating effect on the rice harvest."[13] In addition to drought, severe floods are also highly likely. Flood disasters caused by heavy rainfall are extremely damaging because they destroy not only the plants but also the fields on the hill slopes, and they cause erosion and increase the sandiness of the soil.[14]

Agriculture

Basic Policies and Conditions

I have quoted the German geographer to show that not all North Korea's agricultural problems are the "homemade" result of deforestation and similar activities; some of them indeed have natural causes. It is remarkable to see that most of Lautensach's observations from presocialist times —too little arable land, unfavorable climate, deforestation, and the rising risk and damage of floods—can be found in current debates about North Korean agriculture.[15] This is not to say that the typical inefficiency of socialist systems and their low sensitivity toward environmental issues are not major reasons for the DPRK's difficulties acquiring enough food; however, it would be equally wrong to discard the effects of natural conditions as propaganda. One should also consider that the population of North Korea has almost tripled since 1945, leading to worsening relations between more or less invariable arable land and a growing number of mouths to feed heads of population. This can be overcome only with significant increases in productivity. In this regard, North Korea has obviously failed, although the leadership is aware of the problem. In the 2005 and 2006 New Year joint editorials, published by *Rodong Sinmun* and setting the key priorities for the year, agriculture was characterized as the "main front of economic construction" (*kyŏngje kŏnsŏrŭi chugong chŏnsŏn*), referring to the stance of Kim Il Sung, who was quoted as having said, "Rice means socialism" (*ssarŭn kot sahoejuŭida*).

Food in North Korea is produced mainly in cooperatives; highly productive private plots (kitchen gardens[16]) exist but so far play a minor role, mainly owing to their small size. In a successful attempt to increase the productivity of collectively tilled land, many smaller fields have been transformed and realigned in well laid-out regular plots, a measure that has so far increased the overall paddy production area by about 60,000 hectares. Since 2004 the establishment of private semiformal minico-operatives has been reported, a process overseen by the government.[17] Recent reports (as of 2008) indicate that this development has been partially reversed.

According to Haggard and Noland, only 20 percent of North Korea's land can be cultivated; a similar estimate of 22.4 percent has been provided by Statistics Korea.[18] Combined with rising demand from a growing population and a low food-import volume, this has led to intensive agricultural techniques, such as the utilization of chemical fertilizers and pesticides that have overworked the soil. The Food and Agriculture Organization (FAO) of the United Nations reported that the total area under paddy in 2004 was 583,000 hectares; maize covered 459,000 hectares; potatoes, 89,000 hectares; and other cereals, 60,000 hectares.[19] The total amount of cultivated land according to Statistics Korea in 2009 was 1.91 million hectares in North Korea (compared to 1.73 million hectares in South Korea).[20] The climatic differences between North and South become obvious if one considers that the productive paddy area in the North comprised 609,000 hectares in 2009, whereas in South Korea over one million hectares could be used for rice production on paddy fields.

To gain an idea of the composition of North Korea's agricultural output, consider that in 2004 rice production was measured at 2,370,000 tons; maize, 1,727,000 tons; potatoes, 258,000 tons of cereal equivalent; and other cereals, 119,000 tons. Winter and spring double-crop production added 166,000 tons of winter wheat, 64,000 tons of spring barley, and 255,000 tons of cereal equivalent of spring potatoes. The total cereal production for 2004 was estimated at 5,064,000 tons of rice or rice equivalent.[21]

The DPRK invests an enormous amount of its human resources in agriculture. In 2008 over 8.5 million people, or 36.8 percent of all North Koreans, were employed in this sector (in South Korea the number was 6.6 percent).[22] Each of the approximately 1.67 million cooperative farm households is entitled to a small private garden.[23] A significant proportion of urban dwellers also have access to garden plots. The FAO estimated that North Korea's total household-garden area amounts to 25,000 hectares. A typical pattern of cultivation in these gardens is an early crop of potatoes and green maize, followed by vegetables, such as cabbage, peppers, radishes, and garlic. The estimated production of maize and potatoes on these private plots is 50,000 tons. Production on hill slopes (with an incline of more than 15 degrees) is estimated by the FAO to be roughly 50,000 tons.

Paddy is typically planted in nurseries at the beginning of April and transplanted in late May or early June. To compensate for low soil fertility, seed rates are high. Collectivization was accompanied by an increase in irrigation and the use of industrial inputs. During the 1960s the country pursued the "four modernizations" in agriculture: mechanization, electrification, irrigation, and chemicalization.

According to the North Korean Ministry of Agriculture, over 230,000 nutrient tons of fertilizer were used during 2004.[24] Of the total, 72 percent was provided as humanitarian assistance by the Republic of Korea, the European Union, the FAO, and various nongovernmental organizations (NGOs). Domestic production amounted to 56,524 nutrient tons. Based on FAO data, Haggard and Noland showed that fertilizer consumption has decreased sharply from a level of around 650,000 tons in 1989 to one-third this amount in 2004.[25] This provides one explanation for the food shortage.

Connection to Other Sectors

Agriculture does not exist separately from the other sectors of North Korea's economy. It competes with or depends upon other sectors for inputs of labor, capital, and technology. The availability of these inputs is related to their overall scarcity level, as well as to administrative and political decision making and priority setting. It is no surprise to see that in principle, North Korea's agriculture exhibits the difficulties of a shortage economy as described by Kornai.[26] Although estimates of actual production and demand vary, it is widely agreed that under present conditions, the country is not able to produce a sufficient amount of staple food. However, Ireson argued that in principle, North Korea could achieve food self-sufficiency.[27] Based on FAO calculations, the shortage for 2004 was about 900,000 tons. This deficit has been covered by food aid, concessional trade with China and South Korea, and commercial imports.

Commercial imports are low—too low, I would argue. The reasons are obvious, but they do not form irresolvable problems. As a typical socialist economy, North Korea suffers from a chronic shortage of hard currency. This restricts the import of food and also of crucial inputs such as fertilizer. Import substitution thus becomes a necessity, although officially it is promoted as a deliberately chosen strategy. The need to divert resources to agriculture adversely affects other, potentially more productive sectors of the DPRK's national economy. The relationship also functions in reverse: the overall problematic state of the national economy, including energy production and the chemical industry, negatively affects agriculture because crucial inputs are lacking. This concerns not only fertilizer but also irrigation (electric pumping) and agricultural machinery (plowing, threshing, seeding, transportation). Because of agriculture's dependence on industrial inputs, an industrial crisis more or less directly leads to a food crisis. The DPRK's agriculture is vulnerable to energy crises, oil-price hikes, and an overall recession in the manufacturing sector.

The following data highlight this causality. In 2004 the number of tractors in North Korea was 64,062, of which only 57.5 percent (36,836) were operational. Accordingly, about half the land in the main farming areas is still prepared using draught cattle and human labor, significantly reducing productivity. Not least because farm machinery is in dire condition (owing to a lack of spare parts, fuel, and tires), yields per hectare have dropped about 50 percent since the 1980s, when they were about seven to eight tons.[28] Electricity shortage is a problem of country- and economy-wide dimensions. Despite great progress in the construction of gravity-fed irrigation systems in recent years, most systems still depend on electrically powered pumping stations. The FAO reported that some farms depend for their irrigation on series of ten or more pumping stations and are consequently very vulnerable to water and electricity shortages.

FOOD DISTRIBUTION

The distribution of food in North Korea has received particular attention internationally. Until the mid-1990s, the distribution of staple food was monopolized by the state through the so-called public distribution system (PDS). Cooperative farms sold products to the state at fixed prices that were substantially higher than the actual sales price. In other words, food was heavily subsidized. Because of the famine of 1995–1997, market-type distribution channels have emerged or were strengthened. In 2002 this was turned into an official policy.[29] After a period of a coexistence of state and market distribution, in autumn 2005 the state tried to reintroduce its monopoly on the distribution of staple food. As of 2012, there are no signs of major policy changes, although in 2012 rumors about a reform giving farmers more autonomy in production and marketing (June 28 measures) emerged but could not be confirmed.

The daily grain rations have varied over time and according to occupation and region. In general, farmers and those working in strategic areas, including the military, received relatively high rations. The citizens of the capital city (Pyongyang), too, received preferential treatment, a behavior also observed in other socialist countries. As anecdotal evidence from various sources implies, most North Koreans must complement their state rations by relying on other sources, of which the markets are the most important. This hybrid system—in which a basic amount is supplied by the state and additional demand is covered through the markets—is supposed to cope with the undersupply of food and also provide incentives to producers while maintaining a certain basic level of nondiscriminatory food access.

Markets as such have existed more or less continuously throughout the DPRK's existence. However, since around 2002 they have gained more and more recognition from the state. Their status was upgraded, allowing the sale not only of foodstuffs but also of industrial goods. Their number has grown, and rather than opening only on the first, eleventh, and twenty-first day of each month, as was usual for decades, they were allowed to operate on a much more regular basis. At least one such market exists in each county, city, or district. Vendors pay a stall fee. The authorities regulate vendors' access to these markets; the FAO reports that particularly vulnerable groups, such as unemployed women, are sometimes given preferential access. Since 2005 sources such as Good Friends have reported various state attempts to ban women below a certain age from engaging in trade, obviously because this workforce was missing in the state-owned industries.[30] In March 2009 there were reports that the number of legally tradable items has been substantially reduced and that the prices were fixed.

The attempt by the state and the party to regain control of the economy would not be illogical; having studied the European experience, North Korean leaders are perfectly aware of the connection between economic control and political control. However, also based on the experience of other socialist countries, it is highly doubtful whether, once it has been granted for whatever reason, such liberalization can be reversed without significant fallout in the form of public discontent. The latter would most likely be hidden for fear of political oppression, but it would accumulate over time and form the explosive potential that led to the surprisingly quick disintegration of the seemingly stable socialist societies in Europe. This potential obviously was not present in 1994, when Kim Il Sung died, or during the famine of 1995–1997. However, the public reaction to the next internal or external shock might prove very different, notwithstanding Fahy's argument that famine might not necessarily lead to a political uprising, although common wisdom from developed countries seems to suggest so.[31]

What remains is the remarkable fact that despite the clumsiness of the actual measures, the North Korean state tried to use price as a tool for regulating the economy, which is not to be taken for granted in a socialist system. The prices in the PDS were substantially changed in absolute terms as well as in relation to incomes and procurement prices during the price reform of July 2002 but have, as far as observers know, remained stable ever since.[32] Meanwhile, inflation on the markets has reached levels of up to 200 percent annually,[33] quickly restoring the huge gap between state-set and market prices and undermining one of the reform goals. Another price adjustment to narrow the gap between state and market prices would be the logical consequence. The currency devaluation of December 2009 can be interpreted as such an attempt.[34] This and other measures to curb the influence of the markets have not been very successful; however, they show how concerned if not desperate the North Korean leadership is about the societal effects of the increasingly important nonstate distribution channels.

The actual amount of food needed to sustain North Korea is a sensitive subject of debate. Disagreements abound regarding the overall amount of food, the level of domestic production, and the size of external inputs through official and unofficial channels. Many involved parties, including North Korea, its partners, adversaries, and international NGOs, at least theoretically have incentives to over- or underestimate. In any case, despite almost annual warnings, another major famine like the one in 1995–1997 had not occurred as of late 2012. This is not to say that North Korea's population does not suffer from malnutrition; however, there are indications that the situation is not as severe as is sometimes contended in the media.

Even if one has access to reliable numbers on actual harvests, these must be treated cautiously. As the UN World Food Programme (WFP) argued based on its worldwide experience, significant amounts of grain need to be set aside to be used for next year's seed. More food gets lost during transportation and storage or is used to feed animals or to produce goods such as alcohol. In addition to grain as staple food, other sources (e.g., wild plants, small animals, milk products, fruits, fish) are used; estimating them is usually very difficult without proper access. Haggard and Noland argued that the WFP has overstated the role of starchy food in the North Korean diet by about 20 percent.[35] They also pointed out that even the exact size of the North Korean population is unknown, making calculation of the actual food demand even harder. Estimates of the cereal livestock-feed requirements in North Korea vary from as little as 0.2 million to as high as 1.4 million metric tons. Postharvest losses are estimated at 2 percent–30 percent, again a very large span.

Likewise, the estimates for North Korea's aggregate food demand vary strongly, from 3 million to 7 million metric tons. This is not just an academic question, considering that output estimates for the past years have hovered between 2.5 and 5 million metric tons. It is undisputed that until 1993 this number was much higher.[36] But at what point does a famine start? Haggard and Noland contrasted their own estimates of the food balance (i.e., output minus demand), which have been continuously positive since 1996/1997 except for 2007/2008, with estimates from the UN system (WFP, FAO).[37] The latter see the North Korean food balance as negative throughout the last decade, with the exception of 2005/2006.

Obviously, the DPRK's agriculture is facing major challenges, although the actual magnitude of the food crisis is subject to debate.

Attempts at solving the problem through administrative measures can be observed, but success has been limited. Many but not all difficulties facing North Korean agriculture are homemade. The legal and moral justification of such measures aside, there is little doubt that North Korea has suffered heavily from an international embargo policy.[38] The failure of the light water reactor (LWR) project in the context of the Korean Peninsula Energy Development Organization (KEDO) has dealt a serious blow to the DPRK's economy and its agriculture. North Korea's low payment morale, combined with a lack of strong political supporters, has effectively excluded the option of significant foreign loans, although recently indications have emerged that China is willing to play that role. Based on what was shown previously, I would argue that a sustainable solution to the North Korean food crisis can be found only in industry —as a producer of crucial agricultural inputs, such as fertilizer, energy, and machinery, and as a source of export income in hard currency to be used for food imports.

Industry and Trade

Despite the difficulties inherent in assessing the status of North Korea's agriculture, the utility of available data on that sector of the country's economy is still relatively high. Satellite imaging provides good estimates of arable land, weather observation and comparative studies in South Korea provide clues on the yield per unit, and analysts have a relatively fair understanding of the aggregate calorie demand. A proper evaluation of North Korean industry, however, is much more difficult if not altogether impossible.

Utility of Data on Industry

The major reason for this difficulty is provided by the German example. Ritter and Paqué respectively conducted two of the many studies that confirm how wrong most West German estimates of the value and productive capacity of East German industry were.[39] The main reasons have been the lack of an expressive unit of accounting and the gap between quantity and quality. To apply this to the Korean situation, not only do outsiders have merely a rudimentary understanding of what North Korean factories manufacture, but they also face enormous difficulties establishing what this output is worth and at what cost it is produced. In fact, it is doubtful whether the North Korean authorities themselves know. This will remain unchanged as long as the North Korean currency is neither convertible nor pegged to a convertible currency, such as the Chinese yuan or the US dollar.

In addition, even if one knew how many tractors, TVs, shoes, and so forth North Korean factories produce, one still has no clue what these are worth because they do not have to compete on the world market against similar products. Experience with other formerly socialist countries, information about the level of technological development and sophistication of North Korea, and circumstantial information from visitors about consumer preferences[40] imply a substantially lower value than world-market products, which often have few similarities to the North Korean product beyond the name.

Furthermore, the lack of a reliable accounting unit, the absence of competition, and the typical procurement problems in a centrally planned state-socialist economy make it impossible to know whether single North Korean enterprises are operating on a profit or generating losses. There is no labor market, so labor inputs might be low cost on paper; nevertheless, calculated in terms of opportunity (how much value the same worker could generate at another workplace), the cost of labor will in all likeliness be relatively high. Factories in systems like the North Korean one expend enormous amounts of resources either finding sources from which to procure crucial inputs or manufacturing such inputs on-site because they are hard to find elsewhere.

Overall, I am relatively pessimistic regarding statistics on the DPRK's manufacturing. A few facts seem reliable: equipment is often outdated, abrasive wear is a problem because spare parts are lacking, inputs of energy are below demand, and access to the latest technologies is limited. This is not to say that scholars know nothing; they do have a fairly good understanding of the DPRK's economic structure and of the system as such.

Industrial Structure

Looking back to the last time Korea had a "natural" economic structure, one receives the impression presented in table 3.

Table 3. Regional concentration of industries in Korea, 1945.

	North	South
Consumer goods	20%	80%
Food production	35%	65%
Machinery	35%	65%
Coal	80%	20%
Chemicals	85%	15%
Hydroelectric power	90%	10%
Iron and steel	95%	5%

Source. Jung-en Woo, *Race to the Swift: State and Finance in Korean Industrialization* (New York: Columbia University Press, 1991), 41.

As table 3 shows, the North was industrialized, whereas agriculture and labor intensive industries were positioned in the South. It is worth noting that Japanese colonial policy was then in its later stage, oriented toward assimilation; Korea was to become part of Japan. Thus, the industry that North Korea inherited from the Japanese after liberation in 1945 was considerably developed. To provide just one example, in 1936 Korean production of nitrogen compounds (mainly based in the North around Hamhŭng or Hŭngnam) had reached one-eighth that of the German empire, at that time the largest producer in the world.[41]

North Korea relatively early exhibited features of an industrialized society. Building on the Japanese foundation and benefiting from the politically motivated support of the Soviet Union and its allies, the urbanization rate in North Korea reached levels of around 40 percent as early as the 1960s. Currently, about 60 percent of North Koreans live in an urban environment, a percentage that corresponds with the figure for South Korea in the 1980s.[42]

One can learn another lesson from table 3. Unlike divided Germany, the two parts of Korea were highly complementary economies—in other words, each part had what the other was lacking. This led to difficulties in both Koreas after the division. The North Korean disadvantage in agriculture and light industry initially seemed to be smaller compared to the situation in the South. The DPRK had a higher gross domestic product (GDP) than the Republic of Korea (ROK) did until the late 1960s or even up to the 1980s.[43]

However, it turned out that in the long run, the DPRK's lack of arable land, its unfavorable climate, inefficient socialist management, declining industrial production (including production of fertilizer), an overall shortage of inputs (e.g., workforce, electricity, fuel), and the inability to generate (or assign) enough hard currency to finance the import of food proved to be bigger problems.

This was exacerbated by a typically socialist, if not Stalinist, economic policy favoring heavy and chemical industries at the expense of light industry and agriculture. Initially, there was great success, despite (or because of) the Korean War of 1950–1953, which provided a strong political motivation for the Soviet Union and other socialist countries to invest heavily in the economic well-being of their client at this highly symbolic interface between the two Cold War systems. More than 50 percent of state investment went into the industrial sector during the years 1954–1976, over 80 percent of that amount going into heavy industry. The share of industry in national output rose from 16.8 percent in 1946 to around 56 percent in 1990.[44] However, growth rates declined from about 30–40 percent annually during the 1950s to much lower levels, indicating the predictable end of an extensive growth strategy. Nevertheless, as table 4 shows, the DPRK is still an industrialized economy with a contribution of agriculture to gross national income (GNI) of below 21 percent.

Table 4. South Korean estimates of the composition of North Korea's GNI in 2009 (rounded).

Sector	**Percentage**
Agriculture, forestry, fisheries	20.9%
Industry	34.8%
Gas and electricity	4.1%
Construction	8.0%
Services	32.1%

Source. Statistics Korea, *Pukhanŭi chuyo t'onggye chip'yo*, 50.

I should also note the political factor's role in shaping the structure of North Korea's industry. In the late 1950s, and more intensely in the early 1960s, the North Korean leadership responded to the Sino–Soviet conflict and the subsequent decrease in external inputs with a new allocation policy that focused on self-defense and self-sufficiency. Kim Il Sung had to make a difficult decision between military and political security, on the one hand, and economic prosperity, on the other—and he deliberately chose to the disadvantage of the latter. This is an important historical lesson that renders highly questionable all outside hopes about the effectiveness of economic incentives in coercing North Korea in one direction or another.

North Korean Trade

The one shining exception among economic statistics on North Korea seems to be trade. This is mainly owing to the presence of factors the absence of which makes an assessment of industrial production impossible: trade is conducted and reported mostly in hard currency, and it is taking place in a competitive international environment. The analytical tool of choice is called *reverse statistics*; the DPRK does not report its trade with other countries, but those other countries do. Restrictions exist because not all trade with North Korea is being reported, because in some cases barter trade takes place, because differences between CIF (cost, insurance, freight) and FOB (free on board) calculations must be considered, and because a large part of North Korea's imports is either financed through long-term loans or takes the form of aid and assistance (i.e. unilateral transfers). Nevertheless—in particular, compared to other parts of the economy—scholars' understanding of the DPRK's trade relations is relatively good, if not exceptional.

The very structure of the North Korean economy, as discussed previously, implies a heavy export orientation. Japan, the most advanced East Asian economy, is just two hundred kilometers away. With China, the most dynamic economy and the biggest potential market, the DPRK shares a long land border, including railway connections. Possessing abundant mineral resources, a well-developed heavy and chemical industry, a highly educated workforce,[45] and a substantial need for export revenue to finance imports of technology, machinery, and food, North Korea should be highly active and visible on international markets.

But this is not the case. The reasons for this irregularity are manifold. To begin with, North Korea's centrally planned economy does not produce many goods that are sought after in the international market. On the ideological side, the DPRK leadership has been very reluctant to allow the emergence of interdependencies because they would be the natural consequences of a deeper integration into international trading structures. Ideological and strategic considerations are deep seated; the DPRK even shunned participation in the socialist camp's division of labor and did not join the Council of Mutual Economic Aid (COMECON).

In the past, the DPRK has exhibited a certain reluctance to live up to contractual commitments. The history of bilateral economic cooperation with the DPRK is full of accounts of delayed or cancelled payments, delayed delivery or inferior product quality, and attempts at renegotiating agreements.[46] Clearly, North Korea is not among the most accommodating trading partners.

Among the most significant reasons for the abnormal status of trade are sanctions. These have a long history; they were first issued against North Korea because it was part of the socialist camp, later because of its status as a "rogue state," a violator of human rights, an alleged producer and distributor of illegal goods (narcotics, counterfeit money), a violator of international agreements, a potential proliferator of nuclear materials and technologies, and so on. Sanctions against North Korea affect trade both directly, banning goods and services, and indirectly, through financial sanctions that make sending and receiving payment cumbersome, if not impossible.[47] They also have an important psychological effect, for trading partners fear repercussions even if their activities are perfectly legal.

Table 5 summarizes North Korean trade since 1990. Among the most notable issues is the heavy drop in exports and imports after the collapse of the socialist system in Europe and the Soviet Union. Another remarkable feature of North Korea's foreign trade is its imbalance.[48] It seems that throughout most of its existence, the DPRK has incurred a trade deficit—it imported more than it exported. This is not unusual, but it seems odd for a country like North Korea. A trade deficit implies financing through debt or unilateral transfers. In particular, the latter seems counterintuitive, given the bad international reputation of the DPRK and the many sanctions that have been issued against this country—but only at first glance. A recent study by the Congressional Research Service has confirmed that the United States alone provided the astonishing amount of USD 1.2 billion in aid and assistance to the DPRK in the years 1995–2011.[49] Eberstadt estimated that between 1995 and 2004, the total US transfers to North Korea amounted to USD 1.1 billion.[50] South Korea—not to mention China—until the end of the Roh Moo Hyun presidency in 2008, was another major source of unilateral transfers.

Looking at the regional distribution of North Korea's foreign trade, one finds a clear dominance of the Asia Pacific (87.8 percent of all North Korean trade in 2009), China taking the lead with 78.5 percent of North Korean trade in 2009. Germany followed as a more-than-distant second with 2 percent and was also the most important European trading partner, with a share of 45 percent of DPRK–EU trade. The other top-ten North Korean trading partners were Russia, India, Singapore, Hong Kong, Brazil, Taiwan, Bangladesh, and the Netherlands. Among the most remarkable changes in the past few years have been trade relations with Japan; these were once very strong but as of 2009 have fallen to less than USD 3 million annually (in 2006 the number was over USD 121 million). The bulk of North Korea's exports, almost 42 percent in 2009, were minerals (HS codes 25–27), followed by base metals and articles of base metal (15.3 percent; HS codes 72–83), as well as textiles and textile articles (14.1 percent, HS codes 50–63). The sharpest increase in North Korean exports (+74.4 percent in 2009) took place for vegetable products, most of which go to China. North Korean imports in 2009 were mostly textiles (15.4 percent), minerals (15.0 percent), and machinery (14.7 percent).[51]

Table 5a. North Korea's trade, 1990–2000 (millions USD and %).

	Exports	Change	Imports	Change	Total trade	Change	Balance
1990	1,733	—	2,437	—	4,170	—	-704
1991	945	-45.5	1,639	-32.7	2,584	-38.0	-694
1992	933	-1.3	1,622	-1.0	2,555	1.1	-689
1993	990	6.1	1,656	2.1	2,646	3.6	-666
1994	858	-13.3	1,242	-25.0	2,100	-20.6	-384
1995	736	-14.2	1,316	6.0	2,052	-2.3	-580
1996	727	1.2	1,250	-5.0	1,977	-3.7	-523
1997	905	24.5	1,272	1.8	2,177	10.1	-367
1998	559	-38.2	883	-30.6	1,442	-33.8	-324
1999	515	7.9	965	9.3	1,480	2.6	-450
2000	556	8.0	1,413	46.4	1,969	33.0	-857

Source. Korea Trade and Investment Promotion Agency (KOTRA), *2011 Pukhanŭi taewoemuyŏk tonghyang* [Trends in North Korean trade, 2011], KOTRA Paper 12-018 (Seoul: Korea Trade and Investment Promotion Agency, 2012).

Recently, North Korea has been making efforts to expand foreign trade and international cooperation while at the same time making sure that the state remains in control of these activities. On January 4, 2010, the DPRK designated Rasŏn—the country's first free-trade zone, comprising the northeastern cities of Rajin and Sŏnbong—a "special city."

Table 5b. North Korea's trade, 2001–2011 (millions USD and %).

	Exports	Change	Imports	Change	Total trade	Change	Balance
2001	650	16.9	1,620	14.6	2,270	15.3	-970
2002	735	13.1	1,525	-5.9	2,260	-0.4	-790
2003	777	5.5	1,614	5.9	2,391	5.8	-837
2004	1,020	31.3	1,837	13.8	2,857	19.5	-817
2005	998	-2.1	2,003	9.1	3,002	5.1	-1,005
2006	947	-5.2	2,049	2.3	2,996	-0.2	-1,102
2007	918	-3.0	2,022	-1.3	2,941	-1.8	-1,104
2008	1,130	23.0	2,686	32.7	3,816	29.7	-1,556
2009	1,063	-6.0	2,351	-12.5	3,414	-10.5	-1,288
2010	1,513	42.2	2,660	13.2	4,174	22.2	-1,147
2011	2,788	84.3	3,528	32.6	6,316	51.3	-740

Source. Korea Trade and Investment Promotion Agency (KOTRA), *2011 Pukhanŭi taewoemuyŏk tonghyang* [Trends in North Korean trade, 2011], KOTRA Paper 12-018 (Seoul: Korea Trade and Investment Promotion Agency, 2012).

The area was named an economic free-trade zone in 1991 and touted as "Northeast Asia's Golden Triangle." Kim Jong Il visited the city in December 2009. Russia invested EUR 140 million (USD 202 million) in the Rasŏn project in late 2008, mainly for the restoration of railways.[52] China is allegedly involved in developing the zone's port facilities.

In obvious relation to the upgrading of the Rasŏn zone, on January 20, 2010, the Korean Central News Agency (KCNA) announced the National Defense Commission's plans to launch the State Development Bank in order to fund its development projects and "to provide investment on major projects to be carried out according to state policy." The Pyongyang-based bank would be capable of conducting "transactions with international monetary organizations and commercial banks."

If I were to summarize the main feature of North Korean trade, I would conclude that China is the main partner, minerals are the most important export product, the DPRK has been continuously running a trade deficit, and trade has increased in recent years but has not yet reached pre-1990 levels.

THE DPRK'S ECONOMIC SYSTEM AND POLICIES

Thieme laid out the key components of economic systems: planning, steering, coordination, information, control, and motivation.[53] This section briefly explores how the North Korean leadership has decided to address these challenges.

From the Soviet Model to *Juche*

After 1945 North Korea became a centrally planned economy under the influence of the Soviet Union, and at first, it resembled that system closely. Central planning implies that the free and decentralized interplay of demand and supply, the mechanism that regulates market economies, is replaced by the administration. The latter determines ex ante which products are needed and in what quantities; accordingly, it sets production targets and allocates them to production units. It estimates the needed inputs for production and manages the procurement and distribution of these inputs. This system has a whole array of consequences for monetary and fiscal policy, and despite claims that it is a superior system, in the past it has proved to lead to great inefficiencies.[54]

Such a system was not accepted in North Korea without internal debate—in particular, shortly after 1945. Not all members of the elite regarded the Soviet model as ideal for their country, and with great interest they followed discussions in Eastern Europe and China about alternatives. Kim Il Sung managed to maintain control, not least through a series of purges, including one after a failed coup in August 1956.[55]

However, Kim Il Sung started deviating from the Soviet model when it stopped serving his goals. In particular, the new ideas of collective leadership and peaceful coexistence with the West were not acceptable to him. He was also very skeptical regarding the DPRK's membership in a bloc, for this would have forced him to sacrifice too much of his newly won independence. The issue became pressing after Stalin's death in 1953 and even more so when major differences emerged between the Soviet Union and China. In 1958 North Korea very cautiously emulated the Chinese Great Leap; but Kim Il Sung was not ready to return to the centuries-old relationship of suzerainty. He opted, rather, for his own indigenous model of a state and an ideology, known under the term *juche* (*chuch'e*).

The term is rather clumsily translated "self-reliance" ("self-determination" would be much better), and the style of the lengthy and repetitive official explanations, full of simplistic statements, unpolished rhetoric, and contrived arguments is hardly convincing. One of the best definitions of *juche* is found in the work of Jorganson,[56] who described *juche* as a "culture-specific ethnic nationalism." Along the same lines, Suh called it "nothing more than xenophobic nationalism that has little relevance to communism."[57] In a convincing argument against the mainstream assumption, Myers argued that Kim Il Sung's speech of December 28, 1955, usually cited both within and outside the DPRK as the moment of *juche*'s introduction, has been designated as such only ex post; the actual creation of *juche* as the North Korean ideology took place much later, in the mid-1960s.[58] This is supported by an analysis of press and propaganda.

The core ideas were summarized by Kim Jong Il himself.[59] Not diverging far from Bucharin's way of thinking, he argued that the masses need a powerful ideology in order to become the creators of history, and that they need a leader to guide the way. It was Lenin who first had to put a spin on Marx and Engels's theory to justify starting a revolution in a single country that still had one foot grounded in feudalism. In principle emulating Lenin, Kim Il Sung announced that because Korea was different from any other country, its ideology had to be adjusted accordingly, to fit the specific conditions of Korea. This was effectively an insult to both Moscow and Beijing, and it was understood as such.

Park emphasized that *juche* was primarily a political ideology designed to provide legitimacy to the regime.[60] He also pointed to the close integration of the concepts of nation and leader in the new ideology. Under *juche* North Korea was to go its own way in ideology (*juche*), the economy (*charip*), politics (*chaju*), and defense (*chawi*).[61] Such an approach would inevitably involve self-reliance, but it by no means excludes international cooperation. Rather, overly strong dependence on one side was seen as dangerous, given Korea's past and the attempts at domination made by China and the Soviet Union. Accordingly, diversification and balancing are much more at the center of *juche* than autarky and self-isolation.

Most important, the guiding principle of *juche* is the so-called creative methodology. This aspect was designed to enable Kim Il Sung to continue using the old Marxist-Leninist terminology, which he needed in order to benefit from the powerful global position of this ideology at that time, while also doing something very different. Creativity means flexibility, the opposite of orthodoxy. In essence, it means that there are no fixed rules, except that the leader decides how the principles of the orthodox ideology will be correctly adjusted to fit the situation in his allegedly unique country. This opened the way for almost any policy that the leader deemed appropriate. If the leader decided in 1983 that he wanted to transform his impression from a visit to China into practice, he could simply give the order for a Joint Venture Law in 1984 without needing to even consider a change in the official ideology.

When it became clear to Beijing and Moscow around 1960 that they would not be able to treat the DPRK as one of their satellite states, they stopped—or at least dramatically reduced—assistance. Even though the relationship with these two great allies improved later, external support never reached earlier levels. Accordingly, economic policy in the DPRK came to be oriented mainly toward the utilization of domestic resources and the maximization of external inputs. The former includes massive use of the workforce; the so-called mass line is explicitly mentioned in articles 13 and 14 of the constitution (last amended in 2010).

The Mass Line and Early Perfection Measures

The massive use of workforce is not unproblematic, for a number of reasons. It tends to function well for simple manual labor but much less effectively for more qualified tasks. It tends to function better as a short-term measure but loses its effectiveness if the workforce is given time to learn and adjust. In fact, systematic underperformance has been identified as one of the core features of socialist economies.[62] In addition, transaction and opportunity costs can become restrictively high; one example is the use of engineers for farm labor. They have to be trained, transported, housed, and fed. Meanwhile, they are prevented from fulfilling their original tasks.

In 1958, inspired by China's Great Leap, the *ch'ŏllima* movement was introduced in North Korea.[63] The message was simple: work faster. There are various derivations of this principle, like the "see the morning star movement"—that is, getting up earlier in order to work longer—as well as the various "speed battles" ahead of important events, such as the leaders' birthdays, independence day, party congresses, and so forth. Such speed battles, which have been very common, last up to one hundred or even two hundred days. Often, one such campaign has followed another so that the effect, again, quickly disappeared.

In addition to these quantitative methods, some qualitative approaches have proved more successful. The two most prominent ones are both mentioned in the constitution: the *ch'ŏngsanri* method (article 13) and the *taean* work system (article 33). The *ch'ŏngsanri* method was developed by Kim Il Sung during one of his regular on-the-spot guidance sessions in spring 1960, in response to what he identified as bureaucratism and formalism, the typical effects of a settled, or classic, socialist system. The local party officials provided farmers with ideological instructions that were unrelated to the actual farm work. Acknowledging this, the *ch'ŏngsanri* method was aimed at encouraging closer cooperation between the peasants and the leadership of the cooperatives. Instructions would be more practical, and farmers could easily present their suggestions and complaints to the cadres, who would then respond appropriately and promptly. As in other socialist countries, such lofty ideas quickly collided with the reality of a bureaucratic state that was paternalist and averse to forwarding criticism. In many ways, the *ch'ŏngsanri* method reflects the basic dilemma of a socialist economy: the problems can be identified, but solutions can be developed only within the same systemic constraints that led to the emergence of the difficulties in the first place—and that will continue to create problems unless the system itself is fundamentally and radically changed (the latter being Kornai's definition of reform).[64]

The same principle applied to the industry is the *taean* system, developed during an on-the-spot guidance in a factory for electric appliances in 1961. As for the *ch'ŏngsanri* method, the basic idea is quite rational. Management, engineers, and workers are supposed to cooperate closely without the limits of the barriers erected by their workplace hierarchy. The logical way to do this is via the party, in which all members enjoy equal status and are united around one idea. Institutionalizing the participation of all groups within the factory in the planning and implementation process would ensure that no idea gets lost, no concern remains ignored, and no target is omitted. The overarching principle is "one for all, and all for one" (article 63 of the constitution). This recalls the

Chinese principle of the "three equalities," in which party cadres, technicians, and masses were to merge in one single-hearted unity.

The Dilemma of Motivation

There is one more component of the DPRK's economic system that deserves attention: motivation. What makes people work hard—why are they innovative and productive? As I would argue based on personal experience in various socialist systems and on a study of works like Kornai's *The Socialist System*, the setting of a system of proper and sustainable incentives for maximum productivity is one of the key problems in any socialist economy. The limitations of the socialist system rarely come to the fore more clearly. Workers typically do not have access to goods and services based on their actual work performance, expressed in terms of wages. Rather, they are allotted a standard amount of goods by the state, and they need political and social capital (conformity with state requirements, networks, access) to obtain more. Being productive is, at best, only one way of achieving their material and other goals. A similar logic applies to producers. They typically do not face the danger of market exit, and they do not have to deal with competition. Their problem is to find an economical way to respond to the administration's demands for higher production, which they usually try to achieve by cheating (over- or underreporting), by focusing on quantitative indicators while ignoring quality, or by building networks with the higher levels of administration. Ultimately, unlike market economies, which can use a mix of consumerist incentives and fear of job loss or bankruptcy, socialist economic systems, including North Korea's, have very few if any effective means of motivating workers and producers to strive for maximum productivity. Extensive propaganda and increasingly harsh repression are thus typical expressions of a very basic helplessness.

The State Budgets and Fiscal Policy

Among the few economic data that are regularly provided by the DPRK via its news agency, the KCNA, are the annual state budgets. These are reported by a vice premier during the annual session of the Supreme People's Assembly (SPA), the North Korean parliament. Because macroeconomic information is regarded as a state secret by North Korea, these numbers must be taken with a grain of salt. In addition, since 2003, the budget reports have contained only relative numbers (percentages). Analysis is further complicated by the fact that information is not provided on the same issues each year. Table 6 summarizes the data from the budget reports of 2008–2011.

In typical socialist fashion, the data attest continuous growth and overfulfillment of the plan. Expenditure is slightly below the planned amount, whereas revenue exceeds the plan. The percentage officially allocated to the military is stable and relatively low. A few political priorities can be identified, such as the beautification of the capital, Pyongyang, for the one hundredth anniversary of Kim Il Sung's birthday (celebrated in 2012), and the emphasis on science and technology. The latter belongs in the category of perfection measures—that is, attempts to make the socialist system work.

The key to interpreting the overall budget numbers is understanding their relevance in North Korea. Except for the not insignificant part of the economy owned by the military (the "second economy," not to be confused with the shadow economy), and given the absence of any major private sector, the state economy is more or less *the* economy. The state budget is thus not simply a fiscal instrument; it reflects the flow of inputs and outputs in North Korea. The growth of state budgetary revenue is more or less the civilian part of the DPRK's GDP—or at least the perception thereof that the North Korean leadership has or wants to spread. The gap between budgetary expenditure and revenue is the annual state deficit or surplus.

Table 6a. Comparison of the DPRK state budgets, 2008–2009.

	Plan for 2008	Achieved in 2008	Plan for 2009	Achieved in 2009
State budgetary revenue	+4.0%	101.6% +5.7%	+5.2%	101.7% +7.0%
Profits of state enterprises	+4.7%		+5.8%	
Profits of cooperative organizations	+0.4%		+3.1%	
Fixed asset depreciation			+6.1%	
Real estate rent			+3.6%	
Social insurance			+1.6%	
State budgetary expenditure	+2.5%	99.99%	+7.0%	99.8%
Local budgetary revenue		117.1%		
National budgetary revenue				
National defense	15.8%	15.8%	15.8%	15.8%
Priority sectors of the National economy (metal, power, coal, railway)			+8.7%	
Development of science and technology	+6.1%		+8%	+7.2%
Agriculture	+5.5%	+5.4%	+6.9%	NA
Light industry			+5.6%	
Capital construction			+11.5%	
Popular policies				
Education	+4.2%		+8.2%	
Culture and arts			+3.2%	
Public health	+5.9%		+8%	
Sports			+5.8%	

Source. *Compiled by the author based on data from KCNA* (www.kcna.co.jp).

Table 6b. Comparison of the DPRK state budgets, 2010–2011.

	Plan for 2010	**Achieved in 2010**	**Plan for 2011**
State budgetary revenue	+6.3%	101.3% +7.6%	+7.5%
Profits of state enterprises	+7.7%		78.5%
Profits of cooperative organizations	+4.2%		+3.8%
Fixed asset depreciation	+2.5%		+1.4%
Real estate rent	+2%		+0.7%
Social insurance	+1.9%		+0.4%
State budgetary expenditure	+8.3%	99.9%	+8.9%
Local budgetary revenue			16.1%
National budgetary revenue			83.9%
National defense	15.8%	15.8%	15.8%
Priority sectors of the National economy (metal, power, coal, railway)	+7.3%	+8%	+13.5%
Development of science and technology	+8.5%	+8.1%	+10.1%
Agriculture	+9.4%	+9.4%	+9%
Light industry	+10.1%	+10.9%	+12.9%
Capital construction	+8.6%	+12.9%	+15.1%
Popular policies	+6.2%	+6%	
Education			
Culture and arts			
Public health			
Sports			

Source. *Compiled by the author based on data from KCNA (www.kcna.co.jp).*

What would one expect from North Korea? Continuous growth, of course; plan fulfillment at 100 percent or overfulfillment; and a message to the population that everything is just getting better and better. However, this is only partially true, as figures 1 and 2 show. There are two ways to display the annual growth rates for the main budgetary positions: either apply a base value of 100 (%) to a given year, and then apply growth rates annually (figure 1); or simply look at the changing value of the annual growth estimate (figure 2). Stereotypical knowledge about the "manipulative" North Korean state suggests that one should expect a steadily rising curve for figure 1 and a more or less flat or slightly ascending curve in figure 2.[65]

Figure 1. Cumulative Economic Growth in North Korea according to the DPRK Budget (base year 2004 set as 100, annual rates applied).

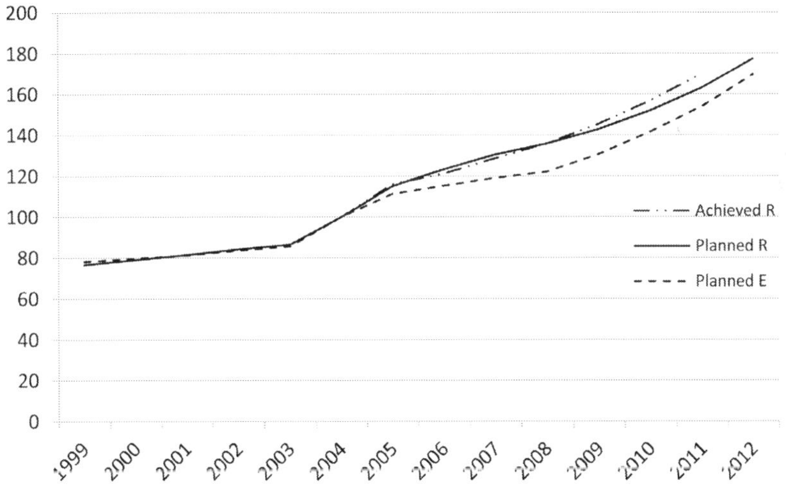

Source. Drawn by the author based on data from KCNA (www.kcna.co.jp).

Figure 1 almost shows what is expected, although one notes the rather sudden increase between 2003 and 2005 and the widening gap between the values for revenue and expenditure after 2005. It also seems that the

North Korean government applies good fiscal discipline because the line for planned expenditures is below the one for revenues.

But if the same data are considered separately rather than cumulatively, a very different picture emerges; figure 2 is quite dynamic, zigzagging up and down. In particular, since 2008 fiscal discipline has apparently been given up; North Korea now deliberately runs a modest deficit, for it plans to spend more than it plans to earn. One sees correlations with political events: the reform period after the June 2000 inter-Korean summit and the July 2002 economic reforms; the reversal after the war on Iraq and in 2005, when the idea of introducing market elements was finally put on hold; the 2008 stroke of Kim Jong Il and the (alleged) continuous growth ever since.

How is one to interpret these data? Taking them as exact GDP growth rates or in any other respect as a precise reflection of reality would be naïve. The value of North Korea's products, of the inputs necessary, and in the end of profitability are not calculable as long as prices are naturally distorted in a centrally planned economy with no money market.

The budget growth rates thus convey something else: the way the North Korean leadership estimates the performance of its economy. Figure 2, with its ups and downs, suggests that this is not just propaganda but more or less the contribution of the North Korean leadership to outsiders' guessing game about numbers. Clearly that is not the final answer on the GDP question, but it is certainly something one should contrast with other insights.

According to figure 2, the self-perception of economic growth was relatively moderate until 2002; suddenly a dramatic increase takes place that reflects the high hopes pinned on the July 2002 economic measures. Was it the failure of these measures or the changed priorities, after the United States fully embarked on its "war against terror" with the 2003 Iraq invasion, that resulted in the drop a year later?

Figure 2. Economic Growth in North Korea According to the DPRK Budget and the Bank of Korea (annual growth rates in %).

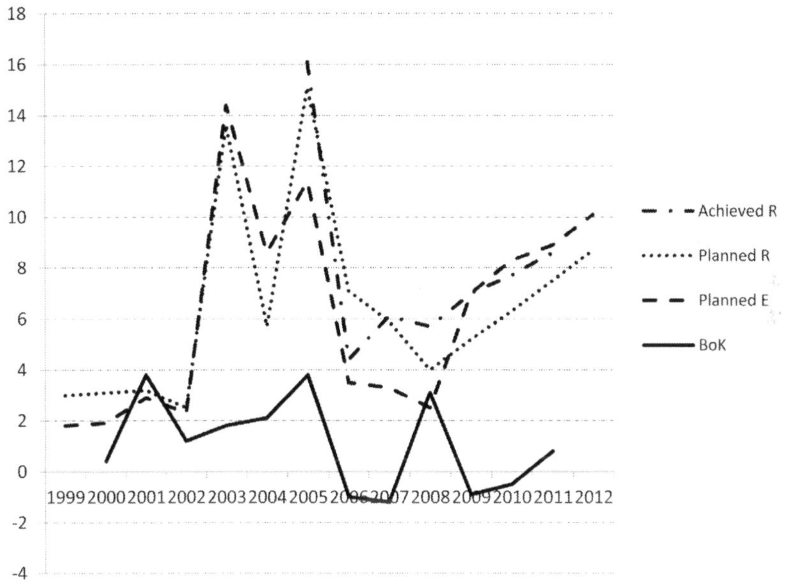

Source. Compiled based on data from KCNA (www.kcna.co.jp).

One can only speculate why 2005 shows another peak of optimism before 2006—the year of the first nuclear test—when expectations of economic performance dropped as suddenly as they had jumped a few years earlier. From 2008 the rates grew more steadily. The reform period and its enthusiasm had faded, and a more conservative outlook seems to have taken hold. This is interesting to note because 2008 was the year of Kim Jong Il's stroke, a time when the leader was probably less effective and others had to take on greater responsibility. Note also that from 2008, achieved revenue is greater than planned revenue—a typical feature of orthodox socialist planning that regards overfulfillment of the plan as a key indicator of success. I have called this *socialist neoconservatism.*[66] Furthermore, from about the same time, planned expenditure grew at a higher rate than planned revenue did. Without absolute numbers, and looking at the opposite relationship between the two indicators in figure 1, one should be careful interpreting this as a deliberate policy of deficit spending. But if the latter is the case, one should ask where the funds to bridge this gap originate. To be extremely speculative, one could even argue that a new reform period is imminent, with official growth rates reaching 2003 levels.

Figure 2 also includes the North Korean GDP growth estimates by the Bank of Korea. In absolute terms, these are much lower than the North Korean data. But remarkably, the correlation coefficient for this South Korean estimate and North Korea's officially announced achieved revenue from 2005 to 2011 is relatively high ($r = 0.65$).[67] In other words, although both sides seem to differ about the amount of growth, at least there is some moderately strong agreement about its general direction.

CHALLENGES

In the North Korean economy, planning is centralized, economic processes are steered and coordinated via the bureaucracy, information about inputs and outputs and control over the economic performance of production units are in the hands of state authorities, and the system of motivation is ineffective. Knowledge and understanding of these mechanisms and their outcomes is crucial to exploring possible alternative policies. Typically, the leadership in socialist systems is keenly aware of the status of its economy but at the same time reluctant to acknowledge the systemic nature of these difficulties. It usually reacts with what Kornai called perfection measures; the *ch'ŏngsanri* method and the *taean* system are examples.

However, such responses do not provide lasting solutions. Many socialist systems have been unable to bear the pressure and have collapsed; only a few, including most prominently China, have found a way to transform their economic systems into de facto incentive-based market economies though they remain officially socialist. Will North Korea be able to repeat the Chinese success, or is it doomed to fail, as its Eastern European counterparts did? As indicated by figure 1, something has happened since about 2002, although it has not lasted. What was it? Will it happen again? In the following chapter, I explore the issue of a systemic change of the North Korean economy.

Endnotes

1. See Rudiger Frank, "Can Economic Theory Demystify North Korea?" *Korea Review of International Studies* 9, no. 1 (2006): 3–26.
2. Oliver E. Williamson, "The New Institutional Economics: Taking Stock, Looking Ahead," *Journal of Economic Literature* 38, no. 3 (2000): 595–613.
3. For a detailed discussion of the applicability of standard economic theory on North Korea, see Frank, "Can Economic Theory Demystify North Korea?"
4. Statistics Korea, *Pukhanŭi chuyo t'onggye chip'yo* [Main statistical indicators of North Korea] (Taejŏn: Korea National Statistics Office, 2011), 104, 106.
5. Hermann Lautensach, *Korea: A Geography Based on the Author's Travel and Literature* (Berlin: Springer Verlag, 1945/1988), 445.
6. Lautensach, *Korea*, 67, 447–449.
7. Drew Thompson, *Silent Partners: Chinese Joint Ventures in North Korea* (Washington, DC: US–Korea Institute, 2011), 53.
8. IFES, *Transfer of Management Rights to Chinese Investment Companies within North Korea* (Seoul: Institute for Far Eastern Studies, 2011).
9. United States Geological Survey, *2007 Minerals Yearbook: North Korea* (Washington, DC: US Department of the Interior, USGS, 2008), http://www.nkeconwatch.com/nk-uploads/usgs-dprk.pdf.
10. Edward Yoon, *Status and Future of the North Korean Minerals Sector* (San Francisco: Nautilus Institute, 2011), 6.
11. Statistics Korea, *Pukhanŭi chuyo t'onggye chip'yo*, 12.
12. Lautensach, *Korea*, 85.
13. Ibid., 93.
14. Ibid., 172.
15. For a more detailed discussion, see Rudiger Frank, "Classical Socialism in North Korea and its Transformation: The Role and the Future of Agriculture," *Harvard Asia Quarterly* 10/2 (2006): 15–33.
16. Kitchen-garden production is mainly for household consumption. About 57 percent of the public distribution system (PDS)–dependent population have kitchen gardens with an average size of 53 square meters; nearly all coop farmers have a kitchen garden, with an average size of 79 square meters. Food and Agriculture Organization of the United Nations, *FAO/*

WFP Crop and Food Supply Assessment Mission to the Democratic People's Republic of Korea (Rome: FAO, 2004).

17. FAO, *FAO/WFP Crop and Food Supply Assessment.*
18. Stephan Haggard and Marcus Noland, *Famine in North Korea: Markets, Aid, and Reform* (New York: Columbia University Press, 2007), 25; Statistics Korea, *Pukhanŭi chuyo t'onggye chip'yo*, 105.
19. FAO, *FAO/WFP Crop and Food Supply Assessment.*
20. Statistics Korea, *Pukhanŭi chuyo t'onggye chip'yo*, 24.
21. FAO, *FAO/WFP Crop and Food Supply Assessment.*
22. Statistics Korea, *Pukhanŭi chuyo t'onggye chip'yo*, 22.
23. According to Statistics Korea, the number was 1.99 million; ibid., 23.
24. See FAO, *FAO/WFP Crop and Food Supply Assessment.*
25. Haggard and Noland, *Famine in North Korea*, 3.
26. Janos Kornai, *The Socialist System: The Political Economy of Communism* (Princeton, NJ: Princeton University Press, 1992).
27. Randall Ireson, *Food Security in North Korea: Designing Realistic Possibilities* (Stanford, CA: Shorenstein APARC, 2006), http://iis-db.stanford.edu/pubs/21046/Ireson_FoodSecurity_2006.pdf.
28. FAO, *FAO/WFP Crop and Food Supply Assessment.*
29. South Korean sources attest a *sijanghwa* ("marketization") since July 2002. Statistics Korea, *Pukhanŭi chuyo t'onggye chip'yo*, 107.
30. Good Friends, http://www.goodfriends.or.kr.
31. Sandra Fahy, "Turning Points in the Experience of Famine: Survivor Testimony from the Democratic People's Republic of Korea" (unpublished manuscript, School of Oriental and African Studies, London, 2008), 2; quoting Sue Lautze, *The Famine in North Korea: Humanitarian Responses in Communist Nations* (Somerville, MA: Feinstein International Famine Center, Tufts University, 1997), 8, http://repository.forcedmigration.org/show_metadata.jsp?pid = fmo:1744.
32. See Cho Myung-chul, *Kyŏngjegwalli kaesŏn choch'i hyŏnhwang p'yŏnggawa kwaje: Pukhan kyŏngje kaehyŏgŭi chŏnmang* [Prospects for North Korea's economic reform: A study on the economic administration adjustment and its performance] (Seoul: Korea Institute for International Economic Policy, 2003).
33. My calculation. See Rudiger Frank, "Economic Reforms in North Korea (1998–2004): Systemic Restrictions, Quantitative Analysis, Ideological Background," *Journal of the Asia Pacific Economy* 10, no. 3 (2005): 278–311.

34. See Rudiger Frank, "Money in Socialist Economies: The Case of North Korea," *Asia-Pacific Journal* (February 2010), http://japanfocus.org/-Ruediger-Frank/3307.
35. Stephan Haggard and Marcus Noland, "Famine in North Korea Redux?" (Peterson Institute. Working Paper WP08-9. Washington, DC: Peterson Institute for International Economics), 5ff.
36. Haggard and Noland, *Famine in North Korea*, 35.
37. Haggard and Noland, "Famine in North Korea Redux?" 25.
38. Rudiger Frank, "The Political Economy of Sanctions against North Korea," *Asian Perspective* 30/3 (2006): 5–36, http://www.asianperspective.org/articles/v30n3-b.pdf.
39. Gerhard A. Ritter, *Der Preis der Deutschen Einheit: Die Wiedervereinigung und die Krise des Sozialstaates* [The price of unity: Unification and the crisis of the welfare state] (München: C. H. Beck, 2007); Karl-Heinz Paqué, *Die Bilanz: Eine wirtschaftliche Analyse der Deutschen Einheit* [German unification: An economic analysis] (München: Hanser Verlag, 2009).
40. I have visited North Korea numerous times since 1991 and have observed a strong preference for imported products. These were mostly made in Japan in the early 1990s, and these were replaced by Chinese products in the twenty-first century. Comments made to me by personal contacts in North Korea point to disesteem for local products.
41. Lautensach, *Korea*, 451; Rudiger Frank, *The GDR and North Korea: The Reconstruction of Hamhŭng, 1954–1962* (Aachen: Shaker, 1996).
42. Statistics Korea, *Pukhanŭi chuyo t'onggye chip'yo*, 20.
43. See Marcus Noland, *Avoiding the Apocalypse: The Future of the Two Koreas* (Washington, DC: Institute for International Economics, 2000), 59ff.
44. Andrea Matles Savada, ed. *North Korea: A Country Study* (Washington, DC: GPO for the Library of Congress, 1993).
45. The literacy rate is close to 100 percent; all children receive a compulsory education from kindergarten through elementary, middle, and high school. In 2009 North Korea had 212 university students per ten thousand citizens (South Korea had 630). Statistics Korea, *Pukhanŭi chuyo t'onggye chip'yo*, 61.
46. Frank, *The GDR and North Korea*.
47. For a discussion of sanctions against the DPRK and their effectiveness, see Frank, "Political Economy." For updated reports on sanctions, see Nikitin, Mary Beth, Emma Chanlett-Avery, Mark Manyin, Dick K.

Nanto, Dianne Rennack, and MiAe Taylor, *Implementation of UN Security Council Resolution 1874* (Special Report, November 11, 2010, Washington, DC, Congressional Research Service, 2010); and Karin Lee and Julia Choi, *North Korea: Unilateral and Multilateral Economic Sanctions and U.S. Department of Treasury Actions, 1955–April 2009* (Washington, DC: National Committee on North Korea, 2009).

48. Nicholas Eberstadt, *The North Korean Economy: Between Crisis and Catastrophe* (New Brunswick: Transaction, 2007), 287, 288, 303. Eberstadt gathered trade data for the period 1977–2005; his analysis confirms the picture shown by table 5—namely, that North Korea's ratio of imports to exports has constantly been above 100 percent.
49. Mark Manyin and Mary Beth Nikitin, *Foreign Assistance to North Korea* (Washington, DC: Congressional Research Service, 2011).
50. Eberstadt, *North Korean Economy*, 287ff.
51. KOTRA, *2009 Pukhanŭi taewoemuyŏk tonghyang* [Trends in North Korean trade, 2009] (KOTRA Paper 10-038 (Seoul: Korea Trade and Investment Promotion Agency, 2010).
52. The actual and the potential roles played by Russia in North Korea are heavily underestimated in the West. See, for example, A. Panin and W. Altov, *Severnaya Koreya: Epocha Kim chen ira na zakate* [North Korea: The Kim Jong Il epoch heading south] (Moscow: Olma Press, 2004).
53. H. Jörg Thieme, "Wirtschaftssysteme," in *Vahlens Kompendium der Wirtschaftstheorie und Wirtschaftspolitik*, Band 1, ed. D. Bender (München: Franz Vahlen, 1992), 1–17.
54. Kornai, *Socialist System.*
55. For more details, see Haksoon Paik, *Pukhan kwŏllyŏgŭi yŏksa: Sasang, chŏngch'esŏng, kujo* [The history of power in North Korea: Ideas, identities, and structures] (Seoul: Hanul Academy, 2010).
56. John Jorganson, "Tan'gun and the Legitimization of a Threatened Dynasty: North Korea's Rediscovery of Tan'gun," *Korea Observer* 27 (1996): 282.
57. Dae-Sook Suh, *Kim Il Sung: The North Korean Leader* (New York, Columbia University Press, 1988), 313.
58. Brian R. Myers, "The Watershed that Wasn't: Re-Evaluating Kim Il Sung's '*Juche* Speech' of 1955," *Acta Koreana* 9/1 (January 2006): 89–115.
59. Kim Jong Il, *On the History of Juche: Treatise Sent to the National Seminar on the Juche Idea Held to Mark the 70th Birthday of the Great Leader Comrade Kim Il Sung, March 31, 1982*, http://www3.cnet-ta.ne.jp/j/juche/

pdf/e-works1.pdf; Kim Jong Il, *The Guiding Principles of the Juche Idea* (1982), http://www3.cnet-ta.ne.jp/j/juche/pdf/e-works4.pdf.

60. Han S. Park, *North Korea: Ideology, Politics, Economy* (Englewood Cliffs, NJ: Prentice-Hall, 1996), 10.
61. See Suh, *Kim Il Sung*, 303ff.
62. Kornai, *Socialist System*.
63. *Ch'ŏllima* means "1000-*ri*-horse" and refers to a magical winged animal that, according to a popular legend, was able to travel a huge distance in just one day.
64. Kornai, *Socialist System*, 386.
65. "Achieved expenditure" has not been considered in the graphs because data are scattered and the value seems to be more or less congruent with planned expenditure for the respective year.
66. Rudiger Frank, "Socialist Neo-Conservatism in North Korea? A Return to Old Principles in the 2008 New Year Joint Editorial," *Napsnet Policy Forum Online* 08-032 (2008), http://www.nautilus.org.
67. Pearson's product-moment coefficient indicates the strength of linear dependence between two variables, ranging from −1 (very strong inverse correlation), to 0 (negligible), to 1 (very strong positive correlation).

Chapter 3

Reforming the North Korean Economy

Understanding Reform and Transformation through the CRE Model

Rudiger Frank

Chronic shortages of food and electricity, an aging transportation network, and an underdeveloped consumer-goods industry are several of the most visible signs of a typically inefficient socialist economy. What are the options and prospects for economic reform in North Korea? What evidence is existent so far, and how can this be integrated into a systematic analysis?

I present the comprehensive reform equation (CRE) model as the analytical core of this chapter. The study examines the successes and failures of the first reform, around 2002, and attempts to understand why there has been a return to orthodox North Korean state socialist positions in ideology and economic policy since about 2005, which I call the neoconservative turn. I believe that this stage will soon be followed by another reform attempt, and thus in the final section of this chapter, I outline a few possible trajectories based on an understanding of the North Korean system, its limitations, and its options. At the end, the reader will hopefully have gained a better understanding of where the North Korean economy comes from and where it is heading.

The Comprehensive Reform Equation

Chapter 2 demonstrates that there is much more information available on North Korea and its economy than is usually assumed. Nevertheless, much still remains in the dark. Against this background, and given that most scholars failed to predict the transformation of socialist systems elsewhere, I suggest caution when discussing the options for reform in North Korea. I thus start from an abstract perspective (box 1) and then add more detail on the single issues.

Despite its many obvious weaknesses and failures, the North Korean system has survived for over sixty years. One reason is that it created not only losers but also winners. By definition, these hold powerful positions within the system. The probability of reforms (p_R), defined as systemic changes rather than perfection measures, is thus determined by the balance of reform support (s_R) and reform opposition (o_R); if the balance is positive, reforms are more likely. Reform support will grow if the expectation of gains from reform (g_R) rises and if the losses from the old system (l_O) increase. This could happen because of a famine, but it could also occur if the leadership's legitimacy is weakened. External pressure (e) can function as a catalyst here. Reform opposition will weaken if the gains from supporting the current system (g_O) decrease or if the anticipated losses (l_R) of a new system are small. The relative weight of the supporters of the old and the new system is expressed by their influence (i_o for opponents and i_s for supporters). All these causalities can be summarized in a set of equations (box 1).

Figure 3. The comprehensive reform equation (CRE) for North Korea.

$p_R = s_R - o_R$	p_R: probability of reform
$s_R = f(e, g_R, l_O) \cdot i_s$	s_R: support of reform
$o_R = f(g_O, l_R) \cdot i_o$	o_R: opposition to reform
$i_o + i_s = 1$	e: external pressure
i_o: share of influence of reform opponents	g_O: gains from the old system
i_s: share of influence of reform supporters	g_R: anticipated gains from reform
	l_O: losses from the old system
	l_R: anticipated losses from reform
$p_R = f(e, g_R, l_O) \cdot i_s - f(g_O, l_R) \cdot i_o$	

Source. Developed by the author.

The quantification of the single variables seems illusory; the value of the CRE model thus lies primarily in the explanation of the systemic relationship of various factors that are in the literature often treated either separately or consecutively without considering their interrelatedness. The next section provides several suggestions for applying the CRE model fruitfully.

Application of the CRE model

Proreform

If the normative goal is to achieve a transformation in North Korea, this means maximizing the absolute value of a positive p_R (probability of reform). Such a goal can of course be achieved by maximizing s_R

(reform support); this seems to be the standard Western strategy. What is often ignored, however, is the option of minimizing opposition to reform (o_R). In particular, minimizing l_R (anticipated losses from reform) seems promising, for it affects the current elite and thus a politically powerful group. The example of Eastern Europe suggests to North Korean cadres that in case of a transformation, they risk losing their social status, if not more. Those who assume that this transformation could be connected to Korean unification are worried about signs of reassurance from Seoul. This includes concerns about property rights (because most former landowners and their descendants live in South Korea and are ready to reclaim their lost property) and the fate of the military, which so far has to fear legal charges after unification.

The policy of economic sanctions against North Korea targeted at reducing access to luxury items, as promoted in the context of United Nations (UN) Security Council resolution 1718 after the nuclear test of 2006, would from this perspective have to be interpreted as an attempt at reducing g_O (gains from the old system), although it is debatable whether the supporters of the regime maintain their support because of the occasional gift of a bottle of cognac.

The functionality of *e* (external pressure) is not necessarily self-explanatory. It can lead to a rally-round-the-flag phenomenon and thus contribute to a stabilization of the old system. Therefore, it seems risky to rely too much on *e* when it comes to reform promotion.

The effect of an increase of l_O (losses from the old system) depends on who is affected, expressed by i_S (share of influence of reform supporters) in my equation. As long as the negative effects of the current system can be minimized by external assistance and by limiting them to less powerful parts of the population, their influence on p_R will be too small to trigger a change. The CRE model can thus be an argument against and in favor of food aid. On the one hand, aid does reduce the negative effects of the current system and thus weakens the drive toward reform; on the other hand, as long as the absence of food aid affects only the less politically powerful parts of North Korea's population, aid will have a minimal effect.

Among the more proactive strategies of reform promotion is the maximization of g_R (anticipated gains from reform). This seems to be the strategy of China when it shows North Korean visitors the success of China's economic policies of the past decades. However, as the experience of the South Korean government implies, not all efforts toward increasing g_R will be welcomed, especially if they are too blunt. In 2008 South Korean president Lee Myung Bak announced a plan called "Vision 3000 through Denuclearization and Openness,"[1] promising to raise the North Korean gross domestic product (GDP) to USD 3,000 per capita if the North fulfilled a number of conditions. The response was sheer outrage; as I can confirm through personal contacts, this was not only an official reaction but also reflected the opinion of at least certain parts of the North Korean population.

A remarkable development to reduce l_R (anticipated losses from reform) and increase g_R (anticipated gains from reform) on the ideological side was the military-first policy (*sŏn'gun chŏngch'i*, usually referred to as *songun*). In addition to the obvious focus on military affairs and the (re)definition of self-defense as the top priority of North Korea, *songun* stressed that the working class was to come second to the military in this new era:

> In the past, it was recognized as an unbreakable formula in socialist politics to put forth the working class. However, the theory and formula that was generated one and a half centuries ago cannot be applicable to today's reality.[2]

In addition to its rather open blow at *The Communist Manifesto* (published in 1848), the ideological catch to such a statement is that though the working class is an economically determined entity, *military* is a political term that can be defined almost at will. Statements like this one prepared the ideological ground for running a market socialist society in the Democratic People's Republic of Korea (DPRK). The reforms would create entrepreneurs—but these are in fact capitalists, by definition enemies of the people, and hence not to be tolerated in a socialist country. This dilemma still exists in China; *songun* would have resolved it for North Korea.

Antireform

To take the opposite perspective, it seems fair to assume that a conservative North Korean government wants to keep p_R (reform probability) strictly negative. It will therefore try to minimize s_R (reform support) by maintaining a certain minimal level of economic performance, actively countering external pressure and minimizing the influence of proreform forces. It will also maximize o_R (reform opposition) by increasing the gains of the current system for key groups of the population, making sure they perceive the losses associated with reform as high and the gains as low, and by ensuring that their relative power is greater than the power of potential proreform forces. The government might also try to reduce the number of those suffering under the current system.

The CRE model can be used to explain why the North Korean system did not collapse despite the many crises it has undergone, including the virtual breakdown of trade after the dissolution of the socialist bloc, the death of Kim Il Sung in 1994, and the famine of 1995–1997. Obviously, the proreform effects of these shocks were either balanced by antireform developments or were not big enough to create a situation in which $s_R > o_R$. The latter option includes the possibility that despite a growth of l_O and e, the uneven distribution of power ($i_o > i_s$) ensured that reform support was small enough to be offset by reform opposition.

This circumstance points to an interesting implication of the CRE model: if all variables are kept constant, the balance between s_R and o_R can be influenced by changing the relation between i_o and i_s. This is how one could interpret, for example, the restrictions on market activities introduced since 2005, including a minimum age for female traders and the currency reform of December 2009, which aimed to expropriate the middle class and force it back into the realm of the state-controlled economy.[3]

Obviously, the CRE model has a large number of practical implications for policy making. I return to this in the final section of this chapter, after a short discussion of the economic policies that can be observed in the past decade.

First Signs of Reform

Providing a full account of the reform process that North Korea has experienced in the past decade is beyond the scope of this chapter.[4] Rather, I demonstrate that such a process has taken place at all, discuss what triggered it, what ended it, and what might lead to another round of reforms. This analysis is based on the assumption that the orthodox North Korean system is unable to provide a sustainable solution to the economic challenges the country is facing, including the food issue.

The first signs of a changed reality in North Korea emerged in connection with the food crisis in 1995–1997, although certain measures, such as the Joint Venture Law, date back to 1984. The state could not keep its part of the societal contract—providing food through the public distribution system (PDS)—and therefore, it seems, in return did not insist on all the rules it had set for its citizens. Among the new freedoms thus acquired were intensified travel to China, mainly by those who lived nearby; a certain relaxation of the harsh restrictions regarding domestic travel within North Korea;[5] and increased tolerance toward the exchange of goods on the farmers' markets.

This must have been a shocking experience for the new leadership under Kim Jong Il, who succeeded his father in 1994, just one year before the crisis. It took Pyongyang a while to come up with a reaction. The first step was a constitutional change in 1998. It not only elevated the deceased Kim Il Sung to the status of eternal president but also included a number of amendments that pointed in the direction of carefully increasing economic freedom and raising the relevance of indirect macroeconomic policy tools for managing the economy (articles 24 and 33). Also in 1998, for the first time since the division, South Korean tourists were allowed into North Korea, arriving via ship in the scenic region of Mt. Kŭmgang. In 2002 this region received separate administrative status, and in 2003 a land route was opened.

In June 2000 the first summit meeting with a South Korean president took place in Pyongyang, during which economic cooperation played a major role and the establishment of an inter-Korean industrial zone near Kaesŏng was decided. The zone was opened in 2004 and by 2009 had resulted in the employment of about 42,000 North Korean workers, who interacted on a daily basis with about 1,000 South Koreans in 117 enterprises.[6]

A few months after the summit, in a rare direct address to his people on January 4, 2001, Kim Jong Il wrote the following in *Rodong Sinmun*:

> Things are not what they used to be in the 1960s. So no one should follow the way people used to do things in the past.... We should make constant efforts to renew the landscape to replace the one which was formed in the past, to meet the requirements of the new era.[7]

Two years later, *Rodong Sinmun*'s report on the budget discussion in parliament stressed that "functionaries for economic guidance shall free themselves from the old viewpoints of the past era."[8] This new ideological trend was particularly remarkable because during the famine Kim Jong Il had made very conservative statements calling for staying the course and not repeating the mistakes made by the comrades in Eastern Europe.[9]

The July 2002 Measures

The most significant step in what I regard as a more or less coordinated reform effort came in July 2002. The measures of July 2002 consisted of a far-reaching price reform, although as far as I know, it was limited to a small number of goods and services. Not only was the degree of the price adjustments significant, but also the relation of prices between the single goods was changed, and a heavy subsidy on rice (measured as the balance between procurement price and retail price) was abolished. Table 7 summarizes the changes.

Table 7. July 2002 changes in North Korea's state-set price system.

	Old (won)	New (won)	Nominal change (times)
Rice (kg)	0.080	44.0	550.00
Corn (kg)	0.490	20.0	40.82
Electricity (kWh)	0.035	1.8	51.43
Bus fare	0.100	2.0	20.00
Basic wages	110.000	2,000.0	18.18
Special wages		6,000.0	54.55
Rice procurement	0.800	40.0	50.00
1 US dollar	2.190	150.0	68.49

Source. Rudiger Frank, "Economic Reforms in North Korea (1998–2004): Systemic Restrictions, Quantitative Analysis, Ideological Background," *Journal of the Asia Pacific Economy* 10, no. 3 (2005): 278–311.

The price reforms corrected a distorted price structure and eliminated a heavy subsidy on food. To a certain degree, elements of a market mechanism were introduced. Wage discrimination led to rewarding harder or more valuable labor with substantially higher wages and even an increase in purchasing power, provided the new wages were indeed paid. This turned out to be a problem, so the reform was ultimately incomplete and triggered hefty inflation that quickly eliminated or distorted all the intended signals.

The reforms included an official devaluation of the domestic currency, a very unusual step for a socialist country. North Korea was preparing to participate more actively in international trade based on a realistic valuation of the won (KPW). This step went hand in hand with the abolition of the so-called foreign exchange certificates. China had done this in 1994—earlier than North Korea, but fifteen years after beginning its own reforms.

The most significant domestic effect of the July 2002 reforms was the legalization of the market on a broad scale, especially for staple food. Obviously following the Chinese example, which had been studied intensively in Pyongyang, improvement of economic efficiency and output levels was to start with agriculture. The effects of introducing decentralized coordination through markets had been impressive in China and in Vietnam. Not only did the output of staple food grow rapidly, but also a large-scale industrial development started with the rural industries, the champions of economic development in China in the 1980s.[10]

These reforms had worked so well in China and Vietnam because of a huge hidden productive potential in agriculture, which at the time of reform was the major sector of both countries' national economies. However, as seen in chapter 2, this could not work in North Korea, where agriculture contributed only about 20 percent to the gross national income (GNI). Productivity gains affected only a minority of the populations positively, whereas the majority had to face higher food prices (and stagnant real incomes). The result was high inflation of about 200 percent annually for staple food on the markets.

Failure of the Reforms

The problems started soon after the introduction of the July 2002 measures. An unprecedented summit meeting between Kim Jong Il and Japan's prime minister, Koizumi Junichiro, in September 2002 was expected to lead directly to the normalization of relations between the two neighbors and to large reparation payments.[11] In return, Kim Jong Il admitted to the previously adamantly denied abduction of Japanese citizens in the 1970s, apologized, and even allowed the repatriation of five survivors. The reaction of the Japanese public, however, made any normalization with the DPRK impossible unless satisfactory evidence was provided concerning the destinies of other possible abductees. Because Pyongyang was not willing or not able to satisfy these demands, bilateral relations cooled and reached an almost historic low, as evidenced by the trade figures as discussed in chapter 2.[12]

North Korea tried to save its reforms by various means, including the hasty opening of a special economic zone on its northeastern border with China, which failed within a matter of days when the furious Chinese, who had not been informed, arrested the head of the zone on charges of tax evasion. An attempt at fighting inflation by introducing bonds in order to reduce the money supply in early 2003—the first time since the Korean War—also failed. In spring 2003, the farmers' markets were renamed "markets," and the range of tradable goods was expanded to include virtually everything, including industrial goods. However, this was already a coping measure and not part of a well-structured reform blueprint. Accordingly, it failed to deliver economic turnaround but nevertheless undermined the state's dominance and threatened social stability. After a few more months, North Korean leaders decided to backpedal and reintroduce the state's dominant coordinating role in the economy.

Seen from a global perspective, North Korea's reform timing was not very fortunate. The United States was preparing for war after 9/11, and a policy of zero tolerance against so-called rogue states limited the degree to which these could hope to be welcomed as economic partners. In desperation, as I would argue, the North Korean leaders returned to a tactic that had been effective in 1994: they played the nuclear card again in October 2002. The blackmail attempt failed this time, worsening the situation by interrupting hopeful signs of international cooperation from the European Union and inviting a new wave of sanctions. Ever since, the international environment has been difficult for North Korea, with the exception of a supportive South Korean government between 1998 and early 2008.

Applying the CRE model presented earlier, one finds that the reforms were triggered by a reduction of g_O (gains from the old system) and a decrease of i_o (share of influence of reform opponents). They failed because g_R (anticipated gains from reform) declined owing to inflation and because the leadership saw its l_R (anticipated losses from reform) grow as the state lost economic and political power to the private sector. With inflation reaching critical levels, one could even argue, for the urban population g_O (gains from the old system) had grown again because it at least provided them a stable amount of food through the PDS. The role of e (external pressure) has in this case clearly proved detrimental to reform probability.

In this situation, the state pulled the emergency brake. It reduced the role of markets, strengthened state distribution, and stepped up an ideological campaign that I call *socialist neoconservatism*, marking a (temporary) return to orthodox prereform positions of North Korean socialism.

Socialist Neoconservatism

One can only speculate on the reasons why such a policy change has happened. There are various possibilities. It could be argued that the reform period, roughly covering the time between the first inter-Korean summit of 2000 and the year 2005, was itself a deviation from the rule and that now one simply sees a return to the normal state of affairs.

The reform could have been a mere perfection measure and thus did not last long. Furthermore, external factors could have played a major role interrupting the reform process. These include the absence of expected normalization-related financial support from Japan, the heightened security concerns because of the US war on terror, the new government in Seoul after 2008, and the heavy burden of economic sanctions, among them the highly symbolic freezing of North Korean assets at Banco Delta Asia in 2005. Finally, domestic factors could have had a major impact. These include a leadership crisis because of Kim Jong Il's health issues, a fight for power between supporters and opponents of reform within the leadership, and the disintegrative effects of the reforms on ideological and political consciousness, as well as on stability. A mix of all these seems the most likely explanation.

Whatever the reasons, my analysis of official media supports the conclusion that North Korea experienced a major political return to orthodox positions. These include the "historic victory" of socialism and its "invincibility," as well as "self-reliance," "independence," and "Korean-style socialism." To illustrate this, I offer a quantitative analysis of articles published on the website of the Korean Central News Agency (KCNA), the country's official news bureau.[13]

Figure 4 shows that the use of *socialism* dropped to almost half of the 1997 levels after 2000 but has risen strongly since 2006. The nationalist term *juche* had reached unprecedented heights by 2010.

Figure 5 illustrates how the policy change was reflected in titles used to address Kim Jong Il on the KCNA website. Contrary to what official propagandists would like to make readers believe, the military titles General (*chang'gun*) and Supreme Commander (*ch'oego saryŏnggwan*) played almost no role. In 2001 one observes a switch from the spiritual title General Secretary (*ch'ongbisŏ*) to the more worldly title Great Leader (*widaehan ryŏngdoja*). In 2006 the trend reversed again.[14]

Figure 4. KCNA articles with the terms *socialism*, *juche*, and *songun* (1997–2010, weighted).

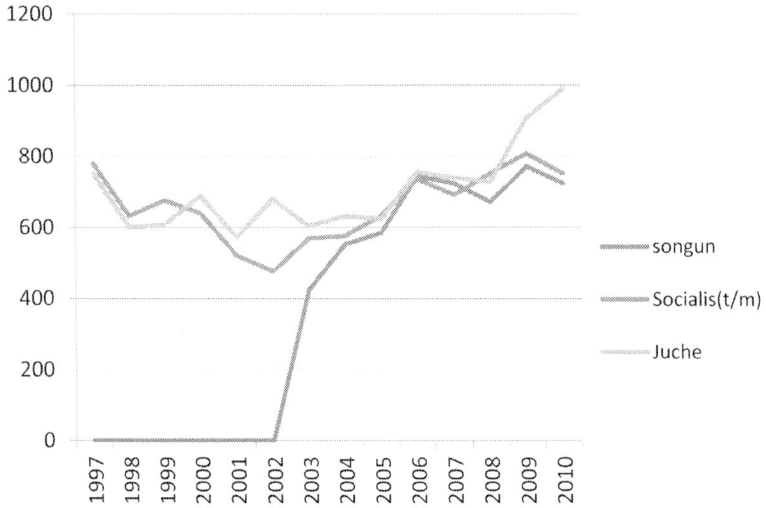

Source. Author's calculations, based on data from KCNA (www.kcna.co.jp).

Among the most significant expressions of the neoconservative trend in North Korea's economic policy was the return to a paradigm that was at least half a century old. In December 2008, Kim Jong Il initiated what I call *ch'ŏllima II*, a movement reminiscent of the North Korean version of the Chinese Great Leap Forward and officially termed the "Great Revolutionary Upsurge" (*hyŏngmyŏngjŏk taegojo*). The original *ch'ŏllima* movement was started by Kim Il Sung during an on-the-spot guidance session at the Kangsŏn Steel Complex in 1958. It was less extreme than the Chinese example but exhibited the typical rationale of classical socialism: in the absence of capital and other resources, labor was to be utilized extensively, bringing into play ideology as a motivator and, less openly stated, the repressive system of the socialist state.

Figure 5. KCNA articles with Kim Jong Il's titles (1997–2010, weighted).

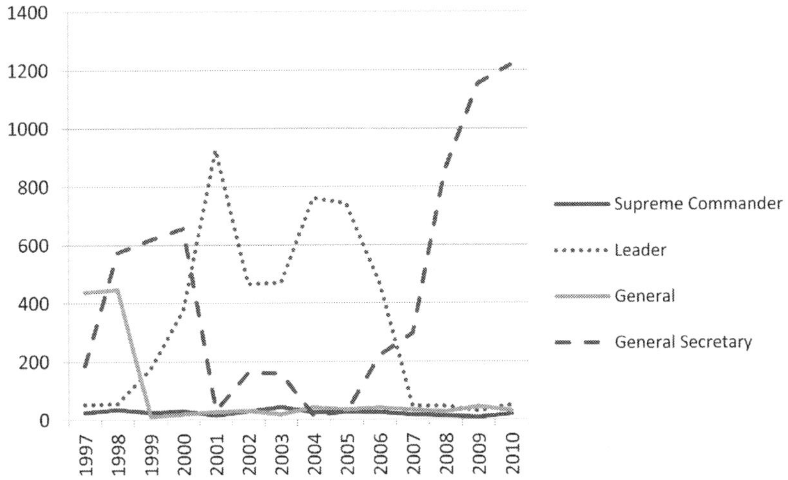

Source. Author's calculations based on data from KCNA (www.kcna.co.jp).

The preparations for such a movement were already visible early in the year 2008. On March 9, *Rodong Sinmun* marked the tenth anniversary of a "work harder campaign" called the Torch of Sŏnggang, initiated by Kim Jong Il during an on-the-spot guidance at the steel mill at Sŏnggang in north Hamgyŏng Province. A few days later, on March 24, *Rodong Sinmun* urged that all people should make a leaping advance in building a socialist economic power, applying the vim and vigor with which they had brought about the "Great Ch'ŏllima Upswing" in the latter half of the 1950s. Readers were informed that through the spirit of *ch'ŏllima*, the work-harder campaign of 1958, North Korea had been able to complete its industrialization in only fourteen years. On May 15, *Rodong Sinmun* stressed that more propaganda and agitation work would help achieve economic success and a leap forward, as in the 1950s and 1970s. On October 20, a KCNA article quoted premier Kim Yong Il as stressing the importance of applying socialist principles in operating the economy and as referring to a thesis by Kim Jong Il on this issue. According to

KCNA, the participants discussed how to "strengthen political control and supervision of economic management, while emphasizing ways of triggering the masses' collective spirit."[15]

On November 22, 2008, KCNA published an editorial to remind readers of the "*kanggye* spirit" shown by Kim Jong Il ten years earlier during the famine, the period known as the Arduous March in North Korea. It praised the people in Chagang Province, who "are not interested in increasing individual wealth," so nobody should "think of whining, dependency on others, fantasies of money and trends pursuing capitalism."[16] In early December, calls to adhere to a socialist economy were renewed. A piece in *Rodong Sinmun* declared that the current situation made sticking to socialist economic principles even more imperative than it had been at any other time. But the key event that launched *ch'ŏllima II* was Kim Jong Il's visit to Kangsŏn, the home of the original *ch'ŏllima*, on December 24, 2008. The workers there adopted a letter that was later used as an example and source of inspiration all over the country.[17] The key phrase in this context is *great (revolutionary) upsurge*, which can be understood as synonymous with *ch'ŏllima II*. Economic nationalism had once again become the policy of the day.

Looking at figure 4, one again notes the reform period 2000–2005 and its end. What is also notable is a decrease in economic nationalist language in 2010. It is yet too early to tell whether this marks a new trend and probably the beginning of a new reform attempt; however, it should at least be noted that—as was to be expected—the *ch'ŏllima II* campaign as a typical perfection measure seems to have lost steam relatively quickly.

Figure 6. KCNA articles with the terms *ch'ŏllima*, *Korean-style socialism*, and *self-reliant/self-reliance* (1997–2010, weighted).

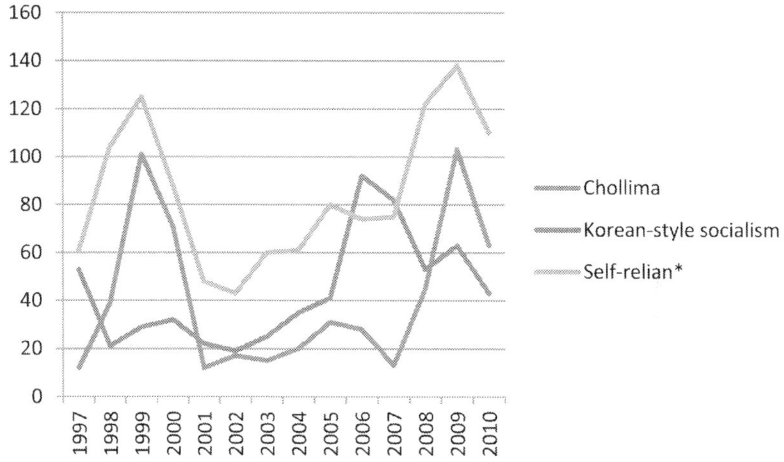

Source. Author's calculations based on data from KCNA (www.kcna.co.jp).

Policy Implications of the CRE Model

An end to the neoconservative drive in North Korea and the start of another round of reforms would help resolve the food situation and positively affect human rights and the nuclear problem.[18] From a long-term perspective, the introduction of a more efficient economic system is the best way to utilize the economic potential of North Korea, as discussed in the first part of this chapter. In this context, the CRE model will be helpful in answering the question of policy recommendations—that is, measures influencing one or more of the CRE model's variables to maximize the probability of reform [$p_R = s_R - o_R - f(e, g_R, l_O)\, i_s - f(g_O, l_R)\, i_o$].

As a general rule, it seems that at this point measures directed at minimizing o_R (opposition to reform) will be more efficient than those meant to maximize s_R (support for reform), assuming that the multiplier i_o is bigger than i_s. Note that o_R does not include external pressure among its determining variables in the CRE model. Rather, anything that reduces

g_O (gains from the old system) or l_R (anticipated losses from reform) or increases g_R (anticipated gains from reform) would be most efficient and should be considered first.

(1) Reduce g_O (gains from the old system). Such gains include material and immaterial benefits for elite members of the North Korean society, such as preferential access to food, an official car, a telephone line, preferential access to good schools for one's children, the opportunity and permits to travel abroad, and access to special stores. The value of these gains would decline not only if they were denied but also if they lost their exclusivity. Power itself is a universally valued perquisite. Following Kornai, one can also expect many members of the "winning group" to be convinced of the moral superiority and scientific correctness of the old system, a circumstance that assigns an intrinsic value to this system's existence.

A look at the list of gains shows that their reduction by outsiders in absolute terms would be technically very difficult. Moreover, it would include actions that are ethically debatable, including sanctions.[19] I therefore suggest to focus on reducing the relative value of g_O by supporting the emergence of alternatives to the perquisites offered by the state. This logic is based on one core idea of new institutional economics: that no transaction is cost-free. Cadres do not receive their benefits for free; they have to spend a good deal of their resources to please the state, always with the high risk of falling from grace. They thus might appreciate more stable and less risky access to these goods and services, which could mean access to sources of monetary income in a market economy. Another way to reduce the relative value of g_O is to increase the overall welfare and access in North Korea, for this would diminish the exclusiveness of the cadres' benefits and hence influence their individual cost-benefit analysis of supporting the system.

From this perspective, strongly supporting trade with North Korea, granting it access to international markets and sources of finance, dropping sanctions, and intensifying assistance and cooperation seem to be promising policies.

(2) Reduce l_R (anticipated losses from reform). Admittedly, it is difficult to anticipate all the effects of reforms on North Korea's economy and society. However, given that the poorer parts of the population are mostly concerned with staple food, heating, and clothing, even a postreform situation that leads to a transformational recession and to a further widening of the inequality gap would not worsen their position.[20] In particular, given the existence of South Korea, one can even expect improvement through social policies, however minimal.

Reducing l_R, therefore, has to focus on the upper group in North Korea's society. These have fairly good access to information and have studied the experience of Eastern Europe and the Soviet Union. They are aware that, depending on the extent of reforms and personal conditions, they might lose their lives, their freedom, their jobs, their prominent positions, their standard of living, their social capital, their life savings, their homes, and so on, if drastic reform were effected. Such views will have to be actively countered through diplomacy and capacity-building measures, admitting initial difficulties but also showing that many supporters of the old system in Europe and the Soviet Union have actually benefited from reform. This includes the facts that no market economy can exist without a strong state and that there is a role for the old bureaucracy to play, provided it is flexible enough to acquire the skills needed for such new tasks. This could be coupled with the offer of providing adequate training.

North Korea's situation is special because it must fear reunification with a dominant partner. In this respect, South Korea has an important role to play in lowering l_R. This concerns issues such as property rights. So far, the North Korean upper social stratum has to fear postunification expropriation based on legal documents supporting claims from the era before 1945 in the hands of former owners and their descendants who now live in the South. Given the National Security Law, supporters of the

North Korean system have to fear legal prosecution. The DPRK military would be less likely to stage a last-ditch effort to prevent reforms that could lead to unification if it were assured by Republic of Korea (ROK) law that military officers would be neither punished nor dismissed if they have conducted their service in a regular way. Members of the East German military, for example, with the exception of political officers, were allowed to change uniforms and were downgraded by only one rank after unification, a demotion that was more than made up for by an attractive salary and a secure job.[21]

(3) Following similar logic, the active increase of g_R (anticipated gains from reform) is one of the most promising and quite obvious policy areas. Such gains would include all the previously made points—namely, material, political, and social incentives. The focus should be on *anticipated*, for fears are still widespread. So far, the most active policy in this regard is being pursued by China: through its presence in North Korea, China reaches the masses, and by showing the North Korean leadership around China, it leaves a deep impression on DPRK leaders, including those at the very top. The invitation of North Koreans abroad would thus be a very effective policy for increasing g_R without requiring clumsy megaphone diplomacy.

(4) The variable l_O (losses from the old system) is one of the factors that would support reform directly. However, it is difficult to show how these losses can be increased without reaching the limits of what is ethically acceptable. In addition, based on Fahy's work, I contend that it would be misleading to expect a worsening economic situation in North Korea to automatically increase support for economic reforms.[22] The only applicable policy, therefore, would be to raise awareness of the old system's deficiencies.

One way to do that is to build on the experience of Eastern Europe. It was not a lack of staple food that triggered reforms there, but rather the fact that too many people had reached the upper limits of an economically inefficient system. An improved economic situation in North Korea might thus be a strong catalyst for change. If such an improvement were reached through intensified international cooperation and the introduction of market mechanisms, then it would be very obvious to North Koreans that for more success and more growth, they should simply follow that path further.

(5) As indicated, the actual effect of external pressure (*e*) is difficult to determine. There is the expectation that in order to trigger a major bottom-up reform movement, North Koreans need only be told how beautiful the world around them is and how dark their own system looks like in comparison. This assumption could turn out to be simplistic and naïve. Therefore, losses (for example, in the form of rally-round-the-flag behavior) inflicted by such measures could outweigh gains. The same is true of diplomatic or military pressure—for example, at the six-party talks, at the UN (on human rights issues), and through military exercises at the North Korean border. Such actions could produce, or actually prop up, the siege mentality that for decades has allowed the North Korean leadership to keep its people under tight control despite harsh living conditions. Economic sanctions, another form of external pressure, have to be applied quickly and massively; otherwise, they will fail to achieve results. And as Gordon argued, sanctions usually hit the weakest parts of society and make control of the country easier for those in power—which is usually the opposite of their original goal.[23]

(6) Another prospective policy field is an increase of the relative influence of reform supporters (i_S). Any policy that either reduces the number of reform opponents (i_O) or increases the number of reform supporters can be expected to raise the probability of reform. Examples include the growth of the influence and the number of nonstate elites, such as a new middle class of business people; a diversification of power within the ruling group by the introduction of a collective leadership system and the emergence of various factions;[24] and the loss of legitimacy through policy failure or corruption. This again points to cooperation as a more promising strategy than pressure.

Conclusion

To summarize the points discussed based on the CRE model, this chapter's analysis of North Korea's economy and its dynamics suggests that a proactive and cooperative approach would be very likely to yield positive results regarding reform. Such an approach affects the economy, domestic politics, and external security. It would increase the probability of a new attempt at pursuing a policy of reform and opening. As the past has shown, the North Korean system is capable of reaching the decision to embark on such a path. Abundant natural resources, a well-educated workforce, a functioning state, a long border with the gigantic economic power China, and the lessons learned in the past decade are excellent conditions for the success of such a policy. However, the past has also demonstrated that internal developments and a lack of proper external support can terminate and even reverse such attempts.

Despite the current prevailing neoconservative trend in ideology and economic policy in the DPRK, there is room for optimism that the next wave of reforms will eventually arrive. In particular the emergence of a new, young leader in December 2011 and his economy-oriented policies can be seen as supportive of such a view. Based on a systematic understanding of the various forces at work through the CRE model, the international community can actively support another reform process.

Endnotes

1. Suh Jae Jean, *The Lee Myung-bak Government's North Korea Policy: A Study on its Historical and Theoretical Foundation* (Seoul: Korea Institute of National Unification, 2009).
2. "2002 Nyŏn kukka yesan chiphaengŭi kyŏlsan'gwa 2003 nyŏn kukga yesane taehan pogo" [Report summing up the execution of the 2002 state budget and on the 2003 state budget], *Rodong Sinmun*, March 26, 2003, http://www.kcna.co.jp/calendar/2003/03/03-27/2003-03-27-002.html.
3. Rudiger Frank, "Money in Socialist Economies: The Case of North Korea," *Asia-Pacific Journal* (February 2010), http://japanfocus.org/-Ruediger-Frank/3307.
4. I define *reform* as a measure in economic policy that would not typically be included in the tool kit of classical socialism, which is based on state central planning for the allocation of goods and services. I deviate from Kornai's terminology insofar as such reforms may not necessarily affect the system directly, leading to its immediate transformation. Reform areas include price setting, production and procurement decisions, and private economic activities. In general terms, the reforms referred to in this chapter influence the balance between state and market in favor of the latter.
5. Typically, travel between counties or cities requires a written permit to pass through checkpoints.
6. Statistics Korea, *Pukhanŭi chuyo t'onggye chip'yo* [Main statistical indicators of North Korea] (Taejŏn: Korea National Statistics Office, 2011), 83.
7. Kim Jong Il, "21seginŭn kŏch'anghan chŏnbyŏnŭi segi, ch'angjoŭi segiida" [The twenty-first century is a century of great change and creation], *Rodong Sinmun*, January 4, 2001, 2.
8. "2002 Nyŏn kukka yesan chiphaengŭi kyŏlsan'gwa 2003 nyŏn kukga yesane taehan pogo" [Report summing up the execution of the 2002 state budget and on the 2003 state budget], *Rodong Sinmun*, March 26, 2003, http://www.kcna.co.jp/calendar/2003/03/03-27/2003-03-27-002.html.
9. Kim Jong Il, *On Preserving the Juche Character and National Character of the Revolution and Construction*, http://www.korea-dpr.com/library/1 11.pdf.

10. George Totten and Zhou Shulian, eds., *China's Economic Reform: Administering the Introduction of the Market Mechanism* (Boulder, CO: Westview Press, 1992).
11. Rumors pointed to about USD 12 billion. They were based on an extrapolation of the amount transferred from Japan to South Korea in connection with their diplomatic normalization in 1965—at that time, USD 800 million.
12. Korea Trade and Investment Promotion Agency (KOTRA), *2009 Pukhanŭi taewoemuyŏk tonghyang* [Trends in North Korean trade, 2009], KOTRA Paper 10-038 (Seoul: Korea Trade and Investment Promotion Agency, 2010).
13. I developed this method in 2008 and have been refining it ever since. First, I counted the number of articles per year that contain certain key words. Given that the overall number of articles each year is different, I have weighted the results by dividing the number of articles with the terms in question by the total number of that year's KCNA articles. I then multiplied the result by 4,000 and thus restored a value on the *y*-axis that comes close to the original numeric dimension. For example: for the term *songun*, I counted 935 articles in 2009, of a total of 4,852 articles. The weighted value for *songun* in 2009 is 935 ÷ 4,852 = 0.1927; I multiplied this result by 4,000 and reached 771 (rounded), which is the numeric value I used in the figure. This procedure was applied to all figures analyzing KCNA articles in this chapter.
14. The peak in references to Kim Jong Il since 2008 has a number of causes, including his health and the succession issue.
15. http://www.kcna.co.jp/calendar/2008/10/10-21/2008-1020-011.html
16. Ibid.
17. KCNA, December 30, 2008, http://www.kcna.co.jp/calendar/2008/12/12-30/2008-1230-006.html.
18. This statement is based on the assumption that human-rights violations are a consequence of repression that is endemic to state-socialist systems, as shown by Janos Kornai, *The Socialist System: The Political Economy of Communism* (Princeton, NJ: Princeton University Press, 1992). I would further argue that the North Korean nuclear program is both a means of extracting aid from the international community and an ideological-political mechanism for coping with the country's unsatisfactory economic situation.

19. Frank Rudiger, "The Political Economy of Sanctions against North Korea," *Asian Perspective* 30, no. 3 (2006): 5–36, http://www.asianperspective.org/articles/v30n3-b.pdf.
20. For more details on the situation in Eastern Europe and expectations for Korea, see Rudiger Frank and Sabine Burghart, *Driving Forces of Socialist Transformation: North Korea and the Experience of Europe and East Asia* (Vienna: Praesens, 2009).
21. See the account by Wolfgang Kappen, "Ubernahme und Eingliederung der Nationalen Volksarmee in die Bundeswehr" [Takeover and integration of the National People's Army into the Federal Armed Forces] (Cologne: Boehlau, 2009), 57–80.
22. Sandra Fahy, "Turning Points in the Experience of Famine: Survivor Testimony from the Democratic People's Republic of Korea" (unpublished manuscript, School of Oriental and African Studies, London, 2008).
23. Joy Gordon, "Economic Sanctions, Just War Doctrine, and the 'Fearful Spectacle of the Civilian Dead,'" *Cross Currents* 49, no. 3 (Fall 1999), www.crosscurrents.org/gordon.htm; see also Frank, "The Political Economy of Sanctions."
24. Perhaps *surfacing* would be more accurate than *emergence*, for it can be assumed that such factions already exist.

Chapter 4

The Marketization of North Korea

The Economic Contradiction at the Heart of Government Policy

Hazel Smith

De facto marketization took place within the Democratic People's Republic of Korea (DPRK), more commonly known as North Korea, after the breakdown of state capacity that was engendered by economic collapse and famine in the early 1990s.[1] The government required large-scale foreign investment that it hoped to obtain from large multilateral donors, such as the World Bank and business investors from the West. Yet the government was also concerned that any "opening" to the West would threaten the legitimacy of the regime, given that Western investment would inevitably be accompanied by a flood of non-government-controlled perspectives and information that would challenge the highly skewed information about the world presented by the government to its people for nearly half a century.[2]

This chapter outlines the marketization that has taken place within the DPRK since 1994/1995 and expands on the policy dilemmas facing the government and its policy responses. Within the limits of the political parameters in which it operated, the government's response to economic problems brought an end to the economic free fall of the 1990s, but it did not make policy choices adequate to bringing about the prosperity and stability it sought. The argument of this chapter is that the government focused on a perceived "information dilemma," and at the same time it ignored growing social inequality based on the semilegal enrichment of the few. The government never developed a viable strategy for managing the tensions that accompanied rapid socioeconomic transformation of DPRK state and society. The subsidiary thesis is that a major potential destabilizing factor for the government was the tension between those sections of the middle and upper echelons that benefited from the new "marketized" economy and those that did not.

MARKETIZATION

The DPRK economy collapsed in the absence of support from the former communist states, which had mostly transformed their societies into capitalist entities by the early 1990s. By 1999/2000 stabilization of the economy had been achieved, albeit with low levels of economic activity. Government policy reconstituted itself around an economic strategy that involved an attempt to find a way to work with the globalized liberal economy. Such a strategy, though not identified as such by the DPRK government, involved accepting an incipient, albeit inherently limited, marketization. This inchoate marketization can be understood as a process of dollarization, fragmentation, and immiseration. By *dollarization*, I mean the effective replacement of the local currency, the won, with hard currency, including but not limited to the US dollar. By *fragmentation*, I mean the process of unequal development—which benefited some, but not the majority—and which can be analyzed with respect to geography and social group. By *immiseration*, I refer to the poor conditions of life for the majority of people—at a time when there was and is little or no social safety net apart from the relatively small amount of assistance provided by international humanitarian organizations.

Government Economic Strategy

The government adopted a twofold approach to its economics. The first aim of the strategy was to encourage foreign investment through offering tax breaks and favorable conditions for joint ventures. A key function of foreign investment was to contribute to the modernization of the economy through the development of information technology as an aid to reindustrialization and economic recovery. The second aim of the economic strategy was to encourage domestic economic entities, such as cooperative farms, businesses, the ministries, and the county administrations, to operate as self-sufficient economic units. The government implicitly acknowledged the marketization from below that had taken place after the famine, when individuals and communities had found non-state-directed solutions to economic problems. The new constitution of 1998 represented an acknowledgment that economic policy was no longer to be underpinned by principles of egalitarianism. Instead, domestic economic entities were encouraged to develop their "comparative advantages"—with the inevitable corollary that those economic units with comparative economic disadvantages would not benefit from the new policy.

By the late 1990s, there were few resources available to support the nationwide public welfare that the state had attempted to provide since its inception in 1948. In addition, the move from collective national provision of basic goods based on some form of a redistributive principle to a constitutional arrangement based on self-help provisions founded on unequal endowments challenged long-established notions of social and community solidarity. Such egalitarian notions had underpinned the strong social bonds that had proved their worth throughout the worst of the famine in the mid-1990s, as starving individuals found themselves surviving only though the extensive mutual support that communities gave their members. DPRK efforts to rebuild within the context of the new economic world in which it found itself thus risked undermining long-established notions of collective responsibility for mutual welfare and at the same time contained the seeds of social fragmentation—and consequently, the potential for political unrest.

Macroeconomic Stabilization

In the early years of the twenty-first century, economic stabilization took place in the absence of trading partners prepared to offer substantial concessional trade in fuel, food, or other commodities, perhaps indicating that the society and the government had learned to apply survival skills within the new globalized world in which the DPRK had now to operate. The country had shown negative gross domestic product (GDP) growth throughout the 1990s, but from 1999 to 2005 GDP growth took place every year, until 2006 and 2007, when GDP entered a second period of negative growth.[3] The absolute figures were, however, very low. Exports rose to just $515 million in 1999/2000, a year-on rise of 8 percent, and imports came to $1.4 billion, an increase of 46.5 percent from the previous year.[4] Total trade grew through the first decade of the twenty-first century, with a slight dip in 2007, but never reached more than $3 billion.[5] The population remained poverty stricken. In 1998 the government estimated average per capita national income at just $457.[6] External sources' estimates did not differ greatly from the government figures, reporting per capita gross national income (GNI) of $573 in 1998, which rose to just $1152 in 2007.[7]

Government acceptance of marketization never presaged much more than a grudging acceptance of social change that it could not prevent but that it tried to control (for example, in the 2002 economic "reforms"). The July 2002 reforms raised official prices, instituted charges for utilities, and sanctioned profit seeking as an appropriate end of enterprises. They did not, however, reflect a wholesale acceptance of private property as a fundamental principle of society, authorize a free labor market, or allow civic freedoms protected by law.

Dollarization

After 1998 hard currency, including the dollar, the Chinese renminbi, the euro, and the Japanese yen, effectively (although not officially) replaced the won as the currency unit used for exchange, as a store of value, and for accounting purposes.[8] Government agencies carried out transactions among themselves using dollars.[9] North Korean nationals needed hard currencies to buy items of any value in local shops and markets. All domestic transactions by foreigners in the country used hard currency. The won now operates as a subsidiary currency for those in the population who do not have access to hard currency.

The government in practice countenanced the dollarization of the economy, which took place in just two years—an extraordinarily short amount of time—between 1998 and 2000. In 1998 it was not possible to give dollars away—for instance, as a tip for good service in restaurants, hotels, and so on. This was because the security services would have questioned any Korean other than those in the higher echelons who was spending foreign currency. From 2000 onward, by contrast, it was possible for poor working people to use dollars—if they could obtain them—throughout the nation. This does not imply that the security forces lost interest in individuals spending dollars. The dollarization of the economy, though comprehensive and tolerated as an economic necessity, is still not legal in the sense of the government's having officially replaced the won with the dollar. There are, however, incentives against prosecuting those engaged in the hard-currency economy, one of which is that those with the most access to hard currency are likely to be those who are already in a privileged or influential position in society, including those working within the security apparatus.

The hard-currency economy developed partly owing to the lack of a developed and reliable banking and credit system. Hard currency enters the country via domestic traders, foreign businesses, international organizations, and foreign governments—some of which choose not to operate through the banking system and instead, partially or fully, operate on a cash basis. South Korean organizations are among those engaged in transactions involving large cash flows—as are international nongovernmental organizations (NGOs).

Fragmentation

Social fragmentation is not manifested in the DPRK as a division between large, easily identifiable, preexisting collective groups and others—for instance, between Pyongyang and the rest of the country, the party and the rest of the population, the army and the nonmilitary, the few who work for profitable enterprises and the majority who work for unproductive factories or for a public service that can no longer pay wages. Instead, social differentiation grew across an axis defined today by those social groups and individuals who have access to hard currency, food, and information and those who do not. Some individuals have access to all three of these valuable commodities, but others may have access to just one of these valuable commodities—perhaps food, for example. Some have access to tens of dollars whereas others may have access to thousands. The individuals benefiting from dollarization are concentrated in certain geographic regions—in the capital and port and northern border towns. They include those who have access to foreigners either directly or indirectly through their work. They include senior personnel in both the party and the state apparatus, but they can also include low-status workers—for example, port personnel and restaurant workers, who labor in establishments that cater to foreigners.

Individuals who have access to food include farmers who have been fortunate enough to work on cooperative farms that have managed to return sufficient harvest to fulfill food needs for farming families.[10] Some rural families have access to "fire fields"—generally pieces of cleared forestland, often on precipitous slopes, that can provide food for two or three agricultural seasons. If a farmer is particularly fortunate, the farm may have generated some surplus, which can be sold in the semilegal farmers' markets that have largely replaced the old public distribution system as sources of food for non-cooperative farm dwellers. It is illegal to sell grain in markets, but farmers that can do so siphon basic grain into non-government-sanctioned private trade networks.

Some individuals in the society also have access to knowledge and information about the outside world. These include senior and middle management in government and the ministries and also workers (e.g., drivers, household employees, restaurant and hotel staff). Local staff members employed in international organizations have continuous access to Internet sources of news about their own country as well as about other countries. Those living in the geographical regions bordering China, too, have for nearly twenty years had access to what is now very substantial and current information—not just about prosperous China but also about modern South Korea. Yanji City, the capital of Yanbian Prefecture, which borders North Korea, is home to nearly a million Korean-speaking Chinese nationals and provides a ready source of information to hundreds of thousands of North Koreans who either cross the border or buy goods from Korean-Chinese traders who regularly visit the DPRK.

Not all individuals benefit to the same extent from access to hard currency, food, and information. Nevertheless, new social divisions are being created along these axes of privilege, thus creating new social strata in the DPRK.

Limits to Growth

Incorporating principles of liberal economic rationality into economic planning and management meant that those provinces, counties, farms, and enterprises that generated surplus--and that since 1998 have been permitted to engage more directly in market transactions--could purchase inputs and basic goods and could redistribute these goods to their constituents. Economic units tended to use these newfound freedoms to engage in more swapping arrangements so that, for instance, a ministry in Pyongyang might offer the use of its trucks in return for obtaining some produce from one of the nearby cooperative farms. Some provinces and counties set up small shops to sell surplus locally or export local produce abroad—for instance, potato starch to China.

In practice, the low level of economic activity throughout the country, combined with limited foreign investment and government policy that was less than enthusiastic in its adoption of market-driven dynamics, militated against these new instruments of economic liberalism as a mechanism for economic growth.

There remain huge aggregate food shortages.[11] Any cooperative farm that manages to produce food exceeding the requirements of its own farmers must relinquish much of that production for sale to the state (at prices determined in won) for national redistribution. Similarly, enterprises that were successful in selling goods abroad and in obtaining foreign currency pay workers in the almost worthless won. Even when enterprises become profitable, benefits to workers remain limited because the economic framework does not legally allow payment to individuals in the hard currency that they need to pay for goods of any value, including the basics, such as food and clothes.

Immiseration

DPRK society fractured along the lines of access to resources (hard currency, food, and information). This division was not even and involved the growth of extreme inequality. Whereas some have benefited, the vast majority of the population continue to live in poverty—facing malnutrition, disease, and hardship as day-to-day conditions of existence.[12]

Rural families, particularly those living in the breadbasket provinces in the south of the country, used to be considered better off than urban families because they have access to land and can grow food. By around 2005, however, these families were also suffering from food deficits because much of their "surplus" grain was expropriated for use by the military and the capital.[13] This is especially true of the northern mountainous counties in North Hamgyong and parts of Ryanggang, where the growing season is short, agricultural land is marginal, and agricultural production even at the best of times has historically been unable to feed local populations. Malnutrition decreased from the high postfamine levels recorded in 1998 but remained unacceptably high and continues to have serious detrimental effects on children and adults, including in Pyongyang.[14] UNICEF reported an under-five mortality rate of fifty-five per thousand in 1996 and a maternal mortality rate of forty-one per thousand.[15] Given the continuing widespread lack of basic drugs and medical equipment, the rise of diseases such as tuberculosis and hepatitis, and the prevalence of diarrhea and acute respiratory illness, the actual mortality rates are likely to have remained high.[16]

Immiseration is prevalent throughout the country. It can be found in Pyongyang as much as in the mountainous remote regions of the north and east of the country. It is entirely related to the inability to grow or purchase food and to obtain basic goods, such as medicine and fuel. This, in turn, is related to the breakdown of the public distribution system that until the early to mid-1990s channeled food, clothes, and other basic goods to the nonfarming population. From 1995 to 2008, international humanitarian organizations and individual governments provided fairly large-scale food and fertilizer aid that enabled most of the population to achieve basic subsistence levels, but this aid never met the national need for medical care, health care, and inputs necessary to rehabilitate the dilapidated and unsafe water and sewage systems that also brought disease to the majority.[17] Urban adults were not entitled to international humanitarian assistance, including food, and had few opportunities to grow their own food. Poverty is quite visible in North Korea's cities—side by side with the observable privilege of the minority with access to hard currency.

Incipient Freedoms and Political Tensions

Marketization from below was accompanied by some increase in individual freedoms—although the interests of the individual always remained subordinate to those of the community and to state priorities. Freedoms were manifested positively—increased freedom of movement, the simple freedom to engage in individual economic decision making—but also negatively. The freedoms brought about by marketization were also manifested in the rise of petty crime, prostitution, smuggling, and gray-area monetary transactions as individuals exercised a newfound ability to operate illegally and outside state control.

Personal mobility is apparent as individuals travel long distances looking for food. Children are sent to different parts of the country to stay with relatives who have access to food. Individuals may now own bicycles, and some have access to cars and other vehicles. Restrictions on travel remain but are confined to the border areas and to zones around Pyongyang. Individuals engage in petty trade on street corners throughout the country and in markets, but these activities are supervised and monitored by government entities. These fragile and limited new freedoms are not yet institutionalized and could be abrogated with any shift in government thinking.

Government encouragement of economic entities to engage in self-help was not accompanied by the institutionalization of economic freedoms. In the urban areas, workers receive valueless won as wages and also receive, theoretically, the more valuable basic food ration. Food rations are allocated to urban workers in the context of what is available and based on the value of the work carried out. In the "lean season"—from January to October, when the harvest has run out—many urban workers must work literally for nothing. Admittedly, in the DPRK of 2012, it is widely accepted that workers should be permitted to be away from the workplace if they find alternative income-generating activities, as long as they can arrange for someone else, maybe a family member, to take their place. This latitude is applied particularly to women, who are culturally expected to take responsibility for food-related activity. In addition, hundreds of thousands of young workers are regularly called away from workplaces to practice for months on end for the frequent mass displays organized for national holidays.

In the rural areas, the government has allowed subwork teams—the lowest level of farm organization—to develop "private" activities, and farm families are now permitted small plots of land. There have been no major changes, however, in the organization of social life in the countryside. This is because the major new freedom—to buy and sell outside the now virtually nonexistent public distribution system—is seen by important groups within the government as a technical and temporary solution addressing the survival needs of the population. The government abandoned the mechanisms of the public distribution system, but it did not abandon its ethos of state control. In addition, much of the rural population values the community bonds that in many counties are hundreds of years old. Likewise, many look to economic recovery to sustain those bonds, not sever them by encouraging workers to leave a farming sector that is already chronically short of labor and lacks the technology that might make up for labor shortages. There is no economic history of rural liberalization in the DPRK that might be held up as a model for organizing an alternative farm economy and society.

In terms of an alternative future social and political organization based on freedom of the individual, the major pressure is likely to come from people who already benefit from loosened state control over individual economic activity. Some may wish to maintain the current system, in which benefits accrue in a nonlegalized, "accidental" manner. Given that the current system does not guarantee security of personal possessions, others might wish to institutionalize the ability to make personal gain. Such a development would imply recognition of the individual's rights in law and would be a step toward recognizing that the state would no longer have primary jurisdiction over every aspect of the individual's life.

POLICY DILEMMAS AND POLICY OPTIONS

Many commentators have recognized the potential of the food and economic crises to threaten stability in the region; many believe, for instance (despite US State Department denials), that the large-scale humanitarian relief from the United States to the DPRK in the 1990s was explicitly designed to prevent a dangerously unpredictable social disintegration.[18]

The DPRK government also fears destabilization. It worries that an uncontrolled influx of information about the West might trigger discontent and precipitate breakdown in law and order, potentially producing an outcome as dangerous to the regime as the acute collapse in food security that resulted in famine in the 1990s. The government has had an economic strategy to introduce information technology as a mechanism to kick-start the country's economy. Information technology, by its nature, brings information, and if much of the new information is contradictory to previous information that the population has received (and perhaps, in the main, believed), this is bound to cause credibility problems for a government that has always relied on its almost complete control of information in order to sustain its legitimacy.[19]

Perhaps, though, this is in fact an imaginary dilemma, and if it is a real problem, it may not be the primary potential challenge to government stability. Not every household in the country will have access to the Internet for a considerable period of time to come. In addition, many in the upper and middle echelons of society already have access to information about the rest of the world and are very capable of making judgments about the relative worth of that information and comparing this new data to what they have been told by the government and by the instruments of the socialization system (education, media, etc.). Information technology and more open means of communication, such as more television programs from abroad, may not make a substantial difference to those struggling for survival in urban and rural areas—particularly if the still strong security apparatus remains in place to police any reaction from the poor.

Neither the DPRK government nor its overseas adversaries have expressed concern about or perhaps even understood the scale of social transformation in the country over the last twenty years. DPRK society is socially fragmented, and economic growth is intrinsically constituted by the rise of influential sectors whose enrichment is based on extralegal or semilicit economic activities. For the government, the scale of fragmentation is perhaps unacknowledged because this form of enrichment is possible only on a large scale for those already in a privileged position. In a state and society without independent legal institutions, it will be difficult to challenge influential senior party and government members who may be benefiting from the incidental effects of marketization in the DPRK.

Overseas interlocutors might need to pay some attention to these hidden but significant fissures within North Korean society. Dissatisfaction with the government is no longer muted, for the mass of the population sees the highly visible wealth of some—side by side with the continuing impoverishment of the many. If this was the only consequence, however, the security apparatus could deal with any unrest through repression. What is much more serious for the government is the split between, on the one hand, those elites in the party, the security apparatus, the army, and so forth, who are raking off hard currency and commodities for personal gain and, on the other hand, those—also among the elite—who either are not in a position to do so or choose to behave in a more ethical manner.

The government could opt to deal with these new divisions in DPRK society by building a legal and administrative system—as China has done—to restrict the opportunities for wealth accumulation through gray-area activities. To do this, it would have to fully accept that it cannot reverse its de facto entry into the international liberal economy and that the best it can do is manage effectively the interpenetration of its economy in the global liberal political economy. The big question is whether key sectors within the government can back away from the opportunities for personal enrichment so as to tackle the necessary establishment and enforcement of rules that separate personal activities from state activities. Such rules would involve the introduction of a legal, political, and economic framework that provides transparency, accountability, and the rule of law. Inasmuch as this would prevent some individuals from making arbitrary use of the lack of a legal framework for personal accumulation, it would also serve to provide legal protections for individuals against the state.

Conclusion

DPRK society has suffered the tragedy of famine and subsequent food shortages that have now become chronic. The vast majority of the population still faces major privations, such as hunger, lack of clean water, lack of medicine, and lack of heating in North Korea's extreme winters. The government fears that another shock to the system—brought by a rapid opening to comprehensive knowledge of the outside world—would threaten its credibility. The major threat to the government, however, comes from the social fragmentation brought about by marketization in the DPRK. Influential sectors within the government increasingly benefit, though, from the status quo and see no reason to tackle the social cleavages I have characterized as framed by dollarization, fragmentation, and immiseration.

The government thus faces a catch-22. If it does not crack down on corruption, the elites will become polarized, and the government will not be able to rely on an undivided security apparatus to keep order. If the government does tackle the problem, it will have to institute political change that will deny the state the authority it has hitherto exercised over every aspect of the population's life—and thus undermine the foundations of state rule.

Endnotes

1. For detailed background, see Hazel Smith, "La Corée du Nord vers l'économie de marché: Faux et vrais dilemmas," *Critique Internationale* (April 2002): 6–14; Hazel Smith, *Hungry for Peace: International Security, Humanitarian Assistance and Social Change in North Korea* (Washington, DC: United States Institute of Peace Press, 2005), 337; Hazel Smith, "Crime and Economic Instability: The Real Security Threat from North Korea and What to Do about It," *International Relations of the Asia Pacific* 5, no. 2 (2005): 235–249; Hazel Smith, "North Korea: Market Opportunity, Poverty, and the Provinces," *New Political Economy* 14, no. 3 (June 2009): 231–256. Recent treatments of marketization in the DPRK following the famine of the early 1990s include Sung Chull Kim, *North Korea Under Kim Jong Il: From Consolidation to Systemic Dissonance* (Albany: State University of New York Press, 2006); Georgy Toloraya, *The Economic Future of North Korea: Will the Market Rule?* Academic Paper Series on North Korea, vol. 1 (Washington, DC: Korea Economic Institute, 2008), 35, available from http://www.keia.org/Publications/OnKorea/2008/08Toloraya.pdf.
2. For an insightful and balanced perspective on the issue of regime legitimacy in the DPRK, see Han S. Park, "Human Needs, Human Rights, and Regime Legitimacy: The North Korean Anomaly," in Chung-in Moon, *Understanding Regime Dynamics in North Korea* (Seoul: Yonsei University Press, 1998), 221–235. See also the still useful Han S. Park, ed., *North Korea: Ideology, Politics, Economy* (Englewood Cliffs, NJ: Prentice Hall, 1996).
3. Korea Economic Institute, *North Korea's Economy* (Washington, DC: Korea Economic Institute, 2008).
4. *Joosong Ilbo*, June 4, 2001, reported in NAPSNet Daily Report, June 5, 2001, www.nautilus.org/napsnet/dr/0106/JUN05.html.
5. Korea Economic Institute, *North Korea's Economy.*
6. Pyongyang Chamber of Commerce, *Country Report,* mimeo. (Pyongyang: Chamber of Commerce, 2001).
7. Korea Economic Institute, *North Korea's Economy.*
8. Much of this paragraph draws on my own experiences living and working in the DPRK May–June 1998, October–December 1999, and September 2000–September 2001.

9. Anthony Michell, "The Current North Korean Economy," in *Economic Integration of the Korean Peninsula*, ed. Marcus Noland (Washington, DC: Institute for International Economics, 1998), 152.
10. Hazel Smith, "North Korea: Market Opportunity."
11. Basic aggregate food shortages remained at over 20 percent of annual requirements. See Hazel Smith, "Food Security: The Case for Multisectoral and Multilateral Cooperation," in *Reconstituting Korean Security*, ed. Hazel Smith (Tokyo: United Nations Press, 2007), 82–102. For harvest figures and the food deficit for 2001/2002, see, for example, Food and Agriculture Organization of the United Nations (FAO), *FAO/WFP Crop and Food Supply Assessment Mission to the Democratic People's Republic of Korea* (Rome: FAO, 2001).
12. For an analysis of conditions throughout the country regarding health, nutrition, education, and water and sanitation, see United Nations Children's Fund (UNICEF), *An Analysis of the Situation of Children and Women in the Democratic People's Republic of Korea, 2000* (Pyongyang: UNICEF, 1999).
13. Hazel Smith, "North Korea: Market Opportunity."
14. Central Bureau of Statistics (DPRK), *2004 Nutrition Assessment: Report of Survey Results*, mimeo. (Pyongyang: Institute of Child Nutrition, 2005).
15. UNICEF, *Analysis of the Situation.*
16. For a discussion of problems for human development in the DPRK, see United Nations Development Programme (UNDP), *Second Country Cooperation Framework for the DPRK, 2001–2003* (New York: UNDP, 2001).
17. For a description of the types and extent of humanitarian need and resources required, see United Nations Office of the Coordination of Humanitarian Assistance (UNOCHA), *Consolidated Inter-Agency Appeal for the DPRK, 2001* (Geneva: UNOCHA, 2000).
18. There has been a debate within the United States government on this issue. An early draft of a congressional General Accounting Office (GAO) document had to be amended when the US State Department protested the assumption of a linkage between humanitarian assistance to the DPRK and broader security issues. See GAO, *Foreign Assistance: North Korea Restricts Food Aid Monitoring* (Washington, DC: GAO, 1999), www.gao.gov.
19. It is difficult to tell, even for foreigners with Korean-language skills, what people do or do not believe in the DPRK. After roughly eighteen months living and working in the DPRK between 1999 and 2001, I found that officials and representatives at the *ri* (village), county, and provincial levels

were very vocal and innovative in their thinking and their responses to the severe food and economic problems they were facing. They did not and could not discuss the broader political issues, except to sometimes mention the negative impact of US sanctions. This does not mean that they did not have strong opinions on the issue—only that they were not willing to share them with foreigners. The main source of information as to the changing beliefs of the population is defector interviews, which need to be treated with methodological care because of their understandable bias and because almost by definition, these interviewees may have faced some of the worst aspects of DPRK society. It would be as foolish, however, to give no credit to their testimony as to allow for its complete representativeness. For an account that, among other things, details the way the population "manages" a system unable to deliver on basic needs, see Kang Chol-hwan and Pierre Rigoulet, *The Aquariums of Pyongyang: Ten years in a North Korean Gulag*, trans. Yair Reiner (Boulder, CO: Perseus, 2001).

Chapter 5

The Army as a Main Pillar of Revolution

Alexander Zhebin

The increased role of the armed forces in the Democratic People's Republic of Korea (DPRK), given the especially dynastic nature of the existing regime, can be seen as another round of the traditional, centuries-old rivalry between the two main branches of the ruling elites in Korea—civil and military. That kind of struggle for the ruler's attention and prestige has flared at varying intensities in Korea under every regime. Each faction has been provided with a place closer to the "throne," depending on the ruler's personal inclinations and on his vision of the hierarchy of threats to his power and to the country's security as a whole.

North Korea's transition to the regime of a besieged fortress, to the use of primarily military methods of managing and organizing the society, has in fact been the response of the ruling elite to the emergency situation the country has been facing at home and abroad since the 1990s. Traditional reliance on the use of force in settling all issues—characteristic of the views and political practices of the North Korean leadership, deeply rooted in a partisan past—encouraged the country's decision to rely on the military as the most organized and effective force to protect the country from external threats, to ensure political stability within, and to avoid a complete collapse of the economy.[1]

SOURCES OF *SONGUN*

The military-first policy, or *songun*, was formally introduced when Kim Jong Il visited one of the military units on the first day of the new year in 1995. Later, the date was moved back to the 1930s in order to support advancement of the policy as the mainstream political course for the country. The primacy of *songun* was explained by, among other reasons, the following "logical" construction: Kim Il Sung had founded the Korean army first, in the 1930s; only much later, in 1945, had he founded the ruling Workers' Party of Korea (WPK) and finally, in 1948, the DPRK.

Several domestic and external factors forced the North Korean leadership to resort to *songun*, thus increasing the role of the armed forces in nonmilitary spheres of the country's life, ranging from economy to culture. In terms of chronology, one major domestic and two important international developments initially pushed the North Korean leadership to engage more actively in turning the country into a military camp and in building up a powerful deterrent—or to put it straightforwardly, the nuclear weapon.

The army's growing role as the regime's main power base was first vividly manifest in the final stage of power transference from Kim Il Sung to Kim Jong Il, which began in the 1990s, when the latter took control of the armed forces. The process underscored a growing tendency to consider the military a main pillar of the regime, even in peaceful times. The choice of this path was not only based on the experience of other countries but also derived from some lessons of history regarding interfaction struggles within the WPK and campaigns against antiparty elements in the 1950s and 1960s. At that time army units stationed near Pyongyang, under the command of generals loyal to Kim Il Sung, helped him and his supporters within the leadership win a majority vote at the WPK Central Committee Plenum in August 1956, when Kim Il Sung's opponents made an unsuccessful attempt to oust him.

The second reason for *songun* was the USSR's demise and the disbanding of the socialist bloc. The North Korean leadership drew grave conclusions from its analysis of events leading to the collapse of socialism in the Soviet Union and most other countries of the former socialist camp. The ruling parties in these countries, it was noted with pointed condemnation in Pyongyang, had been unable to retain power, including control over the armed forces, unable to mobilize society for the protection of socialist gains.

A real shock in North Korea was caused by the fact that the Soviet Union—a former superpower commanding formidable armed forces—collapsed suddenly, without a single shot. Pyongyang leaders believed the primary reason for the collapse of socialism in the USSR and in several other countries was the infiltration of their ruling communist parties' leadership by traitors to socialism who had managed to impose policies depoliticizing and deideologizing the army and security forces.[2] Hence, the North Koreans concluded that the "ideological disarmament of the army destroys socialism" and that "the most vivid example of this [was] the process of the disintegration of socialism in several countries in Eastern Europe."[3] One particular consequence of this conclusion was a drastic upgrading of the role and importance of the Main Political Department (MPD) of the Korean People's Army (KPA). Contrary to the practice that had characterized Kim Il Sung's era, the head of the department—from the mid-1990s, vice marshal Cho Myong Rok (d. 2010)—took the top position in the military hierarchy, above even the minister of the People's Armed Forces, as chief of the KPA general staff.

The third cause behind *songun*, directly linked to the second, comprised the US-led NATO actions in Iraq in the first Gulf War and in the Balkans, coupled with the nuclear crisis on the Korean Peninsula in 1993 and 1994. Pyongyang considered Washington's attempts to effect regime change in a number of countries efforts "to establish by force of arms" a unipolar world in order "to become the world ruler."[4]

Particular concern was aroused in Pyongyang by the United States' explicit attempts, in disregard of the United Nations (UN) Charter and international law, to turn the UN into an instrument of America's violence and arbitrariness. Having lost its main military and political ally, the Soviet Union, in the early 1990s, and becoming increasingly uncertain about unconditional support from another major ally, China, the DPRK began to realize through the very convincing examples provided by events in Europe and the Middle East that under the emerging new world order, appeals to international law were unlikely to be effective if they were not backed by force.[5] Facing the West's new strategy of humanitarian intervention, shocked by drastically changing relations with two major allies (both Russia and China established diplomatic ties with South Korea), and submerged in doubt concerning its own ruling party's ability to maintain control, the North Korean regime had virtually no option but to seek support from the most disciplined and organized armed force in the country—the KPA.

By all accounts, this was not an easy decision for the ruling WPK's top leaders. Memories of dealing with the so-called military-bureaucratic group in the 1960s were still rather vivid. For this reason it was quite natural to expect differing opinions within the DPRK on what course should be taken in the situation. The statement of the first vice chair of the National Defense Committee (NDC) and chief of the KPA MPD, Cho Myong Rok, made in December 2001 at the meeting commemorating the tenth anniversary of Kim Jong Il's nomination as supreme commander of the KPA, was very revealing in this regard. The army chief political officer claimed that after Kim Il Sung's death, by the end of 1994, the new leader (Kim Jong Il) had been left alone to face a great many "internal and external problems." However, ignoring advice from some unnamed high-ranking officials, Kim had appealed for help dealing with those problems not to the working class but to the army, the strongest, most disciplined, and most conscientious sector of society.[6]

Saving the Economy

The middle of the 1990s brought about a new expansion of the military's role. Among major reasons for this was, of course, Kim Il Sung's death. His charisma and enormous authority, maintained up to the last days of his life, had ensured the stability of the entire power structure. His death in 1994 not only precipitated political consequences but also was immediately followed by unprecedented natural calamities in 1995 and 1996—a devastating famine that proved disastrous for the country's economy and for the way of life of the absolute majority of the North Korean population.

The role of the whole set of economic and social factors is usually neglected or, at best, underestimated when analyzing the origins of the military-first policy. However, the drastic deterioration of economic conditions as a result of natural disasters in 1995–1996 had serious political and social implications. Natural calamities and the authorities' inability to deal with them effectively revealed all the shortcomings and chronic diseases of the North Korean economic and social systems. The North Korean government and the state as a whole were unable to fulfill their constitutional obligations before the people—unable, first of all, to ensure the normal functioning of the distribution system for major rationed consumer goods and foodstuffs. The significance of this development can hardly be overestimated, for the collapse of the public distribution system (PDS) was tantamount to the authorities' loss of an important instrument of social control over the population.

Collapse of the economy's civil sector led to the lumpenization of a massive part of the urban population, especially the working class. Disrupted industrial production owing to lack of electricity and raw materials was exacerbated by natural disasters. Hidden and open unemployment swept major cities. As a result, the WPK's social base was drastically weakened. Ruling elites concluded that under such circumstances, relying on the ruling party as the main pillar of the regime would be too risky. There was no sound option except to rely on the most disciplined group of North Korean society—the army and secret services. Pyongyang thus decided, under conditions of worsening economic crisis and mounting pressure from the United States and South Korea (which were seeking to achieve an "opening" of North Korea and ultimately its "soft landing"), that avoiding a situation paralleling that of Romania or East Germany could be ensured only through the solid long-term alliance of the political leadership and the military wing of the ruling elite.

This alliance was not difficult to implement. Top military leaders, notably the minister of the People's Armed Forces and the KPA chief of general staff, as a rule, were members of the Politburo of the WPK CC. The military was heavily represented in the WPK CC itself, as well as in the Supreme People's Assembly (SPA)—North Korea's parliament. The SPA of the Ninth Convocation (elected in 1990) had sixty-two military MPs of the total 687; in the Tenth Convocation (elected in 1998), their representation increased to 107 MPs of the 687 SPA deputies. One finds a similar situation in the WPK's local party committees and legislative caucuses. The practice has led to close links among the ruling party, the government, and the economic and military bureaucracy. The alliance matured and was strengthened during several decades of joint work on solving pending economic and social problems and preparing the northern half of the republic (i.e., the territory now under DPRK control) to repeal foreign threats and achieve the "liberation" of South

Korea, frequently dubbed the temporarily occupied southern half of the republic.

During the process of aligning political and military power, civilian and military leaders have accumulated considerable experience interacting in response to major economic problems. Almost all the so-called monumental creations of the WPK era—the gateway to the estuary of the Taedong River, which flows into the Yellow Sea; the major highway connecting Pyongyang with Wonsan on the east coast of the country and with Kaesong near the demilitarized zone between North and South Korea; hydroelectric power stations, railways, and tunnels—were constructed with the broad and often decisive involvement of the military units, in some cases up to several divisions.

Since the 1990s, sending large groups of demobilized soldiers to undertake enterprises involving heavy and dangerous labor conditions, deploying them to construction sites and to rural areas has become an ever more widespread practice. Allegedly, officers and soldiers do this on their own initiative, deciding to continue their service on the economic front, and remain there as long as necessary to fulfill the task assigned them. This practice allows the authorities to significantly reduce government expenditures on labor wages and on the development of social infrastructure. Moreover, the military has always played a significant role in disaster-relief operations. Their help was also essential for agriculture. But during the most difficult period, 1995–1996, the role of the military in both spheres proved to be a decisive one.

Songun: Cure for All Diseases

With the proclamation of the military-first policy in 1995, the call for simultaneous defense and economic construction, launched for the first time in the DPRK in the 1960s, was revived. But in reality, as had happened three decades earlier, top priority was again given to the military-industrial complex. The line was confirmed annually in joint editorials published annually on January 1 by the party, the army, and youth newspapers.[7]

Editorials for 2010–2012 placed emphasis on improving the lives of the people, light industry, and agriculture, but the ongoing nuclear and missile programs demanded at least the same proportion of North Korea's resources. After the failed Sputnik launch and the nuclear tests conducted in 2009, the country faced unprecedentedly severe international sanctions.[8] The decision to promote *songun* as a major political course led to certain changes in the country's constitution and government structure. The Socialist Constitution of the DPRK was revised twice (in 1998 and 2009) in order to increase significantly the status of the NDC and the powers of its chairman.[9] The chairman of the NDC was officially named the supreme leader of the DPRK.[10]

Kim Jong Il took the lead in the campaign and used it to solidify his control over the armed forces. After his father's death he focused primarily on replacing top- and middle-level commanding officers. The new appointees' devotion to the new leader would have been based, not least of all, on a personal appreciation for the higher ranks and positions. The tradition has long been established to announce massive promotions to the next military rank on the occasion of major national holidays—Kim Il Sung's and Kim Jong Il's birthdays, the anniversaries of the founding of the WPK and the armed forces. According to Kim Jong Il's orders, over 1,100 officers were promoted to the rank of general or saw their general's rank upgraded (from major-general to lieutenant-general, etc.). Candidates for promotion were, as a rule, introduced to Kim Jong Il in person during his frequent visits to various military units. Further, generals and officers received increased payment and food rations. They enjoyed priority in acquiring housing, furniture, and household appliances. In order to improve the food supply for noncommissioned officers (NCOs) and soldiers, the military has developed military-run farms specializing in growing vegetables and breeding poultry, pigs, and even fish. Visits to these farms became almost an obligatory point of Kim Jong Il's on-site leadership of military units.

A powerful campaign was also launched across the country to "create an atmosphere ... under which priority should be given to military affairs, to strengthen the nationwide defense system, and ... to develop the tradition of the unity between the army and the people."[11] The WPK's officials and economic management staff were called on to follow the style and methods of army officers. Military morale and even military culture samples were declared exemplary and enjoyed widespread approval. In particular, the campaign emphasized the inadmissibility of "carelessness, laxity, any manifestations of bourgeois pacifism." All party members and people were exhorted to acquire "the right view of the revolutionary war"—most notably, it does not need to be feared—and to undergo military training.[12]

North Korea's armed forces have apparently been gradually prepared to fight against not only external but also internal enemies. Along with confronting class enemies, who according to North Korea's propaganda included "imperialists" and their "accomplices" in South Korea, the KPA was also given the task of destroying the "enemies of the people." The breadth of this notion's coverage is well known from the history of many countries, including North Korea itself. According to the new course the armed forces were given the functions performed previously by the Ministry of People's Security and border guards. This was particularly noticeable in areas adjacent to China, where the army has become a major barrier preventing both the exodus of North Korean refugees and illegal border trade. The number of military patrols across the country greatly increased. Their routine duties included, in particular, checking the documents of citizens in trains, at railway stations, and at roadside checkpoints when entering or leaving cities and towns. As a result, the military was able to increase its influence in the formulation and implementation of domestic and foreign policy, as well as to expand its direct control over the everyday lives of the North Korean people.

Restructuring the society according to a military model and dividing the country and its population into the armed forces and home fronts, which should operate according to military laws, rendered any deep economic and social reforms difficult—and even unnecessary.

Building the Unity of Army and People

Undoubtedly, not everybody was happy with these developments. In order to persuade a less enthusiastic part of the population, authorities propagated a thesis that under the conditions specific to the DPRK, which builds socialism "under siege of imperialism," the powerful revolutionary armed forces were a necessary prerequisite for a successful life of the people, the party, and the state. In this sense, the propaganda machine claimed, "the army is the people, the state and the party."[13]

Within the armed forces, too, special efforts were undertaken to convince the rank-and-file soldiers that the notions of "defending the country" and of "protecting our system" and the leader were equivalent. Military political officers were instructed to maintain proper contact between the WPK organizations in military units and young soldiers. These efforts seem to lend credence to reports that in present-day North Korea, the youth exhibit an evident lack of "revolutionary ideas and enthusiasm" and thus need intensified political education.

The campaign to improve relations between officers and soldiers and to ensure unity between the army and the people also became an important area of the WPK's political-educational activity in military units. The protracted economic crisis, the chronic shortage of material resources—especially food— adversely affected both the situation within the military and the relations between the armed forces and the civilian population, enterprises, and public offices. Therefore, state media began giving wider publicity to all "good examples" of assistance provided by army units to collective farms and individual civilians coping with natural disasters. In addition, the media constantly covered a campaign launched in the early 1990s by authorities among the people to encourage them to send various gifts and aid to army units—warm clothing and socks, daily necessities items, stationery, and so forth, with accompanying letters designed to encourage and support soldiers in fulfilling their military duties.

According to Kim Jong Il's directive given in 1992, the honorary title Exemplary County of Army and People Unity was established.[14] The title was supposed to be awarded to towns and counties that had achieved the most prominent successes in the national movement. A number of other campaigns designed to establish and promote the military way of life and military culture in society were initiated, including a movement under the slogan "My factory [shop, cooperative farm, school, etc.] is my [military] position." The campaign aimed to strengthen the weakened discipline within the state-run enterprises and various public offices.

Who Is Number One?

Since the implementation of the military-first policy, a major question foreign observers have tried to answer is whether the army or the party dominates the DPRK's political system. Several facts emerging from quite recent events allow one, in my opinion, to arrive at a definite answer to this question.

First, the announcement of Kim Jong Il's death was signed by North Korea's top party and state bodies in the following order: the WPK Central Committee, the WPK Central Military Commission, the NDC, the presidium of the SPA, and the DPRK cabinet. Second, Kim Jong Un's succession process started by awarding him the position within the party, not in the NDC. At the third WPK conference, held in 2010, he was elected vice chair of the WPK CMC but remained outside the NDC until April 2012. Third, the 2012 New Year joint editorial mentioned, in particular, that all soldiers must "accept wholeheartedly the ideas of the Party" and defend the party's Central Committee, headed by Kim Jong

Un, at a "cost of life." The New Year joint editorials of both 2012 and 2011 unambiguously indicate that although the army is a "pillar" and even "the main driving force" of the revolution, it performs this role "in accordance with the will and intention of the Party."[15] These directions fully coincide with relevant directives given by Kim Jong Il at various meetings with the WPK and with government officials during the last decade.[16]

The most prominent evidence of top WPK leaders' firm intention to control the military is their awarding military ranks to three high-ranking party officials with no military background: Chan Song Taek; his wife, Kim Kyung Hee; and Choe Ryong Hae. The latter also attained membership in the Presidium of the Politburo, became deputy chair of the CMC, and was appointed to the key military position of chief of the KPA Main Political Department, thus being upgraded to the number-one place in the KPA's military hierarchy. Further, three other high-ranking officials from the same KPA department were elected to full Politburo membership and received appointments as Minister of the People's Armed Forces, First Deputy, and Minister for Protection of State Security, respectively. Their promotion, along with the removal of Ri Yong Ho on July 15, 2012, signified that that the civilian branch of the ruling elite had recovered control from the military one.

Although at the fourth WPK conference the Politburo's vacant seats were filled mainly by those three individuals and several other generals, this is not military rule but rather rule with help from the military—that is, rule that relies on the military. The cautious position of the top brass themselves can perhaps be explained by the fact that in the DPRK, as well as in other former socialist countries, the military has traditionally been involved in political life. They participated in the election, and they served as members of the central and local party committees and government organs. Therefore, they realize very well not only the scope of the problems the country is facing but also the responsibility that they would bear if they assumed direct leadership of the country.

Generally, the experience of the former socialist countries in the 1980s and 1990s has shown that top military commanders, though holding conservative views, have tended to take a largely passive stance toward unfolding events. There is no reason to expect that they could initiate any major changes, especially any directed toward liberalization of the regime. But in Eastern Europe, military leaders also proved incapable of playing a leading role in any coup aimed at preserving the obsolete order. As long as, in accordance with the adopted policies, allocation of even those very limited resources available in the DPRK provides top military commanders and officer corps with high social status and markedly better food and consumer-goods supplies (compared to the resources granted other social groups), the armed forces as a whole look set to remain loyal to the regime and continue performing the role of its main pillar.

Successful Results, Uncertain Future

Thus, the army's role at present and in the short-term perspective appears to include three main functions. First, it undertakes the deterrence of external threats, above all preventing the realization of regime-change scenarios with due consideration of the lessons provided by events in the Balkans, Iraq, and Libya. The most important element of deterrence against any possible enemy has become manipulation through use of a nuclear and missile trump card. Second, the army protects the existing DPRK regime from domestic "class enemies." It seems that the military's involvement in maintaining public order in the country, as well as its assistance to border-security forces in preventing a mass exodus of refugees and curbing other manifestations of social instability, will continue in the coming years. Finally, the military actively participates in the construction of industrial objects and large infrastructure facilities. The significance of the army's involvement in these activities can be easily comprehended: it comprises a disciplined and inexpensive labor force, ever more important under the current difficult socioeconomic conditions and in the face of the physical and moral fatigue characterizing the country's economically active population.

It seems that the rationale for the choice of the *songun* policy was that reorganization of the whole society according to a military order—the introduction of the so-called revolutionary military spirit in the management of the economy, culture, and the people's daily life—would ensure more order, discipline, and control in the society. This order, in turn, would facilitate rapid response to emerging issues, raise the personal responsibility of officials, and ensure that people continue to tolerate low living standards and other hardships.

There are certain grounds for admitting that opting for the military-first policy in a crisis situation, such as the one the DPRK is now facing, in view of the policy's objectives—retaining power and maintaining political and social stability—has proved successful. It is more difficult to answer the question whether the policy will be able to mobilize the support necessary for a program, if there is to be any, of economic modernization. The military organization is able to rather quickly translate orders down the chain of command and ensure their execution. However, it may prove unsuitable for the harmonization of different interests, the search for compromises, and the mobilization of broad support for a creative political course.[17]

The military-first policy remains a strategic course that Pyongyang's leadership ought to follow indefinitely—so long as there is "imperialism" and "the revolution continues." It seems that in the foreseeable future, the fate of North Korean-style socialism will be directly linked to the level of the country's military might, which is now seen as synonymous with the country's national power. The authorities have declared their determination to pursue the strategic line aimed at massive military buildup regardless of any changes in situation, including a shift in the levels of tension or détente in international relations, and irrespective of any hard or soft approach to North Korea taken by the imperialist nations. The task is not to depart from the course for the sake of solving current economic and social problems because, according to official propaganda, a failed economy can be restored, but losing a war means destroying the very foundations of the country.[18]

The demand that all efforts concentrate on strengthening defense capabilities made it impossible to fulfill the task set by the DPRK's leaders —namely, building "in the near future" an "economically powerful nation." The aim should have been achieved by the one hundredth anniversary of Kim Il Sung's birth. However, the task has evidently remained unfulfilled. On the contrary, the existence of the rather acute food problem was officially recognized.[19] The point is that the priority allocations of financial and material resources for the military virtually exclude the possibility not only of restructuring the economy but also of reaching even the minimum targets of normalization of production at a high level in all sectors of the economy. The first public speech by Kim Jong Un, made on April 15, 2012, confirms adherence to this "farsighted strategy." The new leader called on his audience to "eternally glorify the dignity of military-first Korea"—and to "first, second and third," strengthen the army "in every way."[20]

Such policy directives could seriously complicate the settlement of the nuclear issue on the Korean Peninsula and hinder the normalization of inter-Korean relations because, in fact, the course envisages North Korea keeping its nuclear deterrent under any circumstances. As the negative consequences of this line mount, the army may come to be perceived in society as a conservative and even reactionary force hindering the country from overcoming its current economic difficulties and from achieving the promised prosperity. This perception, in turn, potentially bears serious consequences for political stability in the DPRK.

Endnotes

1. *Rodong Sinmun*, April 25, 1997.
2. Great Leader Kim Jong Il's *Original Idea on Leading a Revolution by Giving Priority to a Military-first Policy* (Pyongyang: Social Science Publishing House, 2002), 25.
3. *Rodong Sinmun*, June 16, 1999.
4. Great Leader Kim Jong Il's *Original Idea on Leading a Revolution by Giving Priority to a Military-first Policy*, 25.
5. Ibid., 34.
6. *Rodong Sinmun*, December 26, 2001.
7. See editorials printed in *Rodong Sinmun* each January 1 for the years 1996–2009.
8. http://www.ncnk.org/index_html.
9. *Socialist Constitution of the Democratic People's Republic of Korea* (Pyongyang: Foreign Languages Publishing House, 1998), 22–24.
10. Ibid., 22.
11. *Rodong Sinmun*, January 1, 1996.
12. *Rodong Sinmun*, June 16, 1999.
13. Kim Jong Il, *Konhwagukyn pulphy vireky chin chuchhey sahwechuy kukaida* [The republic: Socialist state of *juche* possessing invincible power], KCNA, October 10, 2008.
14. Kim Jong Il, *Inminkundaeui kanhwahamy kunsaryl chunsihanun sahwejok kiphunyl seuldae tahayo* [On strengthening the People's Army and creating the *songun* atmosphere in society], talk with responsible officials of the WPK CC, February 4, 1992 (Pyongyang: WPK Publishing House, 1999),13.
15. *Rodong Sinmun*, January 1, 2012.
16. Kim Jong Il, "*Songun* Revolution Line Is Our Epoch's Great Revolutionary Line, Our Revolution's All-Winning Banner," talk with responsible officials of the WPK Central Committee, January 29, 2003 (Pyongyang: Foreign Languages Publishing House, 2011), 3–6.
17. Gabriel A. Almond, G. Bingham Powell, Kaare Strom, and Russell J. Dalton, *Comparative Politics Today: A World View* (Moscow: Aspect, 2002), 179–180.
18. *Rodong Sinmun*, June 16, 1999.
19. *Rodong Sinmun*, January 1, 2012.

20. *Rodong Sinmun*, April 16, 2012.

Chapter 6

North Korea and Good Governance

Contradiction in Terms or Faulty Perspective?[1]

Geir Helgesen

North Korea and good governance—why this comparison? For the last twenty years, Western aid agencies, both public and private, have increasingly focused on good governance as a precondition for economic support to developing nations. What does this have to do with North Korea? In the past, nothing at all. The Soviet Union and China did not insist on any preconditions beyond some sort of formal political-ideological loyalty before assisting countries. Now, however, after the collapse of the communist bloc and the ensuing economic and political disasters that hit North Korea in the 1990s, it means almost everything.

North Korea needs international assistance: not only humanitarian aid but also development assistance. It could probably carry on without, but it would in that case be forced to retreat into almost total isolation, as well as to further strengthen its military-first policy and maintain or increase its ideological brainwashing efforts. Since it became clear to the leadership that economic growth involves opening up to the world, this is what the government has tried to achieve: a cautious glasnost with numerous exceptions and an obvious intent that the present leadership remain in power. Today it seems clear that the system will be forced to carry out reforms in order to survive. However, in doing so, the present shape of the government will, of necessity, undergo change.

Although unconditional development support to North Korea is expected to promote a change of society that most likely would pull the given regime in a positive direction, potential Western donors request some sort of guarantee that this will happen before they enter the scene and contribute to changing the North Korean political landscape. This leaves both North Korea itself and those states with sufficient economic power and technical capacity to assist in regenerating the North Korean economy at a stand-off. North Korea requests assistance yet opposes change (or, in its own vocabulary, "ideological pollution"), whereas any potential donor demands a clearly stated willingness to change before that donor is ready to act. Western powers, in particular, make this demand based on their understanding of good governance, which includes fundamental liberal ideas, such as freedom of association and expression, an independent judiciary, and an impartial law-enforcement institution. It is not unthinkable that their economic presence would in fact produce a number of the changes they deem so important, yet the Western powers hesitate.

At present, *North Korea* and *good governance* may seem to be contradictory phrases. There is hardly any other country on earth with an image as bleak. In media coverage, North Korea is referred to as a Stalinist dictatorship. Certain extremely rare occasions counter this image, such as the New York Philharmonic Orchestra's recent visit to Pyongyang. Otherwise, the news from the nation is mainly negative and often frightening. Most reports talk of clandestine nuclear programs and testing, the development of missiles and other military equipment, economic collapse, malnutrition and hunger, inhumane prisons, and dreadful labor camps. The list could easily be continued but need not be in order to present an illustration of North Korea's international face. It is not pretty. All this is seen by most foreign observers as the result of communist dictatorship, repression, a cult of leadership—a dreadful regime that must seem intolerable to any sane and democratically minded person.[2]

North Korea's foreign relations add to the ugly picture, which is dominated by the division of the peninsula and the continuous fight with South Korea over political legitimacy. In particular, the definitively hostile relationship between North Korea and the United States does not allow the authorities in Pyongyang much space in which to maneuver. With the collapse of the international communist alternative to the capitalist market economy, North Korea (with a few other small economies) was left an isolated island in an unfriendly ocean, and the leadership in Pyongyang confronted two main challenges: national security and economic development.[3] These two challenges were interdependent, but at the same time they seemed incompatible. Translating them into a military-first policy and practical-gain socialism[4] only brought on further international condemnation. North Korea secured itself a position below the scale in those international ranking systems that measure quality of life, human rights, and democracy. Although North Korea has suffered several setbacks since 1990 and has not always responded in a way acceptable to the outside world, is its bleak image the only possible one? Could there be other perspectives, other models of measurement, that are more relevant to the specific case? This possibility is discussed in the following pages.

THE TIMING OF THE GOOD GOVERNANCE CONCEPT

Good governance is increasingly presented—for example, by the United Nations (UN)—as a politically neutral or nonideological approach, something that naturally serves as the basis for development assistance.[5] Still, it is difficult not to see the growth of this concept as a consequence of and reaction to the collapse of Soviet-style communism. It is hardly a coincidence that this approach became central to aid agencies at the time when communism was collapsing; the World Bank published on good governance for the first time in the year the Soviet Union disintegrated.[6]

The end of the Cold War overlapped with the beginning of political thinking in a global context, and it seems clear that with the closing of the communist alternative, liberal democracy and human rights became central themes in the West's approach to the Rest. In essence, this new Western self-confidence emphasized the expanding role of market forces and the constraining role of the state.[7] Of particular importance to developing countries all over the world is the American interpretation and implementation of the good governance formula. Not only is the United States, for the time being, the only so-called superpower, thus influencing lesser powers, such as the European Union (EU), in regard to their foreign and aid policies, but the United States also has a decisive say in institutions that include the World Bank and the International Monetary Fund; this is why many developing countries may be extra responsive to foreign-policy statements coming from Washington.

In 2002 George W. Bush announced his goal of increasing US development assistance to foreign nations by 50 percent, to be distributed to nations that, in the president's words, "govern justly, invest in their people, and encourage economic freedom."[8] To decide which nations meet these standards, undersecretary of state for global affairs Paula Dobriansky wrote, "a new Millennium Challenge Corporation will use specific indicators of performance. A crucial indicator will be evidence that a country practices good and just governance."[9] *Good and just* means democracy in its Western form—free and fair elections, an independent judiciary, the rule of law, freedom of speech and the press, respect for human rights and property rights. In the words of the undersecretary, "practicing these principles of good and just governance results in a free and open society where people can pursue their hopes and dreams. This will facilitate the creation of robust and open economies, which are trusted by investors and financial institutions."[10] No one poses the question whether the people populating "the economy" should be given reasons to trust the incoming investors and financial institutions.

The ideal of good governance that is promoted comprises participation, rule of law, transparency, responsiveness, consensus orientation, equity and inclusiveness, and finally, efficiency and accountability.[11] The problem is that these (to most observers) purely plus-words have not yet produced significant positive change, although their implementation has been attempted in a great number of countries over the last two decades.[12] The reason might be what some critics call an overemphasis on technicalities, combined with Western intellectual hegemony and an ensuing inattentiveness to cultural differences. If so, it may all have to do with an effort to spread "Anglo-American institutions of governance ... based on the assumption that the developed countries have the best institutions, which should be embedded across the world irrespective of cultural and historical conditions."[13] From this perspective, good governance might well be seen as a continued effort to maintain Western hegemony or as another way of legitimizing the logic of the market as a cure-all.

It seems fair to claim that the good governance concept used in the development literature and propagated by different UN institutions is substantially different from that which increasingly guides the development assistance of rich Western donor countries and institutions. In the former, this concept may be nuanced by efforts to include particular national—or, as I prefer to call them, cultural—circumstances. In the tool kit of the latter, however, the concept is more fixed. It is understood as universally applicable and as the main key to development.

From this perspective, good governance includes the expanding role of market forces and the constraining role of the state, and this "has become a political and economic conditionality that is inseparable from debates about appropriate bilateral and multilateral financing for developing and formerly socialist bloc countries."[14] Relating this to North Korea is not difficult. My interviews of North Korean civil servants give the clear impression that they see this medicine as better suited for the doctor than for the patient; in their view, this is a way to promote regime change by peaceful means,[15] and this is exactly what the leadership in Pyongyang wants to avoid.

The World Bank has defined bad governance as "personalization of power, lack of human rights, endemic corruption and un-elected and unaccountable government."[16] Apart from the corruption,[17] this may sum up a widely accepted characterization of the North Korean regime: the incarnation of bad governance. Is there, then, in the case of North Korea, a bridge leading from bad to good—or at least better—governance, or is one stuck with a fundamental contradiction in terms regarding North Korea and good governance? The distance may be too far by any known standards, and flexibility on either side has until now been a rare commodity.

This said, changes are not unimaginable, and some may be under way. For one thing, the ideology of the market as the cure-all remedy is no longer sacrosanct, not even in those major financial institutions with headquarters in Washington. The ideas that the state is a parasite and that everything the state can do, the market can do better, have in many instances proved wrong. There is now a growing consensus in the field that the state is a necessary player, "that an efficient, thriving market economy and civil society require an effective and strong government."[18] Instead of less government in a minimalist state, what may be needed is an effective state and more appropriate government.[19] This, combined with a less essentialist attitude regarding the good governance recipe on the part of the donors[20] and with an acceptance of local differences and acknowledgment of the capacity of existing institutions,[21] should be received as interesting news in Pyongyang, where the authorities struggle with the problem of adjusting the economy without too much political change. Whether this change of perspective in major international organizations will benefit North Korea is another question.

Good Governance: Asian Experiences

Although good governance usually is presented as a precondition for economic development, in a rich variety of Asian examples the order has been the opposite. India and China are the major instances: India, often called the world's biggest democracy, still suffers from great social disparities and widespread poverty. China, where democracy still is alien to the regime, has achieved economic progress and an impressive distribution of wealth, although there is still a long way to go.

In North Korea, however, postwar developments south of the thirty-eighth parallel are more relevant. In the 1960s and 1970s, authoritarian governments rooted in the military with strong links to local entrepreneurs and protected by alliances with the United States carried out an economy-first policy without considering labor rights, democratic rights, or human rights. At that time, it was South Korea that closely approximated the World Bank's definition of bad governance, including extensive corruption. In hindsight, the South Korean "forced economic development" can be defended as the only possible way for a third-world latecomer. By pointing at the peaceful political revolution that followed the economic one, eventually leading to democracy, it may now seem easy to defend this project. It was, nevertheless, a brutal experience for a great many people in the South.

A relevant but seldom asked question is this: If it worked in the South, could it not work in the North? Is it too risky given that the regime is undemocratic, sticks to an unclear communist ideology, and is led by a dictator who inherited the position from his father? One main difference between the South Korea of the past and the North Korea of the present is political family succession combined with a "sort of" communist ideology. Another major difference is that the main benefactor of South Korean development is the main adversary regarding development in North Korea, under current conditions. This might be the ultimate hindrance to a breakthrough, and this is exactly why this relationship needs to be reexamined.

In the highly fascinating article "Seeing North Korea Clearly," authors Daniel Pinkston and Philip Saunders suggested that "ideological blinders" and "misleading intellectual constructs" in the US administration hinder a clear understanding of the North Korean regime, its security concerns, and its international policy intentions.[22] When one views the North wearing ideological blinders, everything related to it is shaded negatively, and the leader is seen as an evil person who will never moderate or change his behavior. Other more positive signals cannot be received because they are unexpected and therefore unthinkable and unimaginable.[23] A change of heart will, in this context, often be interpreted as an effort to deceive because this is the enemy (part of the "axis of evil"), and thus its ideas and views cannot be taken at face value. There must be a hidden agenda. Is there a way around this stalemate?

In dealing with North Korea as a political entity, the general perspective taken by foreign ministries and a majority of aid organizations, as well as the entire Western press, is insufficient. It is insufficient (as argued by Pinkston and Saunders) if it fails to reasonably convey messages from the subjects of study—and this is exactly what it does. What I would argue is that there is something essential observers are missing in trying to grasp North Korean reality, and that this is why the image of North Korea remains unchangeably negative and stereotypically bizarre.

A Better Tool for Grasping North Korean Reality

In the Western part of the world, most observers of North Korea take a strongly critical—if not negative—approach. This critical approach very often overemphasizes things belonging to the political or ideological sphere and misses what is particularly Korean because the critics have no categories in their vocabulary for such "deviations."[24] If the mainstream Western picture of North Korea fails to convey an understandable image of a country and a system that actually differ from most other countries and systems,[25] then this picture must be challenged. If descriptions of North Korea as a Stalinist dictatorship run by an aggressive scoundrel are one sided, oversimplified, and out of context, then one cannot expect much insight from them. Many of these conventional accounts are based on a context that is alien to North Korean reality; therefore, it is necessary to shift the perspective.

Is there, then, a reality in North Korea that is different from realities in other parts of the world? Is that which is perceived to be fact in most parts of the world fiction in North Korea? The mainstream critical observer of North Korean affairs may stick to a universalist rational-choice perspective, claiming that people harbor the same sort of aspirations and dreams, no matter where or when, and that maximization of self-interest is the main driving force in any society. Although self-interest obviously appears to be an impressive and almost determining force in modern Western as well as Eastern consumer societies, it hardly suffices as a universal theory explaining social reality and the human mind. The political-culture approach claims that people's subjective understandings of the nature of power, their expectations about authority, and their interpretations of what constitutes legitimacy are key determinants of political development.[26] Sustainable political change presupposes change in these perceptions, and how such changes are generated remains a crucial question. What can be maintained from the outset is that cultures differ and culture matters.[27]

From a Western perspective, the East Asian region has a different and quite distinct culture. China, Korea, and Japan each has its particular characteristics, but in comparison with northern European cultural traits, for instance, they seem quite similar to each other.[28] Culture is not static, of course, and modernization has altered old ways while introducing new ones. This fact notwithstanding, today scholars know that culture—understood as basic values and norms—has a certain inertia. One could say that culture is a conservative force in any society and that cultural change takes place within a given social context. This is the reason Ronald Inglehart's World Values Survey draws a world map based on values. The cultural zones do not exactly follow national borders, but it makes sense to operate with a Confucian East Asia, a Protestant Western Europe, and so forth. To quote Inglehart, "A history of Protestant or Orthodox or Islamic or Confucian traditions gives rise to cultural zones with distinctive value systems that persist after controlling for the effects of economic development."[29]

This cultural persistence applies to societies with highly developed foreign relations, extensive political and cultural borrowing, free travel, and all types of exchange. In the case of North Korea this is different, and the difference magnifies the importance of culture, both traditional and created. This country has been isolated to such an extent that it has been possible for the political authorities to develop and inculcate a certain worldview in the whole population. This worldview has consciously been created by combining aspects of tradition with political-ideological imports, and more often than not, the imports have been presented in familiar terms and contexts. With no alternative views around—and thus no ideological or political-moral challenges—the North Korean official ideology has become the worldview of its people. Any attempt to understand North Korean politics without taking this into consideration is doomed to failure.

It may be a commonplace statement, but in trying to grasp the North Korean reality, a certain combination of identification with and detachment from the subject is needed. Some scholars call this a need for empathy.[30] This kind of understanding does not imply acceptance but an effort to see reality as it is seen by the other—in this case, the North Koreans. Although it is impossible to fully put oneself in the other's place, such efforts are necessary in order to approach the other. To accomplish this task, an awareness that there are different assumptions about reality and different views about what is good and bad, right and wrong, true and false, is helpful. Thereby, an amount of basic relativism is introduced. A recommended angle on this is to use the political-culture approach, of which Lucian Pye was one of the founding fathers. Briefly stated, this approach emphasizes that politics deals with power and that the phenomenon of power is extremely sensitive to cultural differences. Hence, dealing with politics in different parts of the world necessitates awareness of culture as well as of cultural differences. A possible implication of this approach is that a universal practice in governance is simply a contradiction in terms.

A Reintroduction of the Human Mind to International Politics

Studies in international politics were long dominated by a rational-actor perspective that assumed that political leaders act rationally in their quest for power.[31] In the case of North Korea, this perspective takes a peculiar twist, suggesting that leaders of other countries in their relations with North Korea act rationally, whereas the leadership in North Korea is irrational and bound to miscalculate its own situation, eventually producing catastrophic consequences. The Kim Jong Il leadership in Pyongyang outlived this prophecy by more than fifteen years and several catastrophes; not all of them can be ascribed to the leadership's own miscalculated actions.[32] It might therefore be timely to challenge and expand this Western-centric idea and perceive leaders—both in North Korea and in other countries—as cognitive actors. This implies that they are human beings who perceive the world from different positions informed by the sociocultural and psychological traits particular to the social groups to which they belong. This does not mean abandoning rationality but includes the individual as actor in political relations.[33] This cognitive approach suggests that people differ in how they view the world and their role in it, as well as that these patterns of behavior are detectable and understandable.[34] In other words, this perspective is a dismissal of the intellectual tradition that has sought to eliminate psychological phenomena from explanations of human behavior.[35]

Although this is a fascinating issue, an in-depth discussion of the cognitive approach in international politics lies outside the framework of this chapter. However, because North Korea in the eyes of many academics and media observers remains a pariah, it seems relevant to consider whether this approach could contribute to a more nuanced picture. In this context, the cognitive attribution theory is fitting. The attribution theory (or the correspondent inference theory) has been developed within social psychology as a theory concerned with how people explain both their own and others' behavior.[36] A particularly relevant aspect of this theory is the fundamental attribution error, which finds expression in a general tendency to explain one's own behavior as a response to the given situation: "I had to do *x* because of *y*" (*y* being some external circumstance). This behavior is then perceived as situational—and thus rational. When judging others, one tends to see their behavior as dispositional. Their actions are attributable to an internal disposition; they may be insensitive to others or aggressive—and thus irrational.[37] When reinforced by a widespread general tendency to see oneself and one's friends in a positive light and to see those one dislikes in a negative light (termed the *halo effect*), the fundamental attribution error may account for the resilience of enemy images long after the conflicting relationship has ended. It would be strange if the tense and complicated relationship between North Korea and the United States were completely unaffected by attribution errors, presupposing that human actors and the relationship between them play any role whatsoever in international politics. Several studies give convincing evidence pointing in that direction.[38]

Because variations in cognitive dynamics between individuals within the same culture are important, one must assume that cultural differences increase the likelihood of misperception and misunderstanding.[39]

If one consults cross-cultural psychology, it is quite easy to locate studies focusing on similarities and differences in social attribution across cultures. In a study from 2002 published in *Personality and Social Psychology Bulletin*,[40] one conclusion is that East Asian people "believe in the continuous shaping of personality traits by situational influences."[41] According to the authors, the study indicates that people in East Asia view personality as more flexible, whereas people in the West operate with the idea of personality traits as something quite fixed.[42]

This difference is anything but trivial and may have serious political implications, as demonstrated by the icy relationship between American presidents and North Korean leaders. When American president George W. Bush clearly expressed his distaste for the North Korean leader and Washington decided that North Korea belonged to the "axis of evil," naming it a "rogue state," the problem was—and is—that these expressions imply that the situation will never improve. The evil state will never moderate its behavior; the bad leader will never be reasonable. This is the case because people in the Western world have a tendency to see character and personality as fixed. A leader who is considered evil is not expected to change, and therefore, if he is evil enough, there is good reason to get rid of him, by violent means if necessary. For North Korea there is a recent, frightening example in what happened between the United States and Iraq, and this may explain North Korea's military-first doctrine and its nuclear ambitions.

Is a Nuclear North Korea Evil?

How is this "axis of evil" approach received in East Asia? A fascinating study by C. Fred Alford published in 1999 investigates the notion of evil in South Korea.[43] His findings suggest that not only is there a difference in eastern and western perceptions of whether character is seen as fixed or flexible, but there is also a basic difference in how easterners and westerners understand evil. In Alford's words, "when everything one knows about evil, and everything else, is learned and practiced in the family, and relationships modeled on the family, how can one ever call something, or someone, evil?"[44] To operate with evil as a characteristic of a person is close to impossible in a society where all social relations are seen as extended family, even to the extent that strangers are called by terms that refer to family members.[45]

Is this something that has implications for relations with North Korea? According to Alford, it has indeed. "To call North Korea evil," wrote the author, "would be impossibly terrifying for most Koreans, because [South] Koreans cannot create the type of distance from the North that would allow them to alienate evil there.'[46] Far from making a culturally simplified or stereotypical statement, Alford was seriously reflecting on the perceptions he had encountered in Korea. He suggested that in the Korean worldview, there might be no "cultural-receptors" for evil.[47] Alford's study was carried out in the late 1990s, before the nuclear issue exploded on the Korean Peninsula. He nevertheless included this issue as one of his hypothetical questions, phrased as follows: "Would it be evil if North Korea had nuclear weapons?"[48] Almost all his respondents said no, and about half of them said that North Korea would never use nuclear weapons against the South. Some elaborated by saying that "if the North Koreans had nuclear weapons, they would be ours too."[49]

If evil is not exactly the same to all people all over the world, are things any different with the perception of good? And what about power, this central aspect in political affairs—is power a universal concept? One could continue along this line, scrutinizing every single concept and phenomenon of political relevance; this brings forth the question whether good governance can really be a universal concept. Good governance may be characterized as grand contemporary ideology, for it includes both democracy and human rights. One of the fundamental insights stressed in the political-culture approach is that if grand ideologies are to succeed, they must speak to people's basic psychological needs, touch unconscious emotions, and reach what people intuitively feel to be true.[50] If this is the case, right and truth are linked to a local context, and because political systems are developed based on distinctive historical experiences, they will always maintain a strong parochial dimension.[51]

Western Theories and Asian Facts

More than twenty years ago, Lucian Pye emphasized that social scientists in general have been "unaware of how Asian facts might limit the validity of theories based only on Western experience."[52] This statement may still characterize mainstream social science in the West, including studies focusing on Asian issues, although culture-sensitive approaches have become more visible lately and have gained importance.

Studies in political culture, in particular, focus on how people are socialized to understand and relate to different societal aspects that are of importance to the way in which societies are organized and kept together. Thus, the subjective understanding of the nature of power, expectations about authority, and interpretations of legitimacy constitute the fundamentals of a political culture.[53] It goes without saying that perceptions of power, authority, and legitimacy are based on more than mere textbook teachings. In this sense, political socialization is enculturation, a process whereby individuals are taught by their cultures the values and norms relevant for becoming an accepted member of society. When childhood socialization in the family context, formal teaching in educational institutions, and political and ideological propaganda all have a common root and the one is created to reinforce the other, together they may constitute a resilient worldview that can be very difficult to challenge. With regard to North Korea, I have found no better formulation of this phenomenon than the following quotation: "Without interruption in the progression of socialization for several decades, Juche has been able to deeply penetrate and assimilate itself into the mass belief system. The degree of rigidity and saliency of beliefs may have reached a point at which external disturbances may not easily cause psychological dissonance."[54]

North Korea has developed in more isolated conditions than most countries, isolated by others and by choice. It has transformed traditional values and norms without altering some of the inherent concepts and understandings relevant to society and politics. Whereas Confucianism has been removed from teaching, textbooks, and daily political communication as a stated social and moral ideology, it remains a fundamental basis for contemporary ideology as well as for political thinking and action. This has been possible in North Korea because of its isolation. The aforementioned theorist, Fred Alford, claimed that Confucianism in South Korea today has become "metabolized," present in every part of the social body.[55] When the opportunity came about to discuss this matter informally and in private with a North Korean colleague several years ago, he said without hesitation, "Our people are imbued by Confucianism."[56] Such statements could easily be criticized as oversimplified—and thus wrong—given that Korean political cultures, North and South, are far more complex and also include aspects of shamanism, Buddhism, and Christianity, as well as secular influences from Western ideologies.[57] This is true, but it does not alter the fact that North Koreans adhere to a worldview within which their political system imbues with meaning and responds to basic psychological needs and touches unconscious emotions.

To Allow for Change and Accept the Outcome

To see North Korea clearly, one needs to approach the North Korean worldview, not to prove it wrong or to fit it into an enemy perspective in order to justify continued hostilities and refusals to assist in its development, but to understand it. To measure North Korea based on the ideology of good governance is a dead end, a faulty perspective, because it assumes a universal rationality that exists only as wishful thinking while entirely ignoring any perceptions of reality other than those based on Western ideals, values, and norms.

Research in the field has demonstrated beyond doubt that cultures differ and culture matters. Different cultures are not alien entities but rather different ideas and positions on an extended line of continuity. The generalizations of which a culture consists, however, relate to a particular pattern that characterizes a majority of the people under study.[58] Even the most internationalized societies maintain crucial aspects of a parochial political culture, and countries not engaged in close international interaction, such as North Korea, will obviously maintain stronger local and traditional traits.

People are raised to understand and relate to society through specific cultures, and the differences in world outlook that this causes must be taken seriously. In some parts of the world, social morality promotes individual freedoms; in others, people are taught to seek conformity. In some areas power is paternalistic and dependency is a positive trait; in others, power needs to be checked and dependency avoided. One can find spots on the globe where social emotions are a central part of what holds society together; in others, emotions are relegated to a space outside the realm of politics. In some regions, collectivistic traits are prevalent; in others, individualism prevails. Frequently, East Asia and the Western world occupy opposing positions on what could be termed the extended cultural continuum of human affairs.

Are there any recent and relevant examples in which these insights have been found useful in solving or avoiding problems that would otherwise spoil relations? Fortunately, there are many. No self-respecting global business today neglects culturally based differences, and there is a huge industry and much profit involved in contributing varying degrees of input to this ever-growing field of consultancy.

Unfortunately, this culture-sensitive thinking has not yet affected international politics, in which a hegemonic view of universalism prevails.

Good or bad governance depends on the political culture, on the values and norms that guide citizens toward what are considered acceptable common attitudes and behavior. These are not fixed items but rather fluid ones, and change occurs at a slow pace. Isolation may temporarily inhibit change, but contrary to understandings of a few years ago, globalization may inhibit change to an equal degree, for it often scares people by undermining their belief systems.

In North Korea, change has been slow, mainly owing to fear of external forces. A constructive approach to North Korea takes its fears seriously and acknowledges the worldview it has created as an ideology of survival. A sustainable change in North Korea will come from within, as a result of improved and friendly relations with the surrounding world. This should be one very good reason to improve relations with North Korea despite any present disagreements or conflicts regarding practical issues of relevance.

Until now, the lingua franca of diplomatic relations has not been based on culture-sensitive positions, and basic misunderstandings as well as a general lack of trust may have been unavoidable outcomes of this shortcoming. Making allowances for the existence of different worldviews that produce differences in the human psyche is probably one of the main challenges in international relations in the twenty-first century. Relations between North Korea and the outside world can provide a stockpile of data and create a working laboratory for such studies that would probably add important aspects to the concept of good governance.

Endnotes

1. I would like to thank the reviewer, the editorial team at Globis, the Department of International Affairs at the University of Georgia, and—in particular—my research assistant, Ras Tind Nielsen, at the Nordic Institute of Asian Studies at the University of Copenhagen, for their valuable comments and suggestions
2. Daniel A. Pinkston and Philip C. Saunders, "Seeing North Korea Clearly," *Survival* 45, no. 3 (2003): 79–102. The authors wrote that "Bush administration officials have interpreted North Korean economic problems as the inevitable product of a repugnant political system" (84). According to the authors, this is an oversimplification.
3. Haksoon Paik, "North Korea Today: Politics Overloaded and Secularized," in *North Korea: 2005 and Beyond*, ed. Philip W. Yun and Gi-Wook Shin (Stanford, CA: Walter H. Shorenstein Asia-Pacific Research Center, 2006), 38.
4. Ibid., 47.
5. "Major donors and international financial institutions are increasingly basing their aid and loans on the condition that reforms that ensure 'good governance' are undertaken." UN Economic and Social Commission for Asia and the Pacific, http://www.unescap.org.
6. P. Larmour, "State, Society and Governance in Melanesia. Making Sense of Good Governance" (discussion paper, Research School of Pacific and Asian Studies, the Australian National University, Canberra, Australia, 1998), 4.
7. See John Williamson, "A Short History of the Washington Consensus," http://www.iie.com/publications/papers/williamson 0904-2.pdf.
8. Paula Dobriansky, "Principles of Good Governance," *Economic Perspectives* (2003), IIP E-Journals, www.nth.gov.ua/usa/English/trade/ijee0303/dobrians.htm.
9. Ibid.
10. Ibid., 3.
11. UNESCAP, "What Is Good Governance?" 2009, www.unescap.org/pdd/prs/project activities/ongoing/gg/governance.asp.
12. K. Sing, *Aid and Good Governance: A Discussion Paper for the Reality of Aid* (Delhi, India: Public Interest Research Group, 2003), 17.
13. Ibid., 10.

14. T. G. Weiss, "Governance, Good Governance, and Global Governance: Conceptual and Actual Challenges," *Third World Quarterly* 21, no. 5 (2000): 801.
15. Interviews with North Korean civil servants in Pyongyang, 2004 and 2006.
16. Ibid., 801.
17. It is not the experience of international aid organizations present in Pyongyang that corruption is an endemic problem in North Korea.
18. Weiss, "Governance, Good Governance, and Global Governance," 803.
19. Ibid., 804.
20. Merilee S. Grindle, "Good Enough Governance: Poverty Reduction and Reform in Developing Countries," *Governance: An International Journal of Policy, Administration, and Institutions* 17, no. 4 (2004): 525–548.
21. Merilee S. Grindle, "Good Enough Governance Revisited," *Development Policy Review* 25, no. 5 (2007): 562.
22. Pinkston and Saunders, "Seeing North Korea Clearly."
23. Ibid., 87–89.
24. Pinkston and Saunders, "Seeing North Korea Clearly."
25. Bruce Cumings, *North Korea: Another Country* (New York: Free Press, 2004).
26. Lucian W. Pye, *Asian Power and Politics: The Cultural Dimensions of Authority* (Cambridge, MA: Belknap Press of Harvard University Press, 1985), 19.
27. Lawrence E. Harrison and Samuel P. Huntington, eds., *Culture Matters: How Values Shape Human Progress* (New York: Basic Books, 2000).
28. Geir Helgesen and S. R. Thomsen, eds., *Politics, Culture, and Self: East Asian and North European Attitudes* (Copenhagen: NIAS Press, 2006).
29. R. Inglehart and W. E. Baker, "Modernization, Cultural Change, and the Persistence of Traditional Values," *American Sociological Review* 65 (2000): 49.
30. Pinkston and Saunders, "Seeing North Korea Clearly."
31. Jerel A. Rosati, *The Power of Human Cognition in the Study of World Politics* (Malden, MA: Blackwell, 2001).
32. Pinkston and Saunders, "Seeing North Korea Clearly," 85.
33. Rosati, *Power of Human Cognition*, 50.
34. Ibid., 52.
35. J. Mercer, "Rationality and Psychology in International Politics," *International Organization* 59 (Winter 2005): 78.

36. Jerel A. Rosati, "A Cognitive Approach to the Study of Foreign Policy," in *Foreign Policy Analysis: Continuity and Change in Its Second Generation*, ed. Laura Neack, Jeanne A. K. Hey, Patrick Jude Haney (Englewood Cliffs, NJ: Prentice Hall Humanities/Social Science, 1995), 49–70.
37. Mercer, "Rationality and Psychology," 78.
38. See references in Rosati, *Power of Human Cognition*; Rosati examined much of the literature relevant to the discussion of human cognition in the study of world politics.
39. Rosati, *Power of Human Cognition*, 71.
40. A. Norenzayan, I. Choi, and Richard E. Nisbett, "Cultural Similarities and Differences in Social Inference: Evidence From Behavioral Predictions and Lay Theories of Behavior," *Personality and Social Psychology Bulletin* 28, no. 1 (2002): 109–120.
41. Ibid., 118.
42. Ibid., 118–120.
43. C. Fred Alford, *Think No Evil: Korean Values in the Age of Globalization* (Ithaca, NY: Cornell University Press, 1999).
44. Ibid., 98.
45. Ibid., 99.
46. Ibid., 105.
47. Ibid., 103.
48. Ibid., 107.
49. Ibid.
50. Pye, *Asian Power and Politics*, 322.
51. Ibid., 342.
52. Ibid., 9.
53. Ibid., 19.
54. Han S. Park, *North Korea: The Politics of Unconventional Wisdom* (Boulder, CO: Lynne Rienner). *Juche* is the North Korean state ideology emphasizing self-reliance in every possible sphere.
55. Alford, *Think No Evil*, 151.
56. Professor at Kim Il Sung University in conversation with the author, 1987.
57. Geir Helgesen, *Democracy and Authority in Korea: The Cultural Dimension in Korean Politics* (New York: St. Martin's, 1998), 99–120.
58. Richard E. Nisbett, *The Geography of Thought: How Asians and Westerners Think Differently... and Why* (New York: Free Press, 2003).

CHAPTER 7

NORTH KOREA--DEALING WITH IRRATIONALITY

Bruce Cumings

Shortly after Barack Obama took office, North Korea launched another long-range missile, detonated its second atomic bomb, and greeted the new president with a farrago of nonnegotiable demands: We are a nuclear weapons state! We don't care if you want normal relations with us or not! We want light water reactors! Get your troops out of the South![1] This was the same Barack Obama who had campaigned on reaching out to the "rogue states" that George W. Bush had shunned and who memorably said at his inauguration that leaders who "unclench your fist" would find an open hand in Washington. Pyongyang's leaders chose the United States' Memorial Day, May 25, to successfully test a three or four kiloton atomic bomb, thus silencing claims that their first test of a half-kiloton bomb in October 2006 had been a "dud." President Obama declared all this "a grave threat" to the United States and pushed a resolution through the United Nations (UN) Security Council to shadow and possibly intercept North Korean vessels on the high seas. The North then stated that this would be an act of war and threatened to respond with "merciless blows"—proffering its fiercest clenched fist. Somehow the cunning of history had left Barack Obama carrying the water of John Bolton's Proliferation Security Initiative, no doubt to the delight of Dick Cheney.

American television rounded up all the usual images of North Korea: frightening soldiers goose-stepping through Pyongyang, a madman who starves his people at the helm, missiles fired "over Japan" (all missiles are launched toward the east, to take advantage of the earth's rotation), Hawaii possibly at risk (Defense Secretary Gates sent special missile-defense batteries to the islands). A few experts sought to point out that the Bush administration, in its peculiar combination of ideological rigidity and haphazard policy, had contrived to hand over the plutonium with which the North made its bombs, but no one wanted to hear it: a seamless, bipartisan Beltway consensus said that the North's provocations could never be tolerated; something had to be done.[2]

It is too bad that Kim Jong Il could look so sinister when he wanted to; his father's always-smiling visage sometimes made it hard to imagine him shipping enemies off to the gulag or bureaucrats off to the mines. This odd prince perhaps had the face that life rather than nature had given him; like Bush, he had to contend with the knowledge that his fate would have been rather different without daddy's provenance. But his face was perfect for an American media establishment that loves to present its stories and tales about the North with "Dr. Evil" affixed to the cover. But what does one make of a magazine of record with a worldwide, historical reputation for indefatigable fact checking—namely, *The New Yorker*—advertising a major article on the North under the caption "How Crazy is Kim?" American discourse on foreign adversaries has become completely debased; it is a cartoon show playing into the hands of hard-liners, just as it denies the American people the information and knowledge that would enable them to come to reasonable judgments.

How did the United States arrive at this parody of its long history with Pyongyang? In May 1993 the Koreans dumped eight thousand plutonium fuel rods into cooling ponds, nearly causing Bill Clinton to initiate a second Korean War; luckily, Jimmy Carter's intervention brought about a freeze on the North's plutonium facility that lasted eight years. In August 1998 the North Koreans tested their first long-range missile, producing another frenzy of ill-informed punditry, and in 2006 they ran a scenario very similar to the most recent one—testing missiles and their first atomic bomb, choosing American holidays as punctuation (July 4, 2006, was the date of the North's second long-range missile test; it tested seven short-range missiles again on July 4, 2009). Each episode was followed by more mimetic media tropes: evil communists led by a cognac-swilling nutcase, a rogue regime running amok. How is it that a long-running crisis, now rather thoroughly known in its admittedly difficult and intricate detail, is reinvented every couple of years with no discernible learning amid its eternal recurrence?

The answer lies not in Pyongyang but in Washington: since the Berlin Wall fell a Beltway consensus embracing leaders of both parties has adhered to four core axioms: (1) North Korea stands for nothing, has no support from its people, and will soon collapse; (2) American pressure on this regime will either hasten this process (Republicans) or change its behavior (Democrats); (3) if engagement works to get rid of their nuclear weapons, fine—but the end goal here, too, is a "velvet" form of regime change; (4) if engagement does not work, resort to military force is justified to stop the North from becoming a nuclear power. All these assumptions are false and, in light of recent history, irrational.

The Coming Collapse of North Korea

If "know your enemy" is the *sine qua non* of effective warfare and diplomacy, the United States has been badly served by those in Washington who claim expertise on North Korea. The mantra that the Democratic People's Republic of Korea (DPRK) would soon collapse began with Bush I and lasted all through Clinton and Bush II. Iraq war architect Paul Wolfowitz journeyed to Seoul in the aftermath of the apparent American victory over Saddam to opine (in June 2003) that "North Korea is teetering on the brink of collapse." In intervening years, Americans heard General Gary Luck, commander of US forces in Korea, say (in 1997) that "North Korea will disintegrate, possibly in very short order"; the only question was whether it would implode or explode.[3] In this he was merely plagiarizing another US commander in Korea, General Robert Riscassi, who never tired of saying Pyongyang would soon "implode or explode" (Riscassi retired in 1992). Even the American pledge to build two light water reactors to replace the Yongbyon plutonium complex in the 1994 freeze agreement was premised on collapse: because the reactors would not go on stream for a decade, by then they would belong to the Republic of Korea (ROK). What is the statute of limitations on being systematically wrong? But I know from experience that any attempt by outsiders to break through this Beltway groupthink merely results in polite silence and discrete headshaking. That North Korea's collapse is imminent is still the dominant opinion today.[4]

The leading Washington pundit on North Korea is Nicholas Eberstadt, who has been predicting the impending collapse of North Korea since at least June 1990,[5] but his views are best sampled in his 1999 book, *The End of North Korea*. (When a *New York Times* reporter asked John Bolton what the Bush administration's policy was on the DPRK, he strode to his bookshelf and handed him Eberstadt's book: "That's our policy," he said.) Eberstadt's error is fundamental, for he sees the DPRK entirely through the lenses of Soviet and Eastern European communism and therefore cannot grasp the regime's very different history, the pragmatic shrewdness of its post-Soviet foreign policy, and the desperate survival strategies it is willing to undertake—let alone the anticolonial and revolutionary nationalist origins of this regime (and those in Vietnam and China, yielding no break since 1989 in Asian communism, except for the one true Soviet satellite: Mongolia).

In 1997 the CIA invited Eberstadt and other outside experts to join a panel of government officials that concluded that North Korea was likely to collapse within five years. Robert A. Wampler, who obtained this report under the Freedom of Information Act, quoted senior Foreign Service officer David Straub's observation that one expert after another came through the Tokyo embassy in the early 1990s "pontificating on their prognoses for the inevitable collapse of the North Korean regime, giving odds that allowed Pyongyang anywhere from a few months to perhaps two years before falling."[6] Kim Jong Il, the assembled CIA experts thought, was likely to have just "a brief window of time" to cope with all his difficulties before suffering a probable "hard landing." Without major reform, some "catalyst" was certain to come along "that will lead to collapse." The majority of the group doubted that Kim's regime could persist "beyond five years" and opined that it would succumb to a "political implosion." Yet many of them expressed surprise that in spite of the degraded economy and the beginnings of a famine that would soon grow much worse, somehow the "delusionary" (their word) Kim Jong Il "remained firmly in control." Among those outsiders whom the CIA invited to this exercise, apart from Eberstadt, were academics Kenneth Lieberthal and Robert Ross, and Daryl Plunk and James Przystup from the Heritage Foundation. No academic experts on North Korea were there (Lieberthal and Ross are China experts), but more surprising, neither was anyone from the Brookings Institution or the Carnegie Endowment—the liberal anchors of the (remarkably narrow) spectrum of Beltway opinion. Here was the CIA under the Clinton administration reaching out to the political right for guidance on "North Korea's coming collapse."

Successive administrations and Beltway pundits get North Korea so wrong because they know next to nothing about its origins, view it through the lens of Soviet behavior, and cannot come up with any North Korean interests that they deem worthy of respect. For many, it is an outrage that the regime continues to exist at all (this was the dominant opinion during the George W. Bush administration). But in the end, what difference does this make? Is the DPRK going to erase itself because the American Enterprise Institute thinks it should? Eberstadt eventually got tired of predicting the DPRK's collapse and decided to do something about it: in 2004 he argued that America and its allies should waltz in and, as he put it with Reaganesque flourish, "tear down this tyranny."[7] At the time he had excellent backing for such views in vice president Dick Cheney's entourage, especially Paul Wolfowitz, John Bolton, and Robert Joseph (director of nonproliferation at the National Security Council). With the demise of the Bush vision, if one can call it that, enthusiasm for such a course has waned. But it was the preferred policy of hard-liners for several years, amid the internal civil war that shaped Bush's policies on North Korea—where most meetings on North Korea turned into raging shouting matches.[8]

REGIME CHANGE

A recent book that comes highly recommended by the *New York Review of Books* begins with a "fictional scenario," which takes up sixteen pages, about a preemptive strike against every nuclear, military, industrial, and governmental facility in North Korea—another preventive war, in short. Just as in Iraq, dozens of F-117 Stealth fighter-bombers open the campaign by trying to solve Kim Jong Il's perpetual bad hair day through decapitation, followed by phalanxes of F-16 fighters launched from several nearby American aircraft carriers, B-1 and B-52 bombers, and Tomahawk cruise missiles; thousands of JDAM blast munitions and "high-intensity, heat-generating BLU-118Bs" are unleashed, "designed to penetrate reinforced bunkers." Finally, sixty thousand Marines rush in from Okinawa to march on Pyongyang.[9] If the reader finds this war game preposterous, it is entirely prefigured in Bush administration strategies and the Pentagon's real-world war plans. After 9/11 Donald Rumsfeld suggested preemptive nuclear strikes on rogue states,[10] and when it appeared that the invasion of Iraq would move quickly to victory, he demanded revisions in the basic war plan for Korea (called Operations Plan 5030) and also sought money from Congress for new bunker-busting nuclear weapons. The strategy, according to insiders who have read the plan, was "to topple Kim's regime by destabilizing its military forces," so that they would overthrow him and thus accomplish a regime change. The plan was pushed "by many of the same administration hard-liners who advocated regime change in Iraq." Unnamed senior Bush administration officials considered elements of this new plan "so aggressive that they could provoke a war."[11]

Threatening war is also a bipartisan position and hardly new. On NBC's *Meet the Press* on April 3, 1994, defense secretary William Perry said, "We do not want war and will not provoke a war," but if US sanctions "provoke the North Koreans into unleashing a war ... that is a risk that we're taking."[12] Perry's formulation was careful and precise: he and Ashton Carter Jr. had been studying for some time whether a preemptive strike could be carried out against Yongbyon without starting the next Korean War; they concluded that it could not. By mid-June 1994 the Clinton administration "had devised a plan laying out the first steps the US should take to prepare for war," which included stationing ten thousand additional American troops in South Korea, dispatching Apache attack helicopters and various other aircraft, and moving in more Bradley Fighting Vehicles.[13] Furthermore, "to make sure Clinton understood both the human and the monetary costs of a war, the Joint Chiefs had summoned all the regional commanders and four star generals in the service to Washington in late May [1994] to discuss Korea and brief the president."[14] According to US commander in Korea General Gary Luck's estimates, he would need as many as 80,000 to 100,000 body bags in the field for the American soldiers who would die in a new Korean War, and

Korean troop casualties could reach the hundreds of thousands. Moreover, if the North struck Seoul as expected, "the number of civilian casualties would be staggering." The cost of such a war, Luck predicted, would be at least $500 million and could top $1 trillion, far higher than the almost $60 billion spent on Desert Storm. If Perry and Carter were right and the North would have attacked the South after a preemptive strike, the ultimate consequences of that war cannot be known but might have included American attacks using nuclear weapons: think of it—a nuclear war in the name of nonproliferation. But they seem undaunted by all this as they continued to publish editorials calling for preemptive strikes during the Bush administration.[15]

Shortly before the fiftieth anniversary of the Korean War armistice in 2003, Perry gave a harrowing interview to the *Washington Post.* "I think we are losing control" of the situation, he said; the United States was on a "path to war." North Korea might soon have enough nuclear warheads to begin exploding them in tests or exporting them to terrorists. "The nuclear program now underway in North Korea poses an imminent danger of nuclear weapons being detonated in American cities," he charged—an absurdity, in my view, given that in retaliation the United States would have turned the North into "a charcoal briquette" (Colin Powell's expression). But Perry had also concluded that Bush simply would not enter into serious talks with Pyongyang: "my theory is the reason we don't have a policy on this, and we aren't negotiating, is the president himself. I think he has come to the conclusion that Kim Jong Il is evil and loathsome and it is immoral to negotiate with him." He was correct: Bush possessed a stunning combination of utter ignorance about Korea and visceral hatred for his counterpart in Pyongyang. During his first phone call with Kim Dae Jung, who had won the Nobel Peace Prize in 2000, he cupped the phone and looked at an aide: "Who is this guy?" As for Kim Jong Il, in one meeting Bush exclaimed, "We want him to get rid of his nukes, and if he doesn't ... we have to get rid of him!"[16] Thus did an insecure, reclusive dictator and an insecure, impulsive foreign affairs naïf hold the peace of the world in their hands.

The Perry–Bush preemptive scenarios utterly disregarded the conflict situation on the Korean Peninsula: the United States is still technically at war with the North, 1.5 million soldiers are in proximity along the tense demilitarized zone, and the North has been preparing for the next war ever since the last one ended; it is the world's most remarkable garrison state, nearly every adult having undergone military training. The acute danger—which South Korean leaders immediately grasped—was that threatening preemptive strikes on Yongbyon would converge with existing plans for preemption in a crisis initiated by the North, which have been standard operating procedure for the US military for decades. American commanders in the South have long worried about a war accidentally breaking out through a cycle of preemption and counterpreemption. Leaders in Seoul repeatedly sought assurances from Washington that the North would not be attacked over Seoul's veto. It is my understanding that they never received those assurances. Because the North could destroy Seoul in a matter of hours with some ten thousand artillery guns buried in the mountains north of the capital, one can imagine the extreme consternation that the Bush doctrine caused in Seoul. This, too, is irrationality: there never was a military solution in Korea (as the United States should have learned in 1953), and there certainly isn't one now.

The Achievements of Engagement

In 1998 the new president of the ROK, former dissident Kim Dae Jung, overthrew decades of tit-for-tat animosity in which both Koreas sought petty advantages over each other, using endless threats and posturing that assured progress in inter-Korean relations would be glacial, if it ever occurred. By seeking peaceful coexistence, promising not to "absorb" the DPRK on the German model, and offering aid and exchanges toward the goal of mutual reconciliation, he worked a sea change in South Korean attitudes: long inured to propaganda depicting the communists as evil sadists, southerners came to see them as long-lost cousins ruled by errant uncles. Kim also convinced Bill Clinton that Pyongyang would give up its nuclear program and its missiles in return for a new relationship with the United States. The United States could have its cake and eat it, too, President Kim thought, because Pyongyang would not object to the continued stationing of American troops in the South if the United States normalized relations with the DPRK: Why? Kim Jong Il was almost as worried about China and Japan as he was about the United States, and he could be coaxed into new security arrangements within the security system that the United States had built in Northeast Asia since 1945. Washington could lose an enemy and gain a neutral North Korea, if not a friend or an ally—against China, against a revived Russia, and as a check on Japan's future course.[17]

Now examine the *New York Times* on October 11, 2002: a color picture of Clinton meeting General Jo Myong Rok at the White House, Jo being the head of the conglomerate that builds and sells Korean missiles; Madeleine Albright met Kim Jong Il in Pyongyang two weeks later. American and Korean negotiators had developed an agreement to indirectly buy up all their medium and long-range missiles. Clinton was ready to go to Pyongyang to sign the missile agreement, but the stymied election of 2000 prevented it. Still, this is not the behavior of crazy people intent on a nuclear arsenal with which they can attack Honolulu.

A FAILED POLICY FOR A FAILED PRESIDENT

Bush presided over the most asinine Korea policy in history. Colin Powell was famous for saying that invading a country is like going to Pottery Barn and knocking the merchandise to the floor: you broke it, you own it. At the end of 2006 Bush was the fully vested but not very happy owner of a lot of shattered crockery that had resulted from his strategies on Iraq and North Korea. He also contrived to have major problems with not one Korea, but two. After thirty-five years of closely following Korean–American relations, I can think of no time when affairs were allowed to deteriorate so drastically, nor can I think of an administration that struck more dissonant notes with a close ally. Through acts of commission and omission, Bush trampled on the norms and expectations of the historical American relationship with Seoul, while plunging the relationship with Pyongyang into a dangerous stalemate that ultimately resulted in a nuclear-armed North.

Bush took a while to pay any attention to Korea, but in October 2002 he sent long-time State Department officer James Kelly to Pyongyang to accuse the North Koreans of harboring a second nuclear program utilizing highly enriched uranium (HEU), and in the resulting tumult Bush broke the precious piece of pottery called the 1994 Framework Agreement. (Bolton and Joseph had led a campaign to destroy the 1994 agreement from the minute they took office.)[18] The North reacted by leaving the Non-Proliferation Treaty, taking back the plutonium complex—complete with eight thousand plutonium fuel rods that had been neutered in stainless steel casks—and got busy manufacturing an unknown number of nuclear weapons.

What was accomplished, exactly, by Kelly's confronting North Korea? The answer is that it did nothing but make available enough plutonium for five or six atomic bombs. The Koreans paid no penalty for these acts, apart from more of the ostracism and isolation that they have been used to since the regime was formed in 1948. If American negotiators ought to have learned one thing in the 1990s, it is that one does not confront the North Koreans: their instant reaction for the past half-century has been to raise their hackles and tell the confronting party off. That is what they did to Kelly, who returned to Washington empty handed. Kelly's timing was also absurdly provocative: he delivered his message on the heels of Bush's preemptive strike doctrine, announced in September 2002 and targeting the "axis of evil." A few months later came the preventive war against Iraq. As the invasion ensued, Pyongyang said essentially the following, through its Central News Agency: the UN inspected Iraq for years. It succeeded in disarming Iraq. Then the United States decided to invade. US forces would not have invaded if Saddam had possessed nuclear weapons. This is not going to happen to North Korea. Soon the Koreans found myriad ways of talking about their "nuclear deterrent."

As it happened, US intelligence on the North's HEU was no better than it was on Saddam Hussein's weapons of mass destruction, but it took several years to find that out (in fact, the CIA was much less certain than it had been about Iraq, according to Richard Armitage).[19] In early 2007 Joseph DeTrani, a longtime CIA official, informed a Senate committee that intelligence agencies then pegged reports of the North's HEU weapons program at only "the mid-confidence level," jargon for information that can be interpreted in various ways or that is not fully corroborated. (Now they tell us.) Evidence of small purchases of centrifuges (a mere twenty of them, as it turned out, when thousands are needed for production purposes) had been transformed by Washington analysts into "a significant production capability" in 2002; since that time, however, the United States had turned up no evidence of the "large-scale procurements" that would be necessary for an HEU bomb program: the intelligence consensus had now become "the HEU riddle."[20]

Experts know well that HEU is a very difficult technology to master and would require many years of experimentation before a uranium bomb could be built, but that does not stop officials from hyping threats and misleading the public. Furthermore, no one is surprised if North Korea cheats. But the 1994 agreement and the missile deal were based on painstaking verification measures that assured (1) no plutonium bombs and (2) no missile-delivery vehicles. That was their indispensable value. For two decades faulty intelligence and worst-case scenarios have vastly strengthened the North Korean hand in negotiations; why not try realistic analysis for a change?

After the North detonated its first atomic bomb in 2006, Bush's malignant neglect, as if by magic, turned to benign engagement as Washington and Pyongyang worked out yet another denuclearization agreement in February 2007. Remember that Bush did not "reward bad behavior," had always rejected direct talks with North Korea, and had stuck the North in his axis of evil—while hurling various insults at Kim Jong Il ("pygmy") and telling Washington insider Bob Woodward that he "loathed" Kim and wanted to topple his regime. Vice President Dick Cheney had averred in 2004 that the United States did not negotiate with evil but defeated it. Yet the February agreement was hammered out in highly secret direct talks between assistant secretary of state Christopher Hill and foreign minister Kim Gye Gwan in Beijing and Berlin and was then presented to the multilateral six-party talks for ratification (this China-sponsored modality was always a fig leaf for getting Washington and Pyongyang to talk to each other). So finally Bush made a deal—one very much like the 1994 agreement that he had carelessly helped to destroy.

The back-to-the future quality of this agreement can be appreciated in the list of its achievements: mothballing and dismantling the North's plutonium reactors, relaxing sanctions and embargoes that Washington had laid on the North for decades, taking it off the State Department's list of state sponsors of terrorism, readmitting UN nuclear inspectors, getting a peace agreement finally to end the Korean War, and moving toward normalization of relations. All these were accomplished or being negotiated when Bush came into office, but as already mentioned, the Clinton administration had also worked out a plan to indirectly buy out the North's medium- and long-range missiles; it was ready to be signed in 2000 but Bush let it fall between the stools, and today the North retains all its formidable missile capability.

The explanations for this 180-degree reversal include Bush's weak standing after the 2006 congressional elections, the departure of neoconservatives, and Condoleezza Rice's success at putting an end to internal squabbling. But the deeper reason was probably a decision that Iran was the greater proliferation threat: if a Libya-like deal could be reached with North Korea, that would put tremendous pressure on Tehran to negotiate away its nuclear program; or if Bush decided to use force against

Iran (a leading subject of Washington scuttlebutt at the time[21]), the North would have to be neutralized or simply forgotten.

If the Bush administration takes the cake for manufacturing mayhem in the world while getting nowhere amid ignorant policies and ham-handed pratfalls, its reckless behavior depended on good sense and restraint in "crazy" Pyongyang. Imagine, if possible, the perspective of the leader in Pyongyang. The sole superpower warred against him and occupied his territory in 1950 (called *rollback* then, not regime change); it then targeted him with nuclear weapons emplaced in South Korea from 1958 to 1991 and still does so with its naval and air power. This superpower is run by a president who openly speaks of regime change and hates the Korean leader's guts, accompanied by a defense secretary who frankly discusses using nuclear bunker busters to decapitate the Korean: is this not also utter irrationality? Cold logic does not usually govern the start of wars (think of the Germans in 1914 or the Japanese in 1941); it is fortunate that no war has erupted in Korea in recent times. If the Perry/Carter option is exercised (they were talking about it again in 2009), preemptive strikes will set off a catastrophic war in Northeast Asia, millions will die, and the Republicans will pick up the pieces in 2012. That is just how serious President Obama's dilemma appears at this writing.

Greeting President Obama with a now-classic version of its bravado and brinkmanship probably seemed logical to the North Koreans, given that this has worked in the past to get negotiations going. But they miscalculated, I think, in two senses: first, Obama had already proved himself much more receptive to talks with the North than either of his recent predecessors and had on his desk a host of monumental problems unlike any since the Great Depression; giving him some breathing space was crucial. But the North Koreans boxed Obama into a corner in which Bolton's punitive strategy was his only short-run option; now going back to negotiations would signal weakness. Second, how many times can the North Korean leadership count on its dangerous provocations meeting with good sense on the American (or South Korean, or Japanese) side? Kim Jong Il functioned as a poster boy for Rumsfeld, Cheney, and Bolton; he ought to have been paid by the advocates of missile defense, so much did he help their cause (and silence Democratic critics). Dick Cheney has stated bluntly that Obama is encouraging the United States' enemies (by stopping torture and authorizing the closing of Guantanamo); he intervened in the last few months of the Bush administration to halt the progress made since the February 2007 agreement (by linking Pyongyang to murky events in Syria), leaving Obama holding the bag.

Today it seems unlikely that the North can be coaxed back to yet a third denuclearization agreement, and it likewise seems irrational for anyone in Pyongyang to give up its handful of nuclear weapons when the United States still threatens to attack it. But a glimmer of hope appeared on the eve of Obama's visit to Moscow, when he made the unprecedented statement (for a president), "It's naïve for us to think that we can grow our nuclear stockpile ... [and] be able to pressure countries like Iran and North Korea not to pursue nuclear weapons themselves."[22] I believe a peace agreement finally ending the Korean War and an American pledge of no first use of nuclear weapons on the Korean Peninsula, combined with normalization and aid, might convince the North to give up its nukes and missiles. It is still worth trying because the alternative is another deadly blow to the nonproliferation regime.

Conclusion: Psychology 101

How do psychiatrists deal with an angry, violent, insulting, aggravating, recalcitrant, prideful, self-defeating patient? With concern, empathy, understanding, deflection, subtle advice (usually suggesting alternative behavior), the setting of limits on the one hand and the opening of avenues toward change on the other. Think of Tony Soprano and Jennifer Melfy: did she call him a fat, slovenly, self-indulgent, and self-regarding Mafia thug? No, she treated him like a human being in pain who needed help. China has long used a concept, *zixiao*, which is usually translated "cherishing friends from afar" (or "cherishing the lesser"), but it really means not sweating the small stuff when it comes to relations with allied or tributary states, or enemies who are not really threatening. It is a classic hegemonic device to show that the power that everyone recognizes as superior nonetheless shows concern and regard for the smaller or lesser party. English does not have a good equivalent to this (although *magnanimity* comes close), so its speakers use foreign phrases, like *noblesse oblige*. Perhaps someday a magnanimous American president will come along who knows the intricacies of the country's sixty years of dangerous but fruitless confrontation with the DPRK, who will learn how to live in peace with it and put an embassy in Pyongyang so Americans might finally gain some leverage over an antagonist that has been thumbing its nose at them for more than sixty years. Americans aren't there yet.

All the palaver about how crazy the North is, how the country is on the verge of collapse, and how cruel the regime is explains nothing about what has actually happened since 1994: several deals deeply favoring American and world interests, no collapse, and a regime that is indeed cruel—but have US policies ameliorated or changed that cruelty? In another decade, the regime will have been in power as long as the Soviet Union was. What is to be done about that? Now is a good time finally to shed the anachronistic polarized positions and mindset of the Cold War and to move in the direction of a calm, steady, nuanced, and persistent process of rapprochement with Pyongyang. Think of Jennifer Melfy and Tony Soprano.

Endnotes

1. A shorter and earlier version of this paper appeared in Current History 108, no. 719 (September 2009): 284–290.
2. On May 28, 2009, I was interviewed for more than thirty minutes for CNN's *Anderson Cooper 360*, but the only clip used was the few seconds in which I said that Kim Jong Il was not crazy—giving "the other side of the story," after a retired American general had said that Kim clearly was.
3. Chong Bong-uk, ed., *North Korea: Uneasy, Shaky Kim Jong-il Regime* (Seoul: Naewoe Press, 1997), 143.
4. In spring 2009 I attended a number of conferences and meetings in Washington, and heard yet again that the North was deeply embroiled in a "succession struggle" and might therefore "explode or implode."
5. See Nicholas Eberstadt, "The Coming Collapse of North Korea," *Wall Street Journal*, June 25, 1990.
6. Robert A. Wampler introduced the collection with his essay, "North Korea's Collapse? The End is Near—Maybe" (October 26, 2006). I am part of Dr. Wampler's declassification project at the National Security Archive and appreciate his making these documents available to me. The CIA's January 21, 1998, report (on the 1997 conference) is entitled *Exploring the Implications of Alternative North Korean Endgames: Results From a Discussion Panel on Continuing Coexistence Between North and South Korea.* It is mostly declassified except for some redacted names.
7. Nicholas Eberstadt, "Tear Down This Tyranny," *Weekly Standard*, November 29, 2004.
8. The best account of these knock-down, drag-out internal struggles is Mike Chinoy, *Meltdown: The Inside Story of the North Korean Nuclear Crisis* (New York: St. Martin's Press, 2008). Chinoy's deeply informed book exemplifies the ideal that investigative journalism is the first draft of history.
9. Jasper Becker, *Rogue Regime: Kim Jong Il and the Looming Threat of North Korea* (New York: Oxford University Press, 2005).
10. Chinoy, *Meltdown*, 68.
11. Bruce B. Auster and Kevin Whitelaw, "Pentagon Plan 5030: A New Blueprint for Facing Down North Korea," *US News and World Report*, July 21, 2003; see also Chinoy, *Meltdown*, 234.

12. Quoted in *Chicago Tribune*, April 4, 1994.
13. Susan Rosegrant, "Carrots, Sticks, and Question Marks: Negotiating the North Korean Nuclear Crisis," with Michael D. Watkins (unpublished paper, John F. Kennedy School of Government, Harvard University, 1995), 2, 33–35.
14. Ibid.
15. Ibid., 34–35. See also Chinoy, *Meltdown*, 279.
16. Chinoy, *Meltdown*, 50, 298.
17. New Mexico governor Bill Richardson traveled to North Korea in April 2007 and reported on his return that North Korea sees itself eventually as an ally of the United States; in other words, as an ally against China. They see themselves as playing a strategic role as a buffer between the US and China. (It is more likely that Pyongyang hopes to play the United States off against China, much as it did Moscow and Beijing during the long years of the Cold War.)
18. Bush and his advisors claimed that the North had cheated on this agreement, when in fact the eight-year freeze was never broken. UN inspectors were on the ground every day, and all the facilities were sealed and under constant surveillance. On Bolton and Joseph, see Chinoy, *Meltdown*, 44, 61.
19. For a careful review of this case, see Selig Harrison, "Did North Korea Cheat?" *Foreign Affairs* (February 2006); Armitage is quoted in Chinoy, *Meltdown*, 104.
20. David E. Sanger and William J. Broad, "US Concedes Uncertainty on Korean Uranium Effort," *New York Times*, March 1, 2007, A1, A10.
21. Zbigniew Brzezinski is reported to have entered into an argument with Brent Skowcroft at a Washington dinner party after Brzezinski asserted that Bush was planning to strike Iran's nuclear facilities; following much debate, people were asked for a show of hands, and of the eighteen prominent people there—including former Pakistani prime minister Benazir Bhutto—only two supported Skowcroft's demurral. See Steven Clemons, "Why Bush Won't Attack Iran," *Salon.com*, September 19, 2007, www.salon.com/opinion/feature.
22. William J. Broad and David E. Sanger, "Obama's Youth Shaped His Nuclear-Free Vision," *New York Times*, July 4, 2009, A1, A12.

Chapter 8

The Foreign Policy of the DPRK

Alexander Zhebin

Foreign policy in the Democratic People's Republic of Korea (DPRK) during both Kim Il Sung's and Kim Jong Il's eras, contrary to the widespread perception imposed mainly by media of its being unpredictable, irrational, and provocative, in reality demonstrated a surprisingly high level of consistency, pragmatism, and the ability to compromise.

To start with the commonplace, irrational leaders could hardly sustain a country amid all the upheavals of international politics witnessed since the advent of the twenty-first century. Against all odds, the DPRK managed to realize two successful hereditary transfers of power while maintaining political and social stability; the country preserved its sovereignty after the loss of two major allies (the USSR and China) and crossed all the lines in developing missile and nuclear programs while keeping at bay numerous attempts to achieve a "soft landing" of the regime, whose unmatched art of diplomatic maneuvering brought to the negotiating table with the DPRK four major military and economic powers of the modern world—the United States, China, Russia, and Japan. Any impartial observer can hardly deny that for the last two decades North Korea has been rather consistent in its efforts to reach some accommodation or better relations with the United States. Pyongyang's leaders perceive the US policy as a major threat to the regime's existence. They are well aware that without some compromise with the United States on matters of mutual concern, it will be not possible to feel safe and gain access to the foreign financial sources necessary to modernize the country's economy. This chapter provides the reader with my vision of those efforts, as well as with more general principles and mechanisms of foreign policy decision making.

The Mechanism of Foreign Policy Decision Making

Decision making in the field of foreign policy in North Korea during Kim Il Sung's rule was not very different from the system practiced in the Soviet Union and other socialist countries. The essence of this system is that virtually all major issues of international activity were deliberated and decided upon at the level of the top leadership: at Workers' Party of Korea (WPK) congresses, at plenary meetings of the WPK Central Committee, and on an everyday basis, at the meetings of the WPK Central Committee Politburo and Secretariat. When circumstances demand urgent solutions, the general line is coordinated over the phone and later put on paper as a directive for the relevant agencies.

Because the WPK leadership during Kim Il Sung's tenure included, as a rule, the ministers of foreign affairs, defense, and some others, such a system in principle provided an opportunity to deliberate the foreign policy issues on a collegial basis, to avoid subjective approaches, and to take into consideration not only the views of diplomats but also the expertise of other agencies that have interests abroad—and eventually, to make fewer errors.

Preparing foreign policy issues to be set before the WPK's top bodies —the Politburo and the Secretariat—requires an organizational body capable of analyzing the situation objectively, evaluating the positions of various ministries and departments in order to prepare a draft decision that aggregates the entire spectrum of state interests. Ideally, this body should not impose a particular decision on top leadership, even if such a body has all the necessary information. Its mission is to consider alternative solutions, showing their advantages and disadvantages.

Within the WPK Central Committee the International Department performs this role. It is responsible for defining and fine tuning the country's foreign policy. It has been assigned the following tasks: (1) to develop and present to the WPK leadership foreign policy directions or solutions according to decisions made by WPK top bodies—Politburo and Secretariat--or the leader's instructions, and develop the course to be taken vis-à-vis particular countries or events; (2) to report to the WPK leadership on developments in the international arena and, if necessary, to clarify the relevant course of the DPRK; (3) to coordinate the activities of governmental and quasi-governmental entities in the international arena, ensuring unity of the political line and its consistence; (4) to maintain relations with political parties and movements in other countries, seeking their support for DPRK foreign policy; and (5) to select and recommend personnel for the Foreign Service. Thus, the International Department is meant to act as a body to oversee the country's foreign activity as a whole and to prepare feasible policy options for the top leadership. However, in reality the International Department does not prepare alternative options but, as a rule, offers the only solution. This is because before the work starts, International Department officials in most cases know the position of one or several top party officials. Consequently, the task of the department becomes a bit easier because its officials know what is expected from them.

During each stage of the decision-preparation process, the International Department maintains close contacts with the Foreign Ministry and relevant officials in other ministries who are obliged to submit to the International Department all necessary information and reference materials. Therefore, a draft decision put on the agenda of a Central Committee Politburo or Secretariat meeting is, as a rule, a document created by International Department officials utilizing various reference materials, memos, and reports received from several government agencies and departments. In fact, at Politburo or Secretariat meetings a draft may be amended, updated, or supplemented with new proposals. Therefore, the text of the final version may be different from the draft, but this is not always the case. If the WPK leadership is not prepared to take a final decision on the agenda item or if the situation continues to evolve, a decision is postponed and the relevant draft is returned for revision and updating with a deadline for the next deliberation.

In principle, such a system is rather efficient. It enables a large number of people, including scholars and other specialists, to be involved in the creative process and to work out a more adequate foreign policy course. But the effectiveness of the system depends, above all, on the overall situation in the party and in society (including the level of democracy and pluralism in the country), and on how freely party and state officials may express their views, which do not always coincide with the position of the WPK's top leadership.

The conditions for objective policy analysis are very limited in the DPRK. Instead of serious and in-depth study of a problem, ranking officials of the International Department in most cases seek to guess the mood of the WPK leadership and to present their superiors with proposals that correspond to their wishes. Decision making on the most fundamental issues of foreign policy, especially on dealings with the United States and the problem of the reunification of Korea, has been monopolized by a very narrow circle of people within the top WPK leadership. In several cases, the Politburo members in charge of foreign policy—for instance, Ho Dam and Kim Yong Nam—were not familiar with current developments in the field of relations with South Korea.

The North Korean media are not allowed to publicize impartial analyses or exchange of views on foreign policy or unification issues. Scholars, even in their research, are not free to look for alternative ways of addressing international or unification issues. Any discussion is usually centered on the search for the best way to implement the course that has been approved by a high-level party organ. Under such circumstances, certainly, the decision-making system cannot function effectively enough and leaves room for miscalculations and errors. One of the most obvious mistakes was a wrong assessment of the world community's reaction to the DPRK's decision to withdraw from the Non-Proliferation Treaty; incorrect forecasts for the UN Security Council's voting on the DPRK's missile and nuclear tests represent another serious error. It is possible to assume that somebody was held responsible and punished for the miscalculations, but that person was not among top officials of the International Department or the Foreign Ministry.

Another drawback of the decision-making system at the party's organ level is that it is slow. Therefore, in practice, the Politburo deliberates only the most important foreign policy issues. Current affairs regarding the DPRK's reaction to certain events in the international arena, delegations to other countries and the reception of foreign guests, the DPRK's activities abroad, media coverage of world events, and the appointment of ambassadors are all resolved by the WPK Central Committee Secretariat or by the relevant WPK Central Committee secretary.

The frequency of the Politburo and the Secretariat's meetings depends on a number of factors. During Kim Il Sung's last years, the Politburo met once or twice a month, whereas the Secretariat gathered two or three times a month. If one closely examines some measures and proposals taken during that period by North Korea in the sphere of relations with South Korea, it is not difficult to notice fifteen-day intervals between the WPK Politburo's sessions. This was the amount of time necessary for the North's relevant agencies and officials to prepare proposals for deliberation at each Politburo meeting.

It is particularly noteworthy that the DPRK's single-leader system allows for decision making outside the framework of collective bodies, by the leader alone or within a very narrow circle of relevant top officials. This kind of decision making is typical for addressing the most important problems concerning relations with key friends and foes—China, Russia, the United States, South Korea—and regarding the activity of the armed forces, intelligence agencies, and the financial and monetary system.

The WPK Central Committee International Department and the Foreign Ministry are not in charge of North Korea's policy toward South Korea. Rather, they work to garner international support for that policy from friendly nations and other countries and to propagandize the policy abroad. Therefore, International Department and Foreign Ministry officials, as a rule, are not well versed in the political and economic situation in the South and have very limited or no access to South Korean publications. Their evaluations are usually based on North Korean media publications, including material produced by the Korean Central News Agency (KCNA), and on information for restricted use, and are partly derived from telegrams coming from North Korean embassies abroad. An example of this gap is that North Korean diplomats in Moscow did not know that the North and the South, according to the inter-Korean Basic Agreement signed in December 1991, could cooperate in third countries in order to protect the interests of Korean nationals abroad. Lack of knowledge beyond the immediate scope of their duties is characteristic of many North Korean diplomats.

A second characteristic of many North Korean diplomats is that as a rule, they feel very constrained and therefore fear potentially making mistakes. Journalists often attribute to North Korean diplomats such qualities as persistence in defending their views or an unwillingness to express personal opinions. For any diplomat these qualities amount to a sort of professionalism, but the North Korean diplomats' constraints have other roots—the strong centralization of diplomatic work, when every detail of creative intellectual activity is defined from above. A third feature of North Korea diplomacy, a relative passivity, stems from the first two. North Korea's reaction and actions in response to certain international developments directly affecting the country's interests very often come too late to achieve the intended results. There are cases in which North Korean diplomats have demonstrated a striking indifference regarding important information for their country simply because no one had instructed them to collect such information. North Korean diplomats often cancel meetings with foreigners because they have not received permission from Pyongyang or because they consider themselves insufficiently informed about the designated topic.

North Korean diplomats' behavior is likely affected by the country's de facto isolationist foreign policy, under which the volume of information available not only to the population but also to government officials becomes a problem for the survival of the system. To educate officials and the public in the necessary direction, the DPRK's foreign relations history is constantly interpreted in a way that favors the country, especially the North Korean leaders.[1] Such interpretation usually presents a distorted picture of events or a one-sided interpretation of well-known facts and can cause uneasiness and even protests in foreign countries. This kind of literature, including accounts of the foreign policy achievements of DPRK leaders, is usually published with a special mark on the book's cover that limits the volume's distribution to within the country ("not for foreigners"), within the party (for WPK members only), or within the army (for military personnel only).

The International Department employs about forty officials. After former director Kim Yang Gon was transferred to the WPK Central Committee Unification Front Department, the position remained vacant for a rather long time. At the WPK conference held on September 28, 2010, it was confirmed that Kim Yong Il, a former deputy foreign minister, would run the office. He was also elected to alternate membership of the WPK Central Committee's Politburo. The International Department's activity has long been supervised by a WPK Central Committee Politburo full or alternate member, or by a Central Committee secretary. The same conference gave the job supervising the International Department on behalf of the Central Committee's Politburo to former first vice foreign minister Kang Seok Ju.[2] He was appointed a deputy premier of the North Korean cabinet and elected a full Politburo member. For precision's sake it is necessary to clarify that this and other new appointments mentioned were made not at the conference itself but during the newly elected WPK Central Committee's Plenum session, held September 28, 2010.[3]

All deputy directors of the International Department have diplomatic experience, have worked at the DPRK's embassies or other representative agencies abroad, and as a rule speak several foreign languages. At the time of their appointments, they were relatively young, very energetic people. One can single out vice director Pak Kyong Song, who in the past was the section head for the Communist Party of the Soviet Union and Communist Parties of Eastern European countries. Nowadays the vice director is Lee Yong Chol, the section's former senior official.

After the collapse of the Soviet Union and the elimination of socialism from Eastern Europe, the International Department's activity was guided for a very short period (1992–1993) by Choe Tae Bok—at the time a Politburo alternate member (elevated to full membership by the 2010 WPK conference) and WPK Central Committee secretary. The man is known as a modest person with no career ambitions. For a long time he was in the shadows. He graduated from a Soviet technical institute, received a degree as doctor of technical sciences, and was the WPK Central Committee's top official in charge of science and technical progress in the country. Choe Tae Bok belongs to the part of the DPRK technical intelligentsia that believes in real results, not ideology. Choe has never shown any interest in foreign policy and has always frankly acknowledged that he knows very little about the subject. His appointment to the International Department was apparently not his choice. Because of foreign policy failures, primarily the inability to foresee the collapse of the USSR and socialism in Eastern Europe, the International Department's top officials were sacked; these included Hwang Jang Yop (the WPR Central Committee secretary in charge of the International Department and several vice directors), Kwon Min Jung, Kiel Chae Kyong, and Kim Chae Bon. An entirely new person was needed, one not associated with past failures and traditions established in the department. Therefore, the choice came down to Choe Tae Bok. The decision to give the position back to Hwang Jang Yop was among Kim Il Sung's last mistakes.

The International Department works in close contact with the Foreign Ministry. It has been common practice for Foreign Ministry department directors to report at the end of the day to the relevant International Department officials on the work done and to discuss plans for the near future. At the request of the International Department, the Foreign Ministry prepares background material, gives advice, and provides qualified interpreters to work with the WPK delegations going abroad.

A similar style of communication exists at the level of the International Department's vice directors and deputy ministers of the Foreign Ministry. Relations between the head of the International Department and the foreign minister are determined by other criteria—first of all, by the place of these two individuals in the WPK leadership. Because the foreign minister is usually a member of the WPK Central Committee Politburo, in order to retain the party's influence on foreign policy, another Politburo member—who usually simultaneously holds the post of the WPK Central Committee secretary—was entrusted to look after international affairs and the foreign minister's activities, as was the case with Kim Yong Nam, Ho Dam, and Hwang Jang Yop. Kim was concurrently a Politburo member, a deputy premier, and foreign minister; Ho was a Politburo member and the WPK Central Committee Secretary; and Hwang was simply the WPK Central Committee Secretary.

With the accession of Kim Jong Il, the role played by the National Defense Commission (NDC) increased greatly. In most cases the WPK Central Committee Politburo was actually sidestepped and replaced by the NDC in decision making on major policy, including foreign policy issues. Several directors and first vice directors of the WPK Central Committee departments simultaneously acted as the directors of relevant NDC departments. The enlargements of the NDC undertaken by Kim Jong Il in April 2009 and June 2010 suggested that the body had de facto taken over most functions of the Politburo of Kim Il Sung's era. The role of WPK top bodies, including the Politburo, the Secretariat, and the Central Military Commission (CMC), expanded again after the WPK conference held on September 28, 2010. Kim Jong Un's election as deputy chair of the CMC (not the NDC) was the most significant signal of the party's intention to restore its position at the core of the country's political system.

The Ministry of the People's Armed Forces and the Ministry for Protection of State Security do not coordinate their foreign activities with the WPK Central Committee International Department. They can share information with the department in certain cases. Both ministries are under the direct control of the NDC. The Committee for Peaceful Reunification of the Fatherland and the Asia-Pacific Peace Committee are, in fact, state-run agencies. They handle inter-Korean relations and operate under the guidance of the relevant WPK Central Committee departments. The Committee for Cultural Relations with Foreign Countries is a governmental body to coordinate various government agencies' external relations in the fields of culture and art, as well as to organize relevant activity of nongovernmental organizations. The committee's main task is to disseminate *juche* propaganda abroad and seek support from the international community for DPRK foreign and domestic policy. The committee takes a subordinate position compared to the International Department and the Foreign Ministry. The committee's staff consists mainly of former diplomats and people who have experience working with foreigners. The committee engages mostly in signing and implementing plans for cooperation with other countries, receiving and sending delegations abroad, disseminating literature, and organizing conferences, art festivals, and exhibitions at home and abroad.

The Role of Personality in Foreign Policy

The former North Korean leader Kim Jong Il was under the strong influence of his father from childhood, and throughout his life his thinking remained within Kim Il Sung's theoretical framework and life experience.[4] His record of communicating with prominent foreign officials, politicians, and academics was far from impressive. He rarely traveled abroad and had no experience participating in major international summits and negotiations. Some experts suspect that he lacked the critical capacity for self-assessment regarding his own actions and policy. Many foreign observers also doubted his qualities as a possible policy reformer.

During the initial stage of his activity as Kim Il Sung's heir in the 1970s, Kim Jong Il's pronouncements on a number of foreign policy issues contained some signs of radicalism and were uncompromising with respect to South Korea and the United States. However, he never went beyond what Kim Il Sung had said on the same issues in any area. At that time he became the first man in North Korea with the right to interpret and explain the instructions and policy of Kim Il Sung. In this capacity Kim Jong Il was forthright. He, for instance, confirmed suspicions harbored by some foreign policy experts and officials in the USSR that Kim Il Sung's *juche* ideas, from the very beginning, had been conceived as a means of protection against interference by external forces, particularly the influence of "modern revisionists" (a nickname for Khrushchev's policy in the USSR) and liberalism. Kim Il Sung himself managed for a long time to persuade Moscow and Beijing that those ideas were necessary in order for the DPRK to apply creatively the experience of the USSR and the People's Republic of China in socialist construction.

The second phase of Kim Jong Il's activity as heir began somewhere in the mid-1980s, when he started to develop Kim Il Sung's ideas. In this period he focused his work on the theory of art and *juche* philosophy. But in this field, too, Kim Jong Il never went beyond the ideological and political views of his father. Being to a certain extent a radical young man, he could have put forward his own political ideas, which might have brought him credibility at home and abroad. In particular, he had chances to unite the young radicals so as to carry out certain reforms in society—albeit shallow, purely cosmetic ones. These reforms would have been similar to Khrushchev's "thaw" in the 1960s, with some amendments for the Korean specifics. At least at the time, Kim Jong Il was full of energy and eager to act. He could have done something in his own way to initiate changes. Because of a number of factors, however, the transfer of power to Kim Jong Il was delayed and took nearly twenty years. During this time he gradually lost his vigor and enthusiasm for changes. The circle of people with whom he interacted was narrow, and the atmosphere he worked in was far from creative and did not allow for free discussions.

Many things are hard to comprehend about the process of Kim Jong Il's becoming leader of the ruling party. From the middle of the 1980s, he was empowered to run everything, with exception of foreign policy. When meeting high-ranking Soviet officials, Kim Il Sung repeatedly referred to the abilities of Kim Jong Il in arts and propaganda, and he used to say that he had raised a good heir. But he emphasized that his son was not in charge of international affairs. "As long as I am healthy, it is my job," he reiterated.[5] After his election to the WPK Central Committee Politburo in February of 1974, Kim Jong Il, by virtue of his responsibilities, became more involved in deliberation and decision making on foreign policy issues. From time to time he was drawn to participate in foreign policy affairs but remained backstage, watching and listening more than speaking.

Nowadays, official North Korean propaganda claims that Kim Jong Il was a key decision maker on such sensitive foreign policy and national security issues as the seizure of the USS *Pueblo* in January 1968 and the downing of the US EC-131 reconnaissance aircraft in April 1969.[6] It is worth mentioning that both incidents occurred well before he had been promoted to any more or less important position in the WPK Central Committee. Indeed, according to the official biography, Kim Jong Il was appointed the Central Committee department director and elected WPK Central Committee secretary only in 1973.[7] It is difficult to say who authored some foreign policy initiatives in Pyongyang, but it is known that in 1991 Kim Jong Il worked extensively on such issues as the Basic Agreement between the North and the South and the Declaration on Denuclearization of the Korean Peninsula, signed near the end of 1991.

After Kim Il Sung's demise Kim Jong Il started to meet foreign leaders on his own, but such meetings were still rare. Some observers tried to explain this as reflecting the new leader's possible lack of competence dealing with the realities of international life. But there are a number of more realistic accounts, the most convincing of which came from US secretary of state Madeleine Albright. Speaking to journalists in Pyongyang after her six-hour talk with Kim Jong Il in October 2000, she described the man as "a very good listener and a good interlocutor" and added, "He strikes me as very decisive and practical and serious."[8]

Kim Jong Il's hermitic lifestyle remains another mystery. He rarely appeared in public and no doubt disliked speaking before microphones and cameras; he gave almost no interviews and avoided improvisation.[9] His usual style was to talk in private or before members of his inner circle. This was a dangerous trend for a country's leader, for it increased his isolation from reality. Secrecy and the closed manner of his work and lifestyle created an environment for decision making that did not fully take into consideration the variety of interests of society and realities of the world. These circumstances heavily influenced the atmosphere of the relationship between Kim Jong Il and other top officials, as well as the extent to which they could influence decision making in the field of foreign policy.

The consequences of reforms conducted by the CPSU in the USSR and by communist parties in Eastern Europe did not encourage Kim Jong Il to pursue any bold reforms in North Korea. There were some changes in his policy, but those changes were forced by domestic and international circumstances. After losing one of its main allies, the USSR, North Korea had to adjust its foreign activities, primarily relying on its own efforts and capabilities. But on the whole North Korea under Kim Jong Il's leadership managed to survive in a drastically changed international environment. Notwithstanding all costs and errors, during the first decade of the twenty-first century the DPRK succeeded in establishing diplomatic relations with almost every EU country, managed to resume bilateral dialogue with the United States (albeit within the six-party talks framework), and drastically improved relations with South Korea. In 2000 Pyongyang also restored normal relations with former allies Russia and China. The latter, in spite of North Korean missile and nuclear escapades, is still doing its best to keep the country afloat as a buffer against US forward-deployment of forces in East Asia.

Considering various options for North Korea's future development, one should not exclude the possibility that in the case of excessive pressure from outside, the DPRK would prefer self-isolation and a preservation of tensions on the peninsula. The regime has demonstrated repeatedly its capability to maintain internal political stability and to function for a long period of time under conditions of insulation.

What are the internal factors that influence the DPRK's foreign policy today? Rumors about instability, unrest, or revolts in the North remain unconfirmed. Such events usually lead to considerable personnel reshuffling in the central government and at the regional level, as well as to emergency laws and orders. Such developments are not evidenced in North Korea. Western hopes that Kim Jong Il's ailing health would result in a power struggle for the successor's position proved to be nothing more than wishful thinking. The North Korean leadership managed to normalize activities of the WPK top policy-making bodies through two WPK conferences in September 2010 and April 2012. The composition of the WPK Central Committee Politburo, the WPK CMC, and the NDC (the latter was renovated at the SPA session on April 13, 2012) testifies that members of those bodies had been promoted not as competitors but as truthful aids and supporters of Kim Jong Il's heir, Kim Jong Un.

The DPRK's political system appears to be a well-organized structure, like an army, that ensures deep interdependence among people. Such a system is good for survival under extremely unfavorable conditions and generally can be well controlled. It provides the means to ensure virtually complete isolation from the outside world, control public consciousness, and avoid the emergence of dissent. Therefore, the probability of radical reforms in the DPRK in the near future is very low. A possible solution may well be recognition by the authorities of existing economic realities or tacit approval of a "socialist-style market." Besides, any reforms would be announced and officially propagandized as designed to strengthen the existing political and economic order—not to replace it with liberal democracy or something similar.

North Korea's Nuclear Choice: In Search of Survival

The so-called North Korean nuclear problem once seemed almost settled in the twentieth century, but it has again appeared at the epicenter of world politics. To develop an adequate approach to this question, it is necessary to understand essence of the current situation.

The ongoing crisis started with formal accusations from the United States in October 2002 to the effect that North Korea had failed to honor its obligations under the Agreed Framework. The United States preferred to limit its own obligations under the Agreed Framework—a document signed in 1994 by American and North Korean diplomats to resolve a first nuclear crisis on the Korean Peninsula—to two major points: to organize an international consortium, the Korean Peninsula Energy Development Organization (KEDO) to build an atomic power plant with two light water reactors (LWRs) in the DPRK and to supply North Korea with 500,000 tons of fuel oil annually until the first LWR became operational (originally planned for 2003).[10]

In return, Pyongyang was supposed to "freeze" its graphite-moderated reactor and other related facilities in Yongbyon, where it could produce weapons-grade plutonium, stop construction of two more reactors of the same type, retain membership in the Non-Proliferation Treaty, and abide by the inter-Korean Declaration on Denuclearization of the Korean Peninsula (1991).[11]

The United States has claimed that it carried out its obligations but that the DPRK has failed to honor its part of the agreement. In fact, North Korea kept the specified facilities frozen until the end of 2002, and the United States, under a variety of pretexts, delayed construction of the LWRs--though in President Clinton's letter to Kim Jong Il the United States promised to make it alone if KEDO failed to tackle the task.[12] The United States was slow because the Clinton administration hoped for an early collapse of the North Korean regime after Kim Il Sung's demise in July 1994. After coming to the White House, for partisan and ideological reasons the Republicans anathematized the engagement policy toward North Korea that Clinton's Democratic administration had employed.

Since then US officials have preferred to "forget" that the Agreed Framework, along with the so-called nonproliferation clauses, contains a number of US political obligations to the DPRK, including promises to provide formal guarantees that the United States will not use nuclear weapons against North Korea, will not threaten it with such weapons, and will move to "full normalization of political and economic relations."[13] The United States has definitely failed to deliver on its pledges. On the contrary, in 2002 the Bush administration included the DPRK in its "axis of evil" and put North Korea on a list of countries targeted for preemptive, including nuclear, attacks.

Watching all these developments, the North Koreans were not sitting idle. As a trump card for future bargaining or (depending on how events evolved) as a deterrent, they reportedly started the highly enriched uranium (HEU) program to produce materials for nuclear weapons (the plutonium program until December of 2002 had been frozen under the Agreed Framework). According to a US intelligence leak, the DPRK imported the necessary equipment for that purpose from Pakistan in exchange for missile technologies. Nonetheless, Washington was never in a hurry to impose any sanctions on Islamabad in order to punish it for the proven act of proliferating nuclear technologies in exchange for missile workmanship. Pakistan was, however, a de facto nuclear power and an important US ally in the "antiterrorist operation" in Afghanistan.

However, taking advantage of the North Korea's concession in 2002, the United States decided in November 2002 to stop fuel oil deliveries to the DPRK and to finish with the Agreed Framework. In return, North Korea expelled International Atomic Energy Agency (IAEA) inspectors in December 2002, withdrew from the Non-Proliferation Treaty in January 2003, and reactivated the frozen facilities at Yongbyon. During her trip to Asia in February 2009, US secretary of state Hillary Clinton reportedly accepted part of the blame, saying she believed that the Bush administration's decision to walk away from the Agreed Framework helped create the crisis over North Korea's nuclear programs.[14]

The Agreed Framework does not forbid uranium enrichment directly. However, one should accept that the DPRK promised in the document to comply with the Declaration on Denuclearization of the Korean Peninsula, in which both Koreas promised to refrain from processing plutonium and from enriching uranium. If the linkage is legitimate, then the same should be said concerning references in the Agreed Framework to the necessity that both sides abide by principles of the US–DPRK joint statement of June 11, 1993. The document, besides rejecting "use of force or threat of force," calls for the United States and the DPRK "to respect sovereignty," "to not interfere with [each other's] internal affairs," and to continue "dialogue between the governments" of the two countries on a basis of "equality and fairness."[15] The eighteen-month boycott of dialogue with Pyongyang by the Bush administration, threats addressed to the DPRK, public insults of its leaders, hints about introducing a sea blockade, the US course for regime change, and the toughening of sanctions against North Korea—all this contradicted those promises and broke the Agreed Framework. Unfortunately, despite his preelection promises, President Obama has approached North Korea with a firmness that has in fact resembled and sometimes exceeded that of the Bush administration's first-term policy.

US efforts to place responsibility for the collapsed Agreed Framework entirely on North Korea also resulted in the resurrection of old stereotypes, such as Pyongyang's "nuclear blackmail" and "extortion" of oil, food, and other aid from the world community. But the reaction from most world powers to the 2003 US invasion in Iraq demonstrated that it is premature to equate the attitudes of the world community with the policy positions of the United States. Second, the DPRK has demanded that the United States fulfill its obligations under the bilateral agreement. The United States agreed to supply North Korea with fuel oil and to build an atomic power plant in the country because it had no legal grounds for insisting on terminating a national nuclear power program in the DPRK and was compelled to redeem it. The deal was fixed in the Agreed Framework; the demand to pay under the bargain is not blackmail.

As for the peace program of scientific research and the development of an atomic energy sector, the Non-Proliferation Treaty does not forbid any country's conducting nuclear research for peaceful use, but it also obliges nuclear nations to assist nonnuclear states in the field. The founding of KEDO in 1995 and the consent of its members—the United States, Japan, and the Republic of Korea (ROK)—to building the atomic power plant in the DPRK meant nothing but the West's recognition of North Korea's legitimate right to develop atomic power industry, though certainly under IAEA's control.

Another US-imposed stereotype is connected to accusations against the DPRK concerning its violations of international obligations. One of the basic propositions of international law reflected in the Non-Proliferation Treaty (article 10) states that when a country faces a threat to its existence, it has the right to leave any treaty and to use all means available for the protection of its sovereignty and territorial integrity. The North Koreans have taken advantage of this clause. Certainly, an undesirable precedent was created. The DPRK has continued to justify its actions, claiming that it has been pushed to exercise the measure by none other than the United States.[16]

By listing the DPRK in 2002 among the seven countries that were possible targets for American nuclear attacks, the United States broke the letter and the spirit of several international agreements that, together with the Non-Proliferation Treaty, constitute the nonproliferation regime, starting with the obligation of the nuclear states not to threaten nonnuclear countries with nuclear weapons. American accusations directed at the DPRK and other countries concerning their noncompliance with international obligations and international law are not very convincing because Washington's record in the field is not faultless. The United States refused to ratify the Comprehensive Nuclear Test Ban Treaty, unilaterally left the Anti-Ballistic Missile (ABM) Treaty, rescinded its signature under the Kyoto Protocol (a major document to prevent global warming and ensure humanity's future), and refused to join the International Convention on Land Mines or to accept the jurisdiction of the International Criminal Court. Thus, there are enough grounds to draw the conclusion that neither the United States nor the DPRK is without sin. However, on the whole, the list of US violations of the Agreed Framework is much longer than the list of North Korea's.

Until recently North Korea denied the existence of its HEU program. Only on June 13, 2009, in the Foreign Ministry statement, did Pyongyang claim that "enough success has been made in developing uranium enrichment technology to provide nuclear fuel to allow the experimental procedure."[17] At the same time, the statement insisted that "the process of uranium enrichment will be commenced," thus hinting that American allegations about North Korea's running any industrial-scale HEU program are still groundless and should not become a cause for any serious concern, at least at the present stage.[18]

But the Obama administration's "strategic patience" policy toward the DPRK forced Pyongyang to materialize its warning. In November 2010 the North Koreans invited S. Hecker, former director of the Los Alamos laboratory, to visit a newly built uranium enrichment plant containing about two thousand centrifuges. They explained that the plant would produce fuel for the country's ingenious LWR.[19] According to both his conclusion and the report compiled and submitted to the UN sanction committee in January 2011, the centrifuge plant is so far capable of producing only low-grade enriched uranium.[20]

The United States' Korean policy, just as it was at the beginning of the 1990s, is prompted by fear that further détente in Korea, initiated by the first ever inter-Korean summit in 2000 and upgraded by the second one in 2007, would inevitably call into question if not the expediency then the motives of continued foreign military presence on the peninsula. Commenting on both summits, some American observers have expressed such worries. The withdrawal of US troops from South Korea, in the opinion of many experts, would remove a cornerstone of US strategy in Northeast Asia and in the Asia-Pacific area as a whole because the strategy is based on bilateral military alliances with Japan and the ROK and on the forward deployment of the US armed forces in these countries.

A final reconciliation between the two Koreas—as well as normalization of relations between the United States and the DPRK—would deprive Washington of its last more or less serious argument justifying deployment of the theatre missile defense system in East Asia. If the so-called North Korean missile threat were removed, the true plans of the United

States to neutralize China's and Russia's missile and nuclear means of deterrence would be exposed.

At the same time, Pyongyang realizes that a rapid opening of North Korean society to the outside world, including broad exchanges and cooperation with the ROK, is also dangerous to the political and economic foundations of the present system. Therefore, under the present circumstances, the maintenance of a sufficiently high (though controllable) level of tension on the peninsula is an important prerequisite for preserving political stability and social control in North Korea.

The Korean Peninsula in Sino–US Relations

For China, because of its strategic, political, and prestige considerations, liquidation of the DPRK would be absolutely unacceptable—especially if it came a result of a US military attack. Such an outcome would result in American control over the whole Korean Peninsula and the stationing of US armed forces directly on the Sino–Korean border. Beijing cannot afford to sit idly by, watching as the whole Korean Peninsula is turned into a US bridgehead for pressuring China in an already unwinding grandiose rivalry of two of the most powerful economic and (probably) military powers in the world. The loss of the DPRK would seriously undermine China's prestige and international standing in Asia and all over the world. China, probably, would even have to give up its plans to bring back Taiwan.

Those who are trying to force China to exert more pressure on North Korea by exploiting Beijing's fears of facing a nuclear Japan, South Korea, and even Taiwan somehow neglected to mention one "insignificant" circumstance—a nuclear-armed Japan and South Korea would hardly continue to tolerate the US military presence in their territories. But the withdrawal of US troops from the two countries would mean the collapse of the United States' post–World War II strategy in the region.

The prudence demonstrated by the United States so far in Korea can be explained by only one circumstance—unlike in the Middle East, there is a powerful Chinese factor in northeast Asia. The United States, seemingly, is not ready for a serious clash with China over the North Korean nuclear problem. It would be a conflict with a country of one and a half billion people, with another world civilization—the Confucian one—and the Americans would therefore think more than twice before resorting to a military option in Korea. Even so, North Korea can still be used by China as a card in its relations with the United States. It may happen to be more advantageous for Beijing to provide the small North Korean bear, from time to time, with the opportunity to tease the giant American tiger, just to demonstrate to the world first, that the famous Chinese saying about the United States as a "paper tiger" still matters, and second, that even a small Asian country can confront a superpower like the United States with general safety—almost certain safety, if that particular country is China's ally or under China's protection.

In an emergency situation China's protection may be well extended, as has happened before, over the DPRK's territory because for the North Korean leaders and generals it would be preferable by far to restore centuries-old, traditional relations with China rather than find themselves, at best, in South Korean prisons. Beijing, it seems, will continue to utilize all diplomatic methods available, as well as necessary economic resources, to ensure the DPRK's survival. At the same time, China will induce North Korea in every possible way to exercise restraint in foreign policy, especially on the nuclear issue, and to continue with the economic transformation that would lessen the political and economic burden of China's supporting the North Korean regime.

In view of China's position, any military operation, especially on the ground, by the United States and its allies against the DPRK remains highly improbable, and without it the goals of using force against the country are unattainable.

The DPRK's Position: Taking Advantage of the US–China Stalemate

North Korea's bravado—at times apparently reckless—in clashes with the United States, can be explained partly by Pyongyang's understanding that China's geopolitical interests will ultimately compel Beijing to keep the DPRK afloat. The North Koreans have taken advantage of this impasse between the United States and China, and feeling incapable of defending themselves with their obsolete conventional armaments, they have started developing missile and nuclear weapons in order to deter a possible attack. North Korea's nuclear efforts were confirmed in the KGB and the SVR (Russian foreign intelligence service) reports published in the first half of the 1990s.[21]

At the same time, Pyongyang exploited the situation rather skillfully: while confronting the United States, it succeeded in demonstrating its independence from China by defying Beijing's calls to refrain from acts that might aggravate tension on the peninsula, including the latest unsuccessful Sputnik launch on April 13, 2012, which was condemned by many countries as a new ballistic missile test.

It was quite natural for Pyongyang's leaders to insist on keeping their nuclear deterrence arsenal at any price. First of all, the decision accorded fully with North Korea's top policy principle of self-reliance. In the beginning of the 1990s, DPRK leadership felt betrayed by the former USSR and by China's decisions to support simultaneous entry of the North and the South to the UN and to establish diplomatic relations with South Korea without a reciprocal move on the part of the United States and Japan (the idea of cross-recognition of the two Korean states by the United States, Japan, the USSR, and China had been proposed by Henry Kissinger as early as the mid-1970s). Both moves seriously undermined trust between Pyongyang, on one side, and Moscow and Beijing, on the other. Russia and China's support for UN Security Council resolutions condemning North Korea's nuclear tests in 2006 and in 2009 could hardly have promoted any confidence among former allies.

The US-led invasion in the Balkans and the war in Iraq likely provided the final push for the North Korean leadership in deciding to produce nuclear weapons as the only reliable deterrent. Some aspects of the DPRK's behavior after the US attack on Iraq confirmed the most pessimistic predictions made by Russian observers, who had warned well before the Iraq war about its negative influence on attempts to dissuade North Korea from developing a military nuclear program. US policy was aimed almost explicitly at the physical elimination of Saddam Hussein, at the arrest and prosecution not only of Iraq's top leadership but also of midlevel officials, and at the dissolution of the ruling party. Contrary to US expectations, such a course pushed the North Korean ruling elite even harder to acquire at any cost the means of keeping a new-world messiah from using in Korea the same technologies of exporting American values that were applied in Iraq.

As early as immediately after the first round of the six-party talks, held August 27–29, 2003, in Beijing, North Korea started openly claiming that it possessed nuclear weapons and even "was compelled" by the United States "to build up its nuclear deterrent force."[22] Citing the US intention to justify its "hostile policy" toward the DPRK (multinational "naval blockade exercises," attempts to hinder UN humanitarian assistance to Pyongyang), the North Korean ruling party's newspaper, *Rodong Sinmun*, asserted that "the DPRK is left with no option but to go its own way now that it has become clearer that the Bush administration does not have any political willingness to drop its hostile policy toward the DPRK and is getting more undisguised in its moves to disarm the DPRK and isolate and stifle it at any cost."[23]

Commentaries by North Korean media left no doubt that the country's "bold decision" to go nuclear was also motivated by "a political crisis" that the United States was facing within Iraq during the country's occupation, a crisis in which Washington could "hardly get off the hook." According to *Rodong Sinmun*, the "tragic losses the United States has suffered in Iraq since the end of the war have also put the Bush administration in 'hot water.'"[24] Considering the circumstances, North Korean leadership apparently came to the conclusion that because of the awkward position of the United States in the international community, the Bush hawks would not dare unleash another major military conflict, at least not until diplomacy had been given a real chance.

Pyongyang's decreased interest in concluding the nonaggression pact with the United States apparently signaled that after the war in Iraq and especially after events in Libya, the DPRK leadership had determined that the written nonaggression guarantees from the United States would obviously be insufficient to satisfy North Korea's quest for security. Indeed, Kim Jong Un, North Korea's new leader stated in his speech at the military parade in Pyongyang on April 15, 2012, that "the time has gone forever when the enemies threatened and intimidated us with atomic bombs"—unequivocally suggesting that North Korea is determined to sustain its new status as a de facto nuclear state.[25]

Muddling Through Verification

Insistent US demands that the DPRK admit the existence of its HEU program were transformed, as expected, into an appeal to search thoroughly to find it. Thus, the United States attempted to lay a basis under its carefully prepared demands for a rigorous and invasive verification regime, including short-notice challenge inspections of undeclared facilities.

Because an HEU program is much easier to conceal than other types of nuclear programs, by getting the DPRK's confession on the matter the United States now hopes to legitimize its intention to conduct a total search of all eleven or twelve thousand North Korean underground facilities. So far, the Pentagon's maps on this account are painfully incomplete. Exactly this circumstance, according to the *Atlantic*, remains a major obstacle from the military-technical point of view to imposing an Iraq-style solution for the North Korean nuclear problem.[26]

Most of those underground facilities have no apparent relation to nuclear or missile programs. That is why North Korea has no intention of including them in the list of facilities eligible for IAEA inspections. Attempts to impose on Pyongyang Iraq-style inspections, which went as far as searching Saddam Hussein's residences, may be unacceptable to North Korea for many reasons, not least because the DPRK, unlike Iraq, did not lose a war. Moreover, as North Koreans have pointed out, and not without grounds, Iraq's experience proved that the country's consent to inspections did not save it from a US attack.[27] So a major obstacle to agreement, if any is to be realized, at the third stage of the six-party process will certainly be the problem of verification. The issue could prove to be a mine capable of blowing up the most remarkable agreement.

The full scope of the verification demands proposed by the United States to North Korea remains unknown. Some ideas on the issue were proposed by the conservative think tank the Heritage Foundation. According to its analysts, in the North Korean case, a verification regime similar to those of the Strategic Arms Reduction Talks (START), the Intermediate-Range Nuclear Forces (INF), and Conventional Armed Forces in Europe (CFE) Treaties will be needed. They also called for unrestricted IAEA inspections throughout North Korea and the use of special equipment, and they go as far as demanding that the DPRK submit geographic coordinates of all its nuclear-related facilities.[28] Such inspections are supposed to begin even before the normalization of DPRK–US relations. Pyongyang suspects that Washington is inclined to delay normalization indefinitely. For hard-liners in the United States, North Korea's refusal to agree to such a verification regime would be acceptable because it would then be possible to assign all the blame for another failure of diplomacy to the DPRK. However, North Korean statements testify that the country is not going to accept house-search-style inspections.[29]

The United States' direct presence on the peninsula and its overwhelming superiority to the DPRK in every aspect of military and national power makes it practically impossible for Pyongyang to move toward more transparency and toward embracing confidence-building measures on the peninsula without reciprocal and maybe even advance steps on the part of the United States. Arms control and reduction measures can be divided into two categories: operational and structural. The former relate to the armed forces' activity (maneuvers, etc.); the latter have to do with their level and structure. The diplomatic history of the Korean Peninsula testifies that the DPRK, though rather reluctant to promote operational confidence-building measures, was rather active in proposing structural measures. In this respect, one might mention the DPRK government's proposal on July 23, 1987, of a three-stage reduction of the North's and South's armed forces to the level of 100,000 on each side with a simultaneous gradual withdrawal of US troops from South Korea.[30]

Wrong Answers to Old Challenges

Current US behavior on the peninsula—notwithstanding all the positive changes that the six-party process brought about—certainly discourages North Korea from making any irreversible concessions. The Pentagon is sticking to its business-as-usual formula by staging large-scale military drills inherited from or only slightly renovated since the Cold War in South Korea. Those maneuvers, conducted jointly with South Korean forces, have been explained in the past as necessary for deterring a possible North Korean attack. However, according to South Korean newspaper *Dong'a Ilbo*, in August 2012 the drill for the first time included exercises related to an occupation of North Korea, with follow-up steps to stabilize the situation in the country.[31]

In the early days of the Obama administration, US secretary of state Hillary Clinton compared the "tyranny" in the North to democracy in the South, sounding very much like her predecessor, Condoleezza Rice. North Korean leaders may well suspect that some circles in the United States would like to repeat the Iraq script: when all the targets have been put on maps, it will be possible to declare to the international community that "a sentry is tired " and to start "disarmament" in a way the world has already witnessed in Iraq.

The emphasis placed by the United States and its allies on the economic gains the DPRK would enjoy if it complied with its obligations under deals reached in 2005 and 2007 through the six-party talks seems unjustified; moreover, such an approach would lead away from the essence of the problem. For Pyongyang, economic gains are not a decisive argument. In 2003 Seoul offered Pyongyang deliveries of electricity equal to that produced by two LWRs not constructed by KEDO. The North Koreans did not agree.

Although the economic aspects of the settlement are significant, nevertheless it is necessary to remember that the nuclear problem was caused, first of all, by the security crisis on the Korean Peninsula. The problem emerged as an international issue of concern in the early 1990s; it was North Korea's reaction to, on the one hand, losing a major ally (the USSR) and to, on the other, the unilateral use of force by the United States with the purpose of regime change in a number of sovereign countries. The Chinese understand the situation very well. This is why during the US–China strategic dialogue in July 2009 in Beijing, the Chinese tried so hard to persuade their American counterparts to include some measures to alleviate Pyongyang's reasonable security concerns in any package solution to be offered to North Korea.[32]

For the DPRK, after the US-led NATO invasion in Yugoslavia, the United States intervention in Iraq, and especially after events in Libya, security is top priority. Pyongyang is trying to normalize relations with the United States because in this way it hopes to obtain guarantees of its survival—or at least to create conditions under which it would be much more difficult for the United States to use force against the DPRK.

Meanwhile, many people in the United States are inclined to put off such normalization until after the DPRK satisfies US demands concerning human rights, its missile program, the reduction of conventional armaments, the liquidation of its stocks of chemical and biological weapons, and the export of narcotics and counterfeit dollars. Normalization could also be delayed because of Japan's fixation on the abduction issue.

In view of this US position, negotiations, from the DPRK's point of view, are losing any meaning because even the full satisfaction of US demands on nonproliferation issues would not allow Pyongyang to achieve the main objective for the sake of which North Korea has agreed to participate in the talks—normalization of relations with the United States. North Korea's missile launches and nuclear tests in 2006 and 2009 are nothing more than a clear signal of Pyongyang's frustration with Washington's stubborn refusal to work seriously for a mutually acceptable compromise.

As for North Korea's latest failed Sputnik launch, first, the decision to go ahead with it in April 2012 says a great deal about the situation in the DPRK. On the occasion of the one hundredth anniversary of Kim Il Sung's birthday, the plan was to declare the achievement of the goal proclaimed loudly over the past fifteen years—building an economically powerful country. However, a New Year joint editorial in three newspapers, summarizing 2011, recognized the food problem and indicated its urgency. It can be assumed that the desired progress toward planned economic heights, including the provision of food and consumer goods, had failed. And when there is not enough bread, it is inevitable that the regime resort to a propagandistically profitable show in order to demonstrate achievements that put the DPRK on a level with larger countries. Of course, any such launch has a military aspect, but it seems obvious that this time the main load that the rocket *Unha* was expected to lift into space was a political one.

Second, Pyongyang apparently intends to defend resolutely its right to use nuclear energy and outer space for peaceful purposes. This right is enshrined in relevant international treaties and conventions, which are universal in nature. They are widely used by all countries surrounding North Korea. And Pyongyang will never accept attempts to deprive the country of this right. Further, it is worth noting the positive trends that have emerged in the DPRK's approach to implementing its space program. If the 1998 launch was carried out without prior notice, on the eve of the 2009 launch Pyongyang acceded to a number of conventions on the use of outer space for peaceful purposes. In 2012, North Korea publicized the flight path, which takes into account the security concerns of neighboring countries, and even invited scientists and journalists to attend the launch, thus trying to convince the world of its nonmilitary nature.

Given these circumstances, many realistically minded analysts (including Americans) invited treated this invitation seriously. Western experts also drew attention to the ambiguity of some of the wording in the relevant decisions of the UN Security Council—in particular, Resolution 1874 forbidding the DPRK to conduct tests "using the technology of ballistic missiles" but saying nothing about launching satellites. Because the DPRK explicitly sought to conduct the launch in a situation of maximum transparency, the international community faced the challenge of developing a precisely gauged and concerted response to Pyongyang's actions, a reaction that takes into account not only the known gaps in the resolutions of the UN Security Council but also contemporary international realities, as well as North Korea's reaction to similar situations in the past. Whether one likes it or not, an unnecessarily hard response to the satellite launch attempt could have given Pyongyang a convenient excuse to conduct new nuclear tests, the consequences of which could prove disastrous to the nonproliferation regime.

Pyongyang has already sent a clear signal that it intends to make other participants of the six-party talks accept "the Indian model" for the solution of the North Korean nuclear problem. The DPRK was especially encouraged by the Pentagon's mentioning it in some working papers as a nuclear weapons state. The North Koreans were quick to predict that from now on the United States "would pursue nuclear non-proliferation by improving bilateral ties on the basis of recognizing the DPRK's nuclear status and the six-party talks would be likely to turn into nuclear disarmament talks between nuke-haves."[33] According to the DPRK Foreign Ministry Memorandum of April 21, 2010, which can be regarded as North Korea's version of the US Nuclear Posture Review, Pyongyang intends to seek recognition as a nuclear power. As such, the DPRK is ready to join "on an equal basis" international efforts to prevent nuclear proliferation and ensure the security of nuclear materials.[34]

Taking into consideration the nuclear issue's high degree of politicization, as well as the domestic political situations in both the United States and the DPRK—and in other countries directly involved in the settlement of the nuclear problem—it is plausible that the denuclearization of the Korean Peninsula in the short and even the medium term is unlikely to happen. It would be more realistic to talk about preventing the proliferation by the DPRK of nuclear weapons and missiles and relevant technologies. Generally, the fate of the six-party talks and resolution of the nuclear problem will depend mainly on the choice made by the United States—whether Washington limits its demands to Pyongyang to an exclusively nonproliferation agenda or continues attempts to use the talks to promote a regime-change scenario. In the latter case, it is highly unlikely that the DPRK will abandon its powerful deterrent force.

The DPRK on Multilateral Security in Northeast Asia

North Korea's attitudes toward multilateral mechanisms for resolving international conflicts and the maintenance of peace and security have differed throughout history, sometimes rather widely, and in most cases those attitudes are certainly negative. The explanation for this should be sought in the foreign policy concepts of the North Korean leadership and in tactical maneuvers prompted by changes in the security situation on the Korean Peninsula and in the region.

One of the main points of the DPRK's stance on security is the declaration that the Korean Peninsula is a unique place where "the greatest danger of a new thermonuclear war" supposedly exists—a war that, according to such logic, "could erupt at any time" and would "easily" go beyond the peninsula's limits, escalating into World War III. Pyongyang tried to persuade the USSR, other socialist states, and additional friendly countries that "nowadays there are no more urgent and fundamental issues [than] defusing tension and protecting peace in Korea."[35]

To ensure lasting peace in Korea, North Korean authorities believe, reunification is necessary. "Division means a war, unification would mean a national accord ... a united country will not have the seeds of war." Accordingly, North Korean peace initiatives have been aimed at "providing a favorable environment for achieving the reunification of the country" through the removal of the US military presence from the southern part of the peninsula. North Korean–style peace, which the DPRK intended to achieve, was supposed to be a very short transitional period designed to achieve the reunification of the country—on North Korea's terms, of course, which included, "if necessary," "lending assistance to compatriots in the South." Thus, the "crucial importance" of ensuring peace in Korea in the hierarchy of current international issues was an attempt to channel the socialist country's efforts into achieving the North Korean leadership's specific task: uniting North and South on its own terms.[36]

The DPRK does not want to acknowledge that in the current international environment and in the foreseeable future, too, lasting peace on the Korean Peninsula could be achieved through the normalization of relations between the two Korean states on principles of peaceful coexistence. Each Korean state, by the way, strongly rejects the legitimacy of the other, as well as the very possibility of maintaining internationally accepted relations.

The North Korean leadership's reluctance to recognize the Republic of Korea as an equal partner in the quest for peace and good neighborhood relations in the region in the twentieth century was one of the main reasons for Pyongyang's negative attitude regarding the idea of a multilateral mechanism for security and cooperation in Northeast Asia. North Korea's desire to prevent at all costs its principal allies—the USSR and China—from finding such a partner in the ROK and from normalizing relations with South Korea played prominently into North Korea's foreign policy. Pyongyang's unwillingness to accept Seoul as an equal partner and its desire to prevent others from doing so was demonstrated in North Korea's negative response to ROK president Roh Tae Woo's proposal, made in October 1988 at the UN General Assembly, about convening a six-party conference on peace and security in Northeast Asia, with the USSR, the United States, China, Japan, the DPRK, and the ROK forming a permanent consultative body.

Rodong Sinmun, the WPK Central Committee's newspaper, evaluated these proposals as having been made by a "puppet-like" traitor; they represented a "black plan" that aimed to "sell the country" in order to create two Koreas, "to perpetuate division of the Korean nation and forever give South Korean land to imperialists as a springboard for a war of aggression."[37] North Korea criticized the South Korean initiative as a "reprint" of earlier ideas, particularly the six-party talks. Another argument against the establishment of a multilateral security mechanism for Northeast Asia, according to North Korea, was the absence of normal interstate relations between some countries in the region. The situation, according to Pyongyang, would not allow the participants equal footing in discussing regional security issues. Pyongyang also balked at the implicit proposal of "two Koreas." The DPRK did not hide its fears that such a forum would inevitably lead to "cross-contacts" and later to the "cross-recognition" of two Koreas by major world powers and their joining the UN—thus perpetuating the split.[38] Moreover, the DPRK did not like the list of participants in the proposed talks. According to Pyongyang, "there was no reason that Japan participated in the discussion of the Korean problem" because the "bill" had not yet been settled with Japan for crimes committed by the Japanese against the Korean people during Japan's colonial rule in Korea.[39] There is in fact nothing new in North Korea's recent demands to exclude Japan from the six-party talks. On the contrary, this has been quite a consistent policy line for the last twenty years.

It is perhaps surprising that Roh Tae Woo's proposal, according to the South Korean newspaper *Dong'a Ilbo*, was made without prior consultation with the United States. It met with a rather cool response in Washington because it was believed, not without reason, that the collective discussion of the security problems in the region would inevitably put on the agenda the deployment of US troops in South Korea and the removal of US nuclear weapons from South Korea.[40]

As an alternative to the South Korean president's proposal, the North Koreans put forward their own program. Its basic content aimed to resolve the "most important" problem of the time: "to ease tension and military confrontation on the Korean peninsula." The following measures were proposed to attain this goal: (1) realize a large-scale, systematic reduction of the armed forces of North and South Korea, (2) conclude a peace agreement between the DPRK and the United States and withdraw the American troops from the southern part of the peninsula, (3) adopt a declaration of nonaggression between the North and the South, (4) turn the Korean Peninsula into a nuclear-free, peaceful zone, (5) cease military exercises against each other, and (6) establish a confederal state—the Democratic Confederal Republic of Koryo. The proposal was characterized as "the most realistic and rational way to ensure peace on the Korean peninsula."[41]

After North and South Korea signed the Agreement on Reconciliation, Non-aggression, Exchanges, and Cooperation, together with the Declaration on Denuclearization of the Korean Peninsula, in 1991, the second and third paragraphs of the six-point North Korean program were transformed into demands that United States and South Korea abide with these two documents.[42] Incidentally, those who used to claim that everything that came out of Pyongyang, including the North Korean foreign policy initiatives, was unrealistic can now look at the text of the joint declaration signed in June 2000 by leaders of the two Korean states who confirmed the existence of some common ground in their unification proposals.[43]

Though they rejected the idea of six-party talks, the North Koreans at the same time actively promoted the idea of tripartite talks involving the DPRK, the United States, and the ROK. North Korea's consent to South Korea's participation was forced: Pyongyang understood that at that moment, Washington would not agree to bilateral talks with the North; therefore, the DPRK said that it would not oppose the South's presence.

In 1998 North Korea rejected South Korea's idea of adopting (following the example of the Helsinki Act) a joint declaration by six countries on peaceful coexistence, peace, and stability in Northeast Asia. Pyongyang described the proposal as a "stupid" and "dangerous" plan. The North Koreans pointed out that the situation in the late 1990s in Northeast Asia was "quite different" from circumstances in 1975 in Europe. In particular, in Northeast Asia some countries were simply unwilling to recognize others as sovereign states. Besides, the state of war on the peninsula had never formally ended. Under such circumstances, the DPRK argued, adopting such a declaration would be a foolish attempt "to build a house on sand."[44]

For the aforementioned reasons, the DPRK rejected the idea of a multilateral security dialogue—even when Pyongyang participated in four-party talks involving the United States, China, and the ROK. The talks were proposed by the United States and the ROK in April 1996 and took place between 1997 and 1999. Nowadays, there are very few who remember these talks, which faded into oblivion as soon as the quadripartite process created conditions for direct, bilateral US–North Korea dialogue.

Defending its obviously contradictory approach to the four-party and six-party talks at the time, Pyongyang claimed that North Korea was participating in the four-party talks in order to "create a favorable environment for peace on the Korean peninsula and its reunification." The argument went that if the Korean issue were discussed in the six-party format, with countries that "have different interests and only want to fill a vacuum, interfering in the Korean question," this would only lead to endless debate and strengthen the division of the country.[45] Besides, the North Koreans considered Seoul's efforts aimed at the promotion of the establishment of a regional security mechanism as the implementation of directives from "external forces," particularly the United States. Thus, *Rodong Sinmun* claimed that the South Korean authorities were "just colonial puppets who do not have political independence and sovereignty" and compared them with "watch dogs in the colony" seeking to realize "the American imperialists' attempt to establish US dominance in Asia and all over the world."[46]

North Korea's final position on the issue in the 1990s was set forth by the DPRK Foreign Ministry representative in answer to questions from a KCNA correspondent on October 14, 1999. He said that the DPRK "doesn't agree" with the establishment of multilateral organization on security and cooperation in Northeast Asia and considers such a move "completely premature."[47] Citing the traditional arguments against establishing such a mechanism (absence of interstate relations between some countries in the region, hostile relations between some of them), the Foreign Ministry's representative confirmed the DPRK's aims: the immediate withdrawal of American troops, the signing of a peace agreement between the DPRK and the United States, and the peaceful, independent reunification of Korea through dialogue and negotiations. When Korea is united, he argued, "the world's largest hot spot would be eliminated ... and the problem of security in Northeast Asia will no longer stand so urgently as nowadays."[48] One may assume that in the DPRK's view, after its desired normalization of relations with the United States had been achieved through a bilateral track, no multilateral mechanism would be ever needed in Northeast Asia. The representative of the Foreign Ministry also said that the Korean issue was a problem to be solved within the Korean nation, between the interested parties, and that he considered any attempt to establish a multilateral framework a dangerous intention to evade responsibility for a settlement and "to isolate and stifle" the DPRK. All this, in his view, would only complicate the resolution of the problem and aggravate the situation in the region.[49]

In 2003 North Korea, frightened by the quick US victory in Iraq and facing pressure from China, reluctantly agreed to multilateral talks to resolve the nuclear issue. The process of the talks forced North Korea to clarify its views on a possible security mechanism. North Korea's revised position on the issue was again set forth in a statement made by the DPRK Foreign Ministry's representative on July 22, 2005. Having accepted the situation, the North Korean side did not deny the possibility of establishing such a mechanism. However, North Korea's participation in the process, as might be expected, happened to be subject to a number of conditions. North Korea believed that the process of establishing such a mechanism should "under any circumstances" help create a climate of peaceful coexistence between the DPRK and the United States and achieve the peaceful reunification of North and South Korea.[50]

The denuclearization of the Korean Peninsula, the statement says, will be possible only when the DPRK and the United States can successfully cope with the establishment of a multilateral security mechanism.[51] In other words, North Korea directly linked its possible renunciation of nuclear weapons to the normalization of relations with the United States and to a cessation of threats to the regime. Further, North Korea argued that an essential element of such a mechanism should be the elimination of remnants of the Cold War from the peninsula—including the continued presence of US troops in South Korea, joint military exercises, the maintenance of a UN command in Korea, and the deployment of American nuclear weapons in areas adjoining the Korean Peninsula. Replacing the fragile armistice mechanism with a lasting peace mechanism should lead to the end of hostile US policy toward the DPRK, including cessation of the American nuclear threat, which, according to Pyongyang, in fact gave birth to the nuclear issue on the peninsula.

Thus, Pyongyang continues to see the feasibility of participation in any multilateral mechanisms in the context of its fundamental foreign policy goals—normalizing relations with the United States in order to eliminate the military threat to the regime, limiting US interventions in inter-Korean relations, and ensuring unimpeded access to the international economy and finance markets so as to resolve the country's most pressing domestic problem, modernization of the economy.

In principle, one might argue that with the five working groups within the six-party framework, a multilateral security mechanism for Northeast Asia had already been established. Some of the most pressing security problems in the region were discussed in the working groups. Participants of the working group in charge of the search for a new security mechanism in Northeast Asia, headed by Russia, had already held three meetings in which the DPRK's representative participated, discussing basic principles for peace and security in the region. But the ongoing disruption of the six-party process led to the suspension of those discussions.

Since the 1970s North Korea has been quite persistent in efforts to initiate a bilateral dialogue on security issues with the United States. From the very beginning of the six-party talks, Pyongyang felt uneasy about the multilateral process, suspecting (not without grounds) that it had been devised as a tool for exerting collective pressure on North Korea that would force it to give up its nuclear program. The perhaps justifiable but certainly politically motivated UN Security Council condemnation of the North Korean attempt to launch a satellite on April 5, 2009, provided Pyongyang with a good pretext for quitting the six-party talks and once more signaling its interest in direct negotiations with the United States.[52]

North Korea's insistence on obtaining security guarantees from the United States testifies once more to the consistency of North Korean foreign policy. The DPRK hopes that normalization of relations between the two countries will eliminate a major external threat for the regime that is perceived as coming from hostile US policy. The course was launched as early as 1974, when the DPRK SPA sent a letter to the US Congress urging direct bilateral talks to improve relations between two countries. According to Kim Myong Chol, who used to portray himself as an unofficial spokesperson of the DPRK in Japan, Pyongyang could be quite flexible in accommodating US interests in the region. Instead of an immediate withdrawal of American forces, it would settle for the so-called second-best approach, the legalized, neutralized presence of the US troops on the peninsula.[53] In his 1998 essay concerning North Korean policy on the issue, he wrote that Kim Jong Il and his policy planners believed that the neutralization and legitimation of the US military presence in the South would produce practically the same effect as withdrawal. The neutralized American forces would assume a new role as a peacekeeping force in the Far East. Kim Jong Il would have preferred such an avenue of continued American military presence to allowing US disengagement from Korea to set the stage for a replay of a great power rivalry in the Far East.[54]

Although those suggestions were made more than ten years ago, they demonstrate very revealingly how desperately the regime needs reconciliation with the United States and how far Pyongyang is ready to go to attain this goal.

In Search of a Solution

Lack of trust is the most frequently cited reason for slow or no progress toward resolving the current situation on the Korean Peninsula. The traditional political and military methods that have been employed for achieving the Korean settlement have not brought any tangible results so far. Certainly, the participants of the six-party talks managed to reach a number of important agreements; however, the six-party talks failed to prevent the emergence of North Korea as a de facto nuclear state. Finding a solution will necessarily require considering the circumstances caused by new developments at the international, regional, and domestic levels as they relate to the Korean Peninsula.

The lessons drawn by the DPRK leadership from the aftermath of Germany's reunification, the downfall of socialism in Eastern Europe, and the regime-change scenarios imposed by the United States and its allies on the Balkan countries and in Iraq should be considered first of all. A set of confidence-building measures is needed that addresses the concerns and worries of North Korea's ruling elite. A major factor behind the present seemingly solid unity of the North Korean elite is that both hard-liners and pragmatists carefully observed the fate of former Eastern European communist leaders and Iraqi generals. The consequences may be the most disappointing for those who were expecting an internal struggle within the North Korean leadership to lead to the regime's collapse after Kim Il Sung's death or, more recently, following Kim Jong Il's death and Kim Jong Un's subsequent accession to power.

Indeed, those events in Europe, Asia, and the Middle East form a very convincing argument that is employed by those in North Korea who warn against rocking the boat and instead call the people of North Korea "to share life and death with the Leader." The execution of Saddam Hussein and his generals was the most vivid warning to North Korea's leaders to remain united. Both sides—conservatives and technocrats—have realized that any serious infighting or drastic policy change could destabilize the situation beyond their control. It also seems that nowadays no faction (if any exist), in the North Korean leadership wants unification under the South's dominance.

The position receives support from numerous strata of middle and even low-level party and government officials across the country, including top managers of industrial enterprises and agricultural cooperative farms, as well as from the army and security forces officers, whose members would lose everything in the case of North Korea's collapse or soft landing. Unless North Korean officials are provided with clear-cut guarantees of personal safety, adequate social status, and a certain level of well-being after unification, these parts of society will remain reluctant to abandon nuclear weapons and very cautious about moving toward that goal or toward reunification. The further the North and the South move down the road of reconciliation and cooperation in various spheres, the more urgent and unavoidable will be the necessity of addressing the issue of the North Korean ruling elite's place in a reunified Korea.

Meanwhile, the process of economic integration and globalization in Northeast Asia seems to provide new instruments for attaining this aim. Implementing multilateral economic projects in the region may prove a better and more sophisticated confidence-building measure for accelerating this process. Realization of those projects "not only will open new opportunities for business cooperation and economic integration..., but also will serve strengthening of confidence, peace and security in the Asia-Pacific region."[55] It is highly likely that more active involvement of the DPRK in globalization and cooperation processes in Northeast Asia will bring about positive changes in Pyongyang's international behavior. Experience testifies that excessive pressure and coercion have led, in the majority of cases, to greater suspicion and hostility from the DPRK, whereas engagement and respect for certain positions shaped by history's legacies have brought about cooperation and compromise. The realization, then, of those economic projects amid the specific conditions existing nowadays on the peninsula can serve as a major confidence-building measure, especially in view of the fact that the DPRK's nuclear ambitions are motivated by both security concerns and economic troubles. Only real engagement can convince Pyongyang that the international community has taken a road leading to the DPRK's gradual and peaceful integration into the existing international political and economic order instead of one that would force a regime-change scenario on the country.

The DPRK's priority remains dialogue; the country's leadership views this as the only way to attain normal relations with the United States, removing an external threat, and as the means to gain access to investments and assistance from abroad.[56] The latter is vitally important for Pyongyang because only then will it be possible to revive the country's economy. Otherwise, it will be very difficult for the regime to maintain social stability and, ultimately, to survive in a modern world swept by an all-encompassing economic crisis.

THE PROSPECTS OF FOREIGN POLICY

If the United States can work out and offer a comprehensive and realistic package for the solution of the nuclear problem to North Korea, significant changes for the better in the US–DPRK relationship are quite possible. If the package proposed by the United States is really intended to accommodate Pyongyang's reasonable security concerns, it may well be attractive to North Korea. Naturally, such developments would seriously affect Western views of the security system on the Korean Peninsula and would open new opportunities for achieving détente and disarmament.

Worries concerning a hard-line position from the North Korean military on these issues seem to be exaggerated. Even given the military's elevated profile in the DPRK and its more rigid stance in dealing with the United States, it would be unproductive to overestimate its real role and to misread the DPRK's genuine intentions. The military's increased influence can be largely explained by drastically changed domestic circumstances (Kim Il Sung's and Kim Jong Il's deaths, natural disasters, the food crisis) and the shifting international situation (the USSR's disintegration, the collapse of socialism in Eastern Europe, US action in the Balkans and Iraq). Lessons drawn by the North Korean political leadership from these developments have forced them to rely ever more on the armed forces.

However, allegations about North Korea's military threat cannot be taken seriously. Under the present balance of forces on the Korean Peninsula, and given the regional and international environment, incessant warnings that a war could break out at any moment are employed by Pyongyang mainly for purposes of social control and mass mobilization—and more recently, in order to check popular discontent regarding the chronic food shortages. North Korean leaders know very well, especially after the Gulf Wars, the lessons they have studied in depth: their country is incapable of waging a modern offensive war, and no "big brother" is going to come to their rescue this time. But if it is first assured of its own security, Pyongyang may agree to further steps toward nuclear dismantlement. At the same time, this would increase the influence of the United States in the region. In this or in another sequence, these events will occur sooner or later. In this case, North Korea would likely pay less attention to relations with South Korea and Japan in the hope that Seoul and Tokyo would be forced to follow Washington's lead.

It is difficult to expect that the DPRK's unification policy will become more flexible in the short term. Bearing in mind the experience of German reunification, the North will not risk losing control over the process of rapprochement with the South. The South is ahead of the North in population and in economic might. Since the 1990s Seoul has achieved a number of advantages in the international arena. It is no coincidence that the unification concepts proposed by both sides in the 2000s put off final reunification to a rather distant future. New circumstances to justify such concepts are not difficult to find. The acceptance of a multistage process of inter-Korean rapprochement and the inevitability of a long period of coexistence of two Korean states probably could help create a calmer atmosphere on the peninsula.

Pyongyang is not satisfied with the South's new unification policy, which emphasizes reciprocity and thus pressures the North to make concessions, opening its society to outside ideological influence. Therefore, the North prefers to constrain the dialogue and delay implementation of the agreements with the exception of those in the economic and trade spheres. The DPRK needs some time to overcome its internal economic difficulties, and it needs even more to move toward the democratization of its society. It needs time to not only recognize the existence of two states on the peninsula but also to come to terms with it, to get used to that fact, and to try to adjust its policies. The process of reevaluating the realities in the North has barely begun, and nobody knows how it will evolve.

Certainly, there is a temptation to speed up the process of rapprochement, to make North Korea accept rules of the game that favor the United States and South Korea, and to put pressure on Pyongyang from all sides. But this is unlikely to bring about desirable results, for an internal explosion in the North is unlikely. Applying pressure from the outside would only supply North Korean society with additional incentives for conservatism and insulation.

Endnotes

1. *Rodong Sinmun*, February 3, 2008.
2. Kang Seok Ju started his brisk career as a member of the team of consultants organized in the 1980s, following the example of the International Department of the Communist Party of the Soviet Union Central Committee. Kang was one of a group of four to five people that was established to work on strategic issues of international development and on long-term foreign policy objectives. He reportedly proved to be a very bright person and quickly demonstrated his qualities and style of work (cautious, with an ability for in-depth analysis and thorough evaluation of policy options). He quickly won the trust of Kim Jong Il and became a member of the leader's inner circle. During the last twelve years of Kim's life he performed the role of Kim Jong Il's de facto personal representative at the DPRK Foreign Ministry.
3. KCNA, September 28, 2010.
4. Kim Jong Il, "Konhvagukyn pulphy vireky chinin juche y sahvechuy kukaida" [The republic: A socialist state of *juche* possessing invincible force], KCNA, October 10, 2008.
5. Kim Il Sung, in his meeting with deputy chair of the USSR Council of Ministers Yakov Ryabov, March 22, 1986.
6. *Rodong Sinmun*, February 3, 2008.
7. *Kim Jong Il: Biography* (Pyongyang: Science and Encyclopedia United Publishing House, 1993), 2.
8. US secretary of state Madeleine K. Albright, press conference, Koryo Hotel, Pyongyang, North Korea, October 24, 2000 (Washington, DC: US Department of State, Office of the Spokesman, 2000), 3.
9. Kim Jong Il's two interviews with the Russian ITAR-TASS news agency on the eve of his trips to Russia by train are rare exceptions (July 2001, August 2011)
10. See the text of the Agreed Framework in KCNA, October 22, 1994.
11. Ibid.
12. The Korean Peninsula Energy Development Organization (KEDO) was organized in 1995 by the United States, Japan, and South Korea to build those two LWRs. See the text of the letter in KCNA, October 22, 1994.
13. See the text of the Agreed Framework in KCNA, October 22, 1994.
14. *Washington Post*, February 16, 2009.

15. *Rodong Sinmun*, June 12, 1993.
16. KCNA, "DPRK Foreign Ministry Declares Strong Counter-Measures against UNSC's Resolution 1874," June 13, 2009.
17. KCNA, "DPRK Foreign Ministry Declares Strong Counter-Measures against UNSC's Resolution 1874," June 13, 2009.
18. Ibid.
19. S. Hecker, "A Return Trip to North Korea's Yongbyon Nuclear Complex," Center for International Security and Cooperation, Stanford University, November, 20, 2010, http://iis-db.stanford.edu/pubs/23035/HeckerYongbyon.pdf.
20. S. Hecker, "Can the North Korean Nuclear Crisis Be Resolved?" Paper presented at the Conference on Rethinking Nuclear Issues in Northeast Asia, organized by the Institute for Far Eastern Studies/Kyungnam University (IFES) and the Friedrich Naumann Foundation for Freedom (FNF), Seoul, Republic of Korea, March 21, 2012.
21. *Izvestiya*, June 24, 1994; *New Challenges after Cold War: Proliferation of Weapons of Mass Destruction*, SVR Report (Moscow: SVR, 1993), 92–93; *Nuclear Non-Proliferation Treaty: Problems of Extension*, SVR Report (Moscow: SVR, 1995), 26.
22. KCNA, September 10, 2003.
23. *Rodong Sinmun*, September 25, 2003.
24. Ibid.
25. KCNA, "Kim Jong Un Speaks at Military Parade," April 15, 2012.
26. See S. Stossel, "North Korea: The War Game," *Atlantic Online*, July/August 2005.
27. *Rossiiskaya Gazeta*, August 13, 2003.
28. B. Klingner, "Confronting the North Korean Nuclear Threat," the Heritage Foundation report no. 2023 (April 4, 2007), 5, 9.
29. KCNA, "Foreign Ministry Spokesman Blasts US for Putting on Hold Effectuation of Its Measure," September 19, 2008.
30. KCNA, July 23, 1987.
31. *Don'a Ilbo*, September 11, 2012, http://news.donga.com/view.php?id = Print_Donga|3|20120911|49294562|1.
32. http://russian.people.com.cn/31520/6713986.html.
33. *Pyongyang Times*, December 12, 2008.
34. KCNA, April 21, 2010.
35. *Thon'Il Sinbo*, August 1, 1987.
36. *Rodong Sinmun*, August 27, 1987.
37. *Rodong Sinmun*, November 1, 1988.

38. Ibid.
39. Ibid.
40. *Dong'a Ilbo*, November 9, 1988.
41. *Rodong Sinmun*, November 1, 1988.
42. *Rodong Sinmun*, September 29, 1998.
43. "The Joint Declaration by the North and the South," *Rodong Sinmun*, June 15, 2000.
44. KCNA, February 20, 1998.
45. *Rodong Sinmun*, September 29, 1998.
46. *Rodong Sinmun*, November 1, 1998.
47. KCNA, "The DPRK Foreign Ministry's Representative's Statement," October 14, 1999.
48. Ibid.
49. Ibid.
50. KCNA, "The DPRK Foreign Ministry's Representative's Statement," July 22, 2005.
51. Ibid.
52. KCNA, "DPRK Foreign Ministry Spokesman on Unreasonable Call for Resumption of Six-Party Talks," July 27, 2009.
53. Kim Myong Chol, *Kim Jong Il's Peace Policy*, NAPSNET Special Report, Policy Forum online, January 6, 1998.
54. Ibid.
55. "On Russian President Vladimir Putin's Welcome Address to Participants of 'Korean–Russian Friendship Train, 2002,'" publication of the Ministry of Foreign Affairs of the Russian Federation, July 29, 2002, http://president.kremlin.ru.
56. KCNA, "DPRK Foreign Ministry Spokesman on Unreasonable Call for Resumption of Six-Party Talks," July 27, 2009.

Chapter 9

North Korea and the Western World

The Importance of Culture and Emotions in a Conflicting Relationship[1]

Geir Helgesen

Most observers of North Korea paint a uniform highly critical or rather negative picture of the country and its political system. Consequently, as a recent global poll conducted for the BBC World Service concluded, North Korea ranks among the absolutely least popular countries of the world, on a par with Iran and Pakistan.[2] Even if one rightly questions the idea and the quality of such a political "goodness contest," its result reflects what people in general think about the country under scrutiny. This well-known fact may seem trivial, but it is relevant as a premise for the arguments I present in the following pages.

It is not only among lay people that North Korea receives a bad rating. After the collapse of Soviet-style communism, most Western developed countries made acceptance of liberal democracy and human rights a precondition of their support to countries less economically developed. This is still the case, and there is no opening for different versions of people's power, different perceptions of leadership, different relations between the individual and the collective, different judgments of the past, or different dreams of the future. Unfortunately, this is also the case with self-proclaimed objective and neutral bodies dealing with international affairs in the West. An example is the Internet-based not-for-profit Newnations.com, on which site a World Democracy Audit was released in January 2009 that stated the following:

> In East Asia, North Korea continues to drag its feet—indeed there is no progress on democracy at all. The main world spotlight on the "hermit republic" has been on their on-off dismantling of their nuclear capability, although there has been some speculation on the leadership succession. This is since the current tyrant, seen through a thick security smokescreen, has for a while been seriously ill. As we enter 2009, this nuclear dismantling is still "on-off." South Korea meanwhile, has joined Japan as an independent democratic country, as well as an economic power-house.[3]

This assessment is presented not as a judgment but as an objective statement. Newnations.com proclaims on its homepage that "our mission is to further the promotion of liberal democracy and the safeguarding of the environment by the actions of accountable governments. To advance this cause we report, without fear or favour, the affairs of nations that are in transition, their politics, economics, business, finance and human rights —and we tell it how it is, consistently, calmly, and objectively."[4] This clearly illustrates an unfortunate combination of political arrogance and cultural ignorance that seems to be prevalent in the Western world. To borrow a formulation from Daniel A. Bell, "It is widely assumed [in the West] that liberal democracy is something that all rational individuals would want if they could 'get it.'"[5] This perspective does not allow for alternative ways but maintains a missionary approach to deviant cases. In this light, North Korea epitomizes deviance.

For me, a life with Korea began in the early 1980s. I was not well equipped to understand the subjects of my study or why it was tempting to reject their explanations and condemn their ways. Apparently, the Democratic People's Republic of Korea (DPRK) was just another totalitarian system demanding unconditional support from an impoverished population, promising paradise but delivering nothing much but dreams. The headache, however, was that the North Korean people seemed to buy into the dreams, to believe in them, and even to be willing to fight for them, if needed.

Coming to North Korea as a cultural sociologist, I was from the very beginning burdened by an urge to understand what immediately seemed incomprehensible. As readers may know, cultural sociology is a cross-disciplinary approach to the study of the social reality based on the three classic fields of sociology, social anthropology, and social psychology. In North Korea I tried to contextualize and interpret my observations from the Koreans' perspective whenever I was perplexed by alien things and ways. But their perspective was not easily available. I thought then, and I think now, that the official picture of North Korea disseminated by the authorities in Pyongyang is as far from experienced daily life in North Korea as the Western disinformation about that country is. However, North Korean propaganda operates within a frame of understanding that makes sense to most North Koreans. This is the simple reason why it is important to identify the relevant frame of understanding.

My first serious academic work on North Korea, never published, was the thesis *Kimilsung-Country*; it bore the subtitle *The Cult of Personality, a Part of Tradition or an Alien Substance in Korean Culture?*[6] Within its 265 pages I tried to explain the country and its system as a neo-neo-Confucian "theocracy," for this seemed to be a form of government in which the state's supreme civil ruler had a godlike status, and in which government officials operated as if they were divinely guided. Although my first work on North Korea may have lacked theoretical sophistication, I do not regret it, and moreover, I have not fundamentally altered my initial understanding of this peculiar country and system.

North Korea is probably one of the most isolated modern countries on earth, and it has occupied this position longer than any other country. Therefore, North Korea cannot be described well without a consideration of the impact of traditional indigenous moral systems, creeds, and religions. The cosmology of shamanism and Buddhism remains a basis for the extramaterial, or spiritual, world of the Korean people, and Confucianism remains a foundation for social life, for ideology, and for contemporary political thinking and action. This is not the whole story, but it is an important part of it. And it is the part that is invisible and even unimaginable if the observer's mind is tuned in to North Korea as a communist dictatorship and to its leader as the last Stalinist tyrant. North Korea remains isolated, and the conventional understanding of the country abroad ensures that this isolation is maintained. This is the reason why I continue from where I started in the 1980s. To underscore the importance of isolation might be a trivial, self-evident claim, but again this seems to be a definitive factor and therefore important to bear in mind if one wants to understand North Korea in the contemporary world.

Inventing *juche*, the North Korean leadership decided that self-imposed isolation was the best way of preserving national independence. Cut off from all kinds of input from the surrounding world and made targets of an intensive ideological socialization process, the North Korean people became conditioned to a particular outlook on the world, thinking and acting within a certain frame of understanding.[7] The North Korean population has existed in a virtual cave. They have been prepared to function in this given environment and have developed skills that enable them to do so. This is not a judgmental statement but a broad and generalized picture of the facts as I see them. The North Korean people have been extremely well prepared for an impossible situation. Today, however, it is not possible to maintain such a system. The elite in North Korea are aware that continued isolation is untenable. They are clearly also aware that they are unable to survive without opening up and connecting to the outside world. In isolation their dream of "a strong and prosperous country" will never come through. A significant problem, however, is that the results of an effective socialization and education process remain, and they cannot immediately be undone. With reference to the cave analogy, if one has been trained to operate in total darkness, it takes time before one can appreciate sunshine.

As mentioned already, it is not only North Koreans who harbor a distorted picture of the world. It seems clear that the outside world also has a basically flawed perception of North Korea. North Korea is not only the sum of all its many problems—poverty, developmental mistakes, an outdated system, difficult international relations, and more—nor is the West accurately represented by the positions and actions of the George W. Bush administration's hostile policy toward North Korea. However, today it seems clear that relations between North Korea and the United States are pivotal and can be seen as the master key determining North Korea's future—and according to numerous interviews I have conducted, a growing number of North Korean government officials think likewise.

Thus, it has become increasingly clear that to achieve better relations with the world at large, relations with the United States must be improved first. The dominant role of the United States in all the important international organizations and institutions makes mending relations with Washington the indispensable first step toward opening up to the world. And it has become increasingly clear to the leadership in Pyongyang that without significant improvements in relations with the outside world, it will be more than difficult to accomplish the goal of regenerating the economy and to move away from its current disgraceful position as a recipient of international humanitarian aid.

Why then the stalemate? Prolonged animosity between former enemies is well known in many parts of the world, not least in Asia, but the animosity tormenting relations on the Korean Peninsula seems to be of a particularly thorny kind, for a decade of détente and intensive diplomacy between 1997 and 2007 was not enough to reach a sustainable agreement between the parties concerned. How can this comprehensive deadlock be explained? A partial answer is that distrust might be the strongest feeling characterizing relations between North Korea and the surrounding world, equally distributed between the different parties. Focusing on the Korean side only, North as well as South, fear is probably also a prevalent feeling, and suspicion and anger could be added. Negative feelings are thus plentiful—and also easily understandable, taking into consideration recent history and the prevailing tense security situation on the divided peninsula. Still, it is difficult to understand why negative feelings play such a dominant role in the Korean case when in most other similar conflict cases, similar feelings have been overcome, or at least been dealt with functionally, in order to move on.

Animosity as a Mood of Destruction

It is easy to name North Korea as the responsible party in its conflicting relationship with the outside world. Although Pyongyang is anything but innocent, a conflict always has more than one participant. The following paragraphs briefly touch upon one particular aspect of the detrimental US approach to North Korea and point to a more constructive and productive way of dealing with that country.

The need for a changed approach toward North Korea dawned on the George W. Bush administration when US authorities realized that the expected imminent regime change in Pyongyang was little more than wishful thinking, based on inadequate information provided by US intelligence services.[8] Other foreign policy catastrophes engaging US military forces also contributed to a shift in Washington's approach to North Korea.[9] At that point, an agreement with Pyongyang was sought in order to prove to the world and to posterity that president George W. Bush and his staff were able diplomats after all. Unfortunately, this change not only came too late but also lacked sufficient political support in the relevant institutions in the United States to reach the historic solution that probably had been anticipated. Moreover, the new approach suffered because it was only half-heartedly supported by the very people who were supposed to carry this new policy forward, which the following excerpt indicates very clearly.

Late in December 2008, US secretary of state Condoleezza Rice stated in a public setting that only "an idiot" would trust North Korea.[10] The sentence made headlines in the international media, and a Google search in early 2009 yielded 910 hits—that is, 910 repetitions of this sentence in different English-language news outlets all over the world. Translations are not included here, so this honest or angry or amusing outburst has probably been repeated thousands of times in all, as were similar statements from Bush administration officials regarding North Korea and the North Korean leader over the years. "Axis of evil" and "outpost of tyranny" are among the best known denigrating characterizations of North Korea coined in Washington. North Korean responses never had a similarly huge audience—not that the words used were less juicy; rather, North Korea's access to the media is simply more restricted and more difficult, and often, when its propaganda channels send off accusations, such messages will likely be carried here and there as examples of the leadership's continued insanity, aggressiveness, and crazy behavior. Western audiences expect nothing else from that quarter. Hence, the North Koreans often find themselves between two fires, and the more they retaliate, the more they damage their standing.

Rice was addressing a group of foreign policy experts and students when she made the notorious comment: "Nobody was trusting of the North Koreans. I mean, who trusts the North Koreans? You'd have to be an idiot to trust the North Koreans."[11] This she said at the Council of Foreign Relations, and her comments prompted laughter. Rice was referring to the ongoing six-party negotiations. My question is this: How do name calling and street-language influence international negotiations?

The six-party talks reveal a core problem: even when the opposing parties at times agreed on particular topics in the past, this did not move the process forward much because disagreement occurred when attempts were made to implement the agreements. Was the plan implemented exactly as agreed upon or only partly? Timing became a significant issue, as did sequence. Did a given actor meet the agreed-upon deadline, did it pay—or reveal—as much as promised, and did it follow the sequence, item by item? Too little, too late became an often repeated mutual accusation, and when one party was blaming the other for not upholding the agreement, the other party usually pointed at the first party's failure, misunderstanding, ill-will, cheating, and so forth, as the reason for this. Therefore, time and again what had been agreed upon was transformed, often quite rapidly, into fuel for more verbal fighting. In this lengthy process a spiral of mutual accusations created an atmosphere inhospitable to agreements that hold up outside the conference facility after the signatures, the handshakes, and the photo sessions. Why has this case turned out to be so extremely complicated? What is missing from the diplomatic toolboxes? How can it be that skilled diplomats have been negotiating for years and years without reaching a solution?

The comment by the then head of the US Department of State was probably not a blunder. In the United States, North Korea stands as one of the truly evil, notoriously aggressive, and difficult countries on earth, whether this is formulated by the administration, as during the Bush presidency, or not. In this sense the "idiot" comment only reflects the mainstream position on this issue, and Americans, as well as most other Westerners, might have found it refreshing that a high-level government official expressed herself quite straightforwardly. But the reaction to this comment in North Korea was hardly laughter. *Resentment* may well cover the different shades of feeling that this statement most likely provoked in Pyongyang, feelings that include antipathy, anger, bitterness, dislike, and offence.

The importance of trust in international relations is one of the main and most important contributions of the social sciences to the twentieth century. This insight is increasingly also acknowledged in diplomatic practices. The joint statement of the breakthrough meeting of the six-party talks in Beijing on February 13, 2007, indicates that "the Parties reaffirmed that they will take positive steps to increase mutual trust."[12] What, then, are the odds of developing mutual trust and understanding between the adversaries?

Would insights and experiences collected and generalized in the social sciences be of any help? I think so, for robust knowledge based on cross-cultural studies is readily available. Sociology and anthropology have demonstrated that societal institutions and structures differ in the way they are operated by the personnel who populate them; psychology has shown that the basic structures in people's mental maps are affected by cultural traits; political science has made clear that fundamentals in politics, such as power and legitimacy, are perceived differently in different political cultures, often but not always following political-geographical borders. It is also known that although these differences are not static, the process of change can best be measured in decades, if not generations, and sometimes centuries. In the short run these differences are therefore to be reckoned with and taken seriously.

Insights from cross-cultural studies strongly challenge the political correctness prevalent in the West, where liberal democracy still is seen as the final station on the journey of humankind from primitive society to civilization. Westerners are still immersed in end-of-history thinking, even if Francis Fukuyama, who originated this concept after the demise of world communism, later denounced it, having seen signs of a looming crisis in the West. The ongoing crisis, which is also a crisis for neoconservative ideology and political practice, may change mainstream thinking in the West. A positive outcome of this, apart from the necessary transformation from ecologically irresponsible to much more sustainable economies, could be a more humble approach toward countries with different political and economic structures.

It is common knowledge that what may be considered an attractive trait in a given social environment differs from time to time and from place to place. Although it may also differ between social classes, age groups, and gender groups, such differences are usually minor. Proponents of a certain subculture are generally able to read and react to the signals from other subcultural groups within the same basic culture. Therefore, it appears reasonable to maintain that certain basic characteristics are shared within particular cultures. Alongside this approach to culture as "values, attitudes, beliefs, orientations, and underlying assumptions prevalent among people in a society,"[13] it is important to realize that cultures then create different moral and social environments that affect the people who are born into these environments. These different environments may also create and promote different emotional patterns and, apparently, even different links between emotional actions and reactions: what is considered a joke in one place may be received as a deadly offence in another. These simple facts apply to North Korea as well, but so far Western representatives—whether diplomats, politicians, or media pundits—do not seem to acknowledge that North Korea deserves such consideration. However, without it one risks alienating the entire North Korean leadership, consequently pushing them to adopt a hostile position toward the West and thus destroying any possibility of engaging constructively with Pyongyang.

Until now North Korea has been categorized as one of the remaining communist countries and has accordingly been dealt with in terms reserved for enemy states. This approach is based on the following logic: because the communist bloc evidently is crumbling, North Korea must exist on borrowed time. This "rational" thinking has fooled the international community for years and has made up the false assumption underlying Western relations with North Korea. The dramatic changes in the former Soviet Union and in Eastern Europe resulted in a general and widespread expectation that such changes would continue on a global scale. Such expectations, whether expressed or unstated, have had negative consequences—as demonstrated, for example, in the case of the Korean Peninsula Energy Development Organization (KEDO), in which an anticipated regime change in North Korea undermined the possibility of the project's completion.[14] This experience and several others have certainly promoted further distrust.

Instead of seeing the North Korean problem as the last case of the Cold War conflict, it may be fruitful to see it as an anticipation of the events that Samuel Huntington formulated as a new world order after the collapse of communism, when culture would replace ideology "as the magnet of attraction and repulsion."[15] Shifting the focus from ideological differences and related conflicts to cultural differences, which cause another kind of distinction in human behavior, the United States, and with it the Western world, should be able to find new ways of relating to the last hermit "Kim-dom" of East Asia.

Taking a cultural approach implies that the system in North Korea is seen as the outcome of certain conditions. One such condition was the historical postwar division of the greater part of the world into different interest-spheres linked with one of the era's two so-called superpowers. North Korea became a part of the interest-sphere of the Soviet Union. This made up North Korea's given, nonnegotiable external frame. Internally, there was an equally given condition: the political culture, which was not promoted by either of the existing political forces but penetrated every existing political force as a basic and taken-for-granted value system, and which included perceptions about legitimacy and power, the roles of leaders and followers, the role of the individual versus that of the collective, and many other issues that together constitute the majority's worldview. In the case of North Korea the combination of the given international circumstances and the local conditions made way for a system unequalled in the contemporary world. To ignore this and continue to approach North Korea as an adversary with an alien political ideology depicted as the last Stalinist dictatorship is tantamount to ignoring reality.

A Better Approach: Adding Emotional Aspects to the Cultural Perspective

Here, toward the end of this chapter, I attempt to add some new tools to the toolbox that might be useful in trying to understand North Korea. What is needed is a different approach, another focus that enables one to ignore labels that are so well established that they obviously hinder anything like a neutral view of the country and its people, not to mention a view based on empathy. In addition to the politico-cultural approach that still forms the basis of my understanding, I suggest serious consideration of a comparatively new trend in political science that may contribute new insight and a better understanding to this complicated field of studies. My new take on the issue involves including emotions and studying their impact on trust in international relations.[16]

To pay due attention to the importance of culture, understood as basic values and norms, for politics both internal and international is to accept the empirically proved fact that cultural change is an extremely slow process.[17] Further, to suggest that emotions are something to take into consideration when observing international politics[18] is to realize that hostility and hatred, as well as cooperation and friendship, influence people's decisions and actions.

Until now, according to the classic Western approach, politics should be based on reason, and judgments in politics based on something other than reason counted less, if at all. And if international relations were to be considered normal, they had to be governed by logical, rational calculations, whereas emotions were seen as irrational interferences that ideally should be avoided.[19] Increasing transnational communication at all levels suggests, however, that the rational-actor idea is inadequate, and this assumption is backed by research in cross-cultural psychology, political psychology, and neuroscience. In neuroscience, in fact, it has been found that emotions exert an important influence on decision making because "emotional processes take place as an integral part of rational cognitive processing."[20] In other words, to differentiate between reason and emotions is to artificially divide something that should be seen and understood as a single complex phenomenon.

I now briefly touch upon some new findings in neuroscience, together with a recent discussion in the field of international relations inspired by neuroscientific insights,[21] and then relate this to observations of North Korea's international relations.

Culture explains observable differences between larger groups of actors belonging to different parts of the world. A generally agreed-upon fact is that few such differences are attributable to nature, whereas many result from nurture. The main culturally formative forces are the individual's natural and social environments. Although this has explained general differences between members of different societies, critics have been reluctant to accept this level of generalization. It has been easy to point at exceptions to the rule, and accusations of unnecessary and even dangerous stereotyping have loomed large in the discussions. Recently, however, neuroscience has added substance to the empirically tested idea that culture matters, explaining that "the limbic system, which humans share with other mammals, is hardwired to subserve emotions to maximize chances for survival,"[22] but "the more advanced part of the brain, located mostly in the prefrontal cortex, develops from birth in interaction with the environment and grows largely in reaction to learning from the outside world. That is why people differ from culture to culture."[23]

The mammal brain and the cultural brain coexist and perform different functions.[24] The mammal brain regulates bodily functions, including the emotional centers, but the neocortex or the cultural brain is the center of cognition, of rational thought. The neocortex exists only in the human brain and performs the work that attracts particular attention in the social and political sciences, whereas the mammal brain remains the basic and the fastest part of the brain. Metaphorically, one could say that external input passes through the mammal brain on its way to neocortex. The feelings that are aroused in the limbic system during this process affect how the input will be treated in the cultural brain. The importance of the interaction between the old and the new brain is, in politics and international relations, neglected or grossly underestimated. Now it can be empirically proved that in the relations between the two parts of the brain, the old, emotional part plays a primary role in coloring the external input before it is rationally dealt with. It seems, then, untenable to continue to ignore emotions in politics. If rational thinking is the second step and the emotional processing is the first, and if the two are intimately interconnected, then emotions must be seen as a part of rationality, not as a deviation from it.[25]

But that is exactly what large parts of the political science community have done: emotions have been assumed away, seen as a disturbing element in politics, in decision-making processes, and in relations between leaders from different camps and countries, as well as those between leaders and followers.[26] To approach society and politics from a psychological position has been a no-go for years, and critics of the political-culture approach have pointed their critical finger at precisely this spot, claiming that considering emotions is tantamount to psychologizing the social sciences and a deviation from the true scientific approach. The position that assumes away emotions—and thus also culture—is now difficult; further, one would have to neglect a wealth of new scientific insights in order to maintain this position. In three mutually independent academic fields, evidence now dismantles the myth of a universal rationality. In political science Ronald Inglehart and his international World Values Surveys team have empirically mapped the world in cultural zones.[27] In cross-cultural psychology Richard Nisbett and his colleagues have presented convincing evidence for the existence of different modes of mental processing in differing cultures;[28] and in neuroscience Adolphs and Damasio have shown that "higher cognition requires the guidance provided by affective processing."[29] It should, then, be safe to claim that the idea that culture matters from now on includes the insight that emotions matter as well, and that emotions, although personal, are colored by the natural environment and no less by the social environment. Instead of focusing on ideological differences and disagreements in international relations, one should "be able to account for the complex relationships between experience, perception, cognition, culture, and biology."[30]

How can this—if at all—inform observations of relations between North Korea and the Western world? Can these new findings be utilized in the study and practice of international relations?

It was recently demonstrated in experimental work that hostile communication between leaders increases the risk of violent action, especially when such communication is personalized.[31] The lesson from this must be that an American president should refrain from calling a leader of another country a "pygmy" and that the offended leader should refrain from retaliation, calling his political adversary "a brainless alcoholic." When it is known that emotions, such as fear and anger, shape the perceptions of decision makers[32] and thus affect their decisions, what is then more important than to suggest introducing a cultural filter in cross-cultural international political communication? This is necessary because today it is known that emotions have different salience in different cultural settings and that cultural distance affects one's ability to interpret others' emotions.[33]

In her illuminating article "The Passion of World Politics," Neta Crawford wrote, "If one group consistently views another as hostile rather than fearful—and this perception is reinforced by that group's tendency to issue bellicose statements when it feels threatened—spirals of misconceptions seem more likely."[34] She might have been referring to relations between the United States and North Korea.

Crawford further wrote that expressions of empathy may lead to greater flexibility in negotiations, but dehumanization, demonization, and enmity may have the opposite consequences.[35] In other words, what everyone experiences in daily life matters in international politics as well. I do not claim that any of this is brand new under the sun. It has only been forgotten. Immanuel Kant (1724–1804) wrote, "No nation at war with another shall permit such acts of war as shall make mutual trust impossible during some future time of peace.... Some level of trust in the enemy's way of thinking must be preserved even in the midst of war, for otherwise no peace can ever be concluded and the hostilities would become a war of extermination."[36]

One can hardly imagine that mutual trust can be established without a certain level of acceptance between the parties concerned. A point of departure for establishing better relations is thus to acknowledge the legitimacy of the parties involved, to acknowledge things as they are and not as one would like them to be. In this respect, the first signals from the Obama administration were somewhat disappointing. In South Korea, where a new conservative government had retreated from a wide range of agreements with North Korea signed by the two preceding center-left presidents, secretary of state Hillary Clinton said, "Now the Republic of Korea's achievement of democracy and prosperity stands in stark contrast to the tyranny and poverty across the border to the North."[37] This was not the most encouraging message to send a regime with which one is bound to negotiate. Other statements by Secretary Clinton mentioned the insults, provocative words, and threatening actions from North Korea. She underlined the need for continued pressure against North Korea, but not once did she try to contextualize the conflict; not once did she point to positive acts by the North Korean government. Clinton's remarks were a step backward, relative to what Christopher Hill had achieved during the last period of the Bush administration.

During his many meetings with his North Korean counterparts, Hill reportedly developed empathy and was able to see things from the North

Korean perspective. An approach based on empathy is the most creative and productive approach between adversaries, an approach that has proved effective. To be able to put oneself in the other's place is a virtue held in high esteem both in Western Christianity and in Buddhism, the main religion of East Asia. With the advent of the Obama administration, the birth of a new approach to foreign policy was expected in which human dignity, reconciliation, and hope would replace distrust and fear.[38] To attempt a resolution of the conflict between North Korea and its neighbors, including the United States, might be an excellent test case for this new era's international relations. If representatives from North Korea and the United States agreed to disagree, invested a portion of mutual respect in a common future, and focused on areas in which cooperation is possible and needed, East Asia and the whole world would be a better and safer place to be.

ENDNOTES

1. I would like to thank the reviewer, the editorial team at Globis, the Department of International Affairs at the University of Georgia, and—in particular—my research assistant, Ras Tind Nielsen at the Nordic Institute of Asian Studies at the University of Copenhagen, for their valuable comments and suggestions.
2. Kim Sue-young, "More People Negative Toward North Korea," *Korea Times*, October 2, 2009, http://www.koreatimes.co.kr/www/news/include/print.asp?newsIdx = 39286.
3. *Special Reports: World Democracy Audit, 2009*, Newnations.com, http://www.newnations.com/specialreports/worlddemocracyaudit2009.html.
4. Ibid.
5. Daniel A. Bell, *East Meets West: Human Rights and Democracy in East Asia* (Princeton, NJ: Princeton University Press, 2000), 4.
6. Geir Helgesen, *Kimilsung-Country: The Cult of Personality; A Part of Tradition or an Alien Substance in Korean Culture?* MA thesis, Copenhagen University, 1987.
7. Readers seeking a deeper understanding of this should consult Han S. Park, *North Korea: The Politics of Unconventional Wisdom* (Boulder, CO: Lynne Rienner, 2002).
8. Donald Gregg stated, "I refer to North Korea as the longest-running intelligence failure in the history of US espionage." Gregg was US ambassador to South Korea from 1989 to 1993. Prior to that he served in the Central Intelligence Agency and on the National Security Council, and was also a national security adviser to vice president George H. W. Bush. http://www.pbs.org/wgbh/pages/frontline/shows/kim/interviews/gregg.html.
9. These catastrophes were, namely, the failures and prolongation of the Iraq and Afghanistan wars.
10. Reuters, "Rice says only an idiot would trust North Korea," December 19, 2008.
11. Ibid.
12. *Joint Statement of the Six-Party Talks*, February 13, 2007, para. 6, cited at the People's Republic of China MOFA homepage, www.washingtonpost.com/wp-dyn/content/article/2007/02/13/AR2007021300508_2.html.

13. Lawrence E. Harrison and Samuel P. Huntington, eds., *Culture Matters: How Values Shape Human Progress* (New York: Basic Books, 2000), xv.
14. It can hardly be substantiated, but rumors in informed circles persistently maintained that the only reason the United States agreed to provide a light water reactor to North Korea was that the collapse of the country was seen as imminent.
15. Samuel P. Huntington, *The Clash of Civilizations and the Remaking of World Order* (New York: Simon & Schuster, 1996), 138.
16. In this paper I do not differentiate between emotions, affect, moods, or feelings, although I am aware that this is done in the relevant literature in psychology and neuroscience.
17. The World Values Survey has empirically proved that "a history of Protestant or Orthodox or Islamic or Confucian traditions gives rise to cultural zones with distinct value systems that persist after controlling for the effects of economic development." Ronald Inglehart and Wayne E. Baker, "Modernization, Cultural Change, and the Persistence of Traditional Values," *American Sociological Review* 65 (2000): 49.
18. D. Moïsi, "Thc Clash of Emotions," *Foreign Affairs* 86, no. 1 (2007): 8–12.
19. R. McDermott, "The Feeling of Rationality: The Meaning of Neuroscientific Advances for Political Science," *Perspectives on Politics* 2, no. 4 (2004): 691.
20. Ibid., 693.
21. R. Bleiker and Emma Hutchison, "Fear No More: Emotions and World Politics," *Review of International Studies* 34 (2008): 115–135; N. C. Crawford, "The Passion of World Politics: Propositions on Emotion and Emotional Relationships," *International Security* 24, no. 4 (2000): 116–156.
22. McDermott, "Feeling of Rationality," 692.
23. Ibid., 693.
24. This section is based on chapter 2 of David Servan-Schreiber, *Behandling af Stress, Angst og Depression uden medicin eller terapi* [Treating stress, anxiety and depressions without medicine or therapy] (Copenhagen: Gyldendal, 2006).
25. McDermott, "Feeling of Rationality," 693.
26. I do, however recognize the importance of works such as Robert Jervis, *Perception and Misperception in International Politics* (Princeton, NJ: Princeton University Press, 1976).
27. Ronald Inglehart, *Modernization and Postmodernization: Cultural, Economic, and Political Change in Forty-three Societies* (Princeton, NJ: Princeton University Press, 1997).

28. Richard E. Nisbett, *The Geography of Thought: How Asians and Westerners Think Differently... and Why* (New York: Free Press, 2003).
29. R. Adolphs and A. Damasio, "The Interaction of Affect and Cognition: A Neurobiological Approach," in *Handbook of Affect and Social Cognition* (New Jersey: Lawrence Earlbaum), 27–49. Quoted in McDermott, "Feeling of Rationality," 691.
30. Crawford, "Passion of World Politics," 129.
31. McDermott, "Feeling of Rationality," 696.
32. Bleiker and Hutchison, "Fear No More," 122.
33. Crawford, "Passion of World Politics," 131, 133.
34. Ibid., 134.
35. Ibid., 135.
36. Immanuel Kant, "To Perpetual Peace: A Philosophical Sketch," translated by Ted Humphrey (Indianapolis, IN: Hackett Publishing, 2003), quoted in Crawford, "Passion of World Politics," 150.
37. Remarks to the press, with South Korean Foreign Minister Yu, February 20, 2009.
38. The North Koreans paid close attention to Obama's inauguration speech, which created great expectations in Pyongyang for an improved relationship with the United States. Although the Obama administration has yet to fulfill such expectations, one can hope that stronger US engagement in Asia will include more than a visible military presence. Paraphrasing Obama, it is easy to talk to your "friends," but the real challenge is to establish constructive relations with your "enemies."

Chapter 10

Power Succession-- So Far, So Good

Alexander Zhebin

The Democratic People's Republic of Korea (DPRK) is one of the least known and most difficult countries to visit and comprehend for any foreigner. These two circumstances alone have always evoked strong interest in the country. During the last two decades, this attention was intensified first by serious concerns about Pyongyang's nuclear and missile programs, then by numerous rumors about the health of Kim Jong Il, North Korea's former leader—and finally, after his unexpected death, by a surprisingly smooth power transfer to his son Kim Jong Un.

EARLY START ON A BUMPY ROAD

A tsunami of rumors, speculations, and assumptions generated by the long absence of Kim Jong Il from public view during autumn and winter 2008–2009 forced many experts once again to address the issue of power succession in the DPRK. North Korean leadership, as in the mid-1990s, again had to deal with the key issue of a transfer of power to a representative of the third generation of Kim's family under conditions that were very difficult both internationally and domestically. The serious economic problems the country had faced since the beginning of the 1990s were aggravated by natural calamities in the middle of that decade and into the next, and until 2010 remained a major obstacle to initializing a public succession process.

It is well known that in the 1990s unprecedented natural disasters, along with exacerbated chronic economic difficulties, brought about severe food problems. It was reported that the famine caused serious malnutrition and hunger in most of the country's regions. The dire economic situation became one of the main reasons that Kim Jong Il for three years formally kept vacant the posts of head of state and leader of the ruling Workers' Party of Korea (WPK).

Some observers are very often inclined to underestimate the importance of domestic policy considerations for North Korean leaders' decision making. But in reality the situation within the country and the people's living conditions matter significantly when it comes to staging the most important domestic political forums or other events. Kim Il Sung told a high-level Soviet delegation in 1987 that North Korea had to postpone the convocation of the WPK's Seventh Congress, originally scheduled for 1986, because "we had failed to raise the people's well-being to a necessary level."[1]

By all accounts, the severe food—and in more general terms, economic—situation that led to the growing social tension in the country is the major problem Pyongyang faces nowadays. Nonetheless, as in the Soviet

Union, whose political system in the 1930s was very similar to that of the present-day DPRK, ordinary citizens are inclined to put the bulk of blame on local officials, who they believe have failed to properly implement the directives of the leader, as well as on imperialists and their flunkies, who incessantly make attempts to strangle Korean-style socialism.

At the same time, when assessing the severity of the food situation in North Korea, one should always keep in mind that the North Koreans have lived under conditions leading to malnutrition during almost the whole period of the DPRK's history, and even well before 1945. The northern part of the peninsula has never been a granary. Providing decent food supplies to the population was never among top policy priorities, either for local feudal lords or for Japanese colonial authorities. After the country's liberation from the Japanese colonial yoke in 1945, the situation underwent little change. The North Koreans enjoyed very modest rations during almost the whole period of Kim Il Sung's rule. Since his death in 1994, the situation has only become worse.

The political implications of the sagging economy and concurrent developments are quite complex and diverse. The most serious one for the ruling family is that amid a serious drop in the people's living standards and the aggravated economic situation, it was not easy—because of a number of ideological, political, and psychological considerations—to publicly launch a full-fledged process of power transfer from Kim Jong Il to the chosen heir.

There are four, in my opinion, major factors that forced North Korea's leadership to postpone until 2010 an open promotion of Kim Jong Il's successor. The first one stems from Korea's political traditions, which originated and developed within the Confucian cultural arena. The resurrection and growing influence of traditional political values in the region was mentioned by a number of prominent Russian and foreign specialists.[2] The Confucian tradition (though not only it) demands that the heir's promotion should take place in a festive atmosphere, accompanied by good signs from heaven and by the incumbent ruler's acts of generosity—for instance, providing the people with some gifts or leniency. The economic situation during last fifteen years precluded the leader's distribution to his people of any meaningful "presents," and heaven has been sending quite unfortunate signs—the worst ever natural calamities and chronic malnutrition.

In this situation, many people have often remembered with nostalgia a relatively quiet and prosperous period under Kim Il Sung and compared it with the present, wondering whether under the next generation, the next successor of the Kim clan, their lives would become even worse. Economic problems, especially a very complicated food situation, perhaps represented the main hindrance preventing the North Korean leadership from claiming, as when Kim Il Sung promoted Kim Jong Il to the heir's position, that the reign of Kim Jong Il's successor would be "more glorious" than the current epoch, which for the absolute majority of the North Korean population has been far from a brilliant one.[3]

Second, the DPRK's international environment has remained very complicated and, in most cases, unfriendly. The level of external threat to the regime's existence is perceived by Pyongyang as dangerously high. The complicated diplomatic maneuvering among the United States, China, Russia, and Japan and the drastic aggravation of relations with South Korea have left almost no room for any improvisations by political newcomers and demand very seasoned leadership in foreign policy.

The next group of factors relates to the personality and professional qualities of the potential heirs. Until quite recently, none of Kim Jong Il's children was prepared to and capable of—either through authority in the WPK and in the country or through ability to influence the policy-making process—leading the country in the case of the father's physical inability to do the job. This is particularly true concerning the authority they enjoy in the army and security agencies. The last but not the least important reason is that Kim Jong Il himself, it seems, was not sure who among his sons would be able to tackle the mission and justify his confidence. Both Kim Jong Chol and Kim Jong Un were considered too young (in their mid-twenties) to fill the position. Their personalities were far from definitively shaped, to say nothing about their qualities as political leaders and statesmen.

In addition, Kim Jong Il was in no hurry to give up absolute power. He had waited for the top posts so long (more than twenty years elapsed between his official promotion to the heir's position in February 1974 and his father's death in July 1994), and he had not encountered many chances to enjoy his new position because of aggravated domestic problems and increasing international pressure to give up the nuclear programs pursued by North Korea.

Nuclear Tests, Missile Launches: Promoting a Heir

The decision to initiate, though without much ado, a succession process in 2009 was obviously prompted by Kim Jong Il's health condition. It seems that nobody had predicted the leader's stroke in August 2008. Immediately after partial recovery in the beginning of 2009, Kim Jong Il realized that it would be better for him to create a second, reserve center of power that could become operational in case of his physical inability to perform his duties. Kim Jong Il apparently sensed that it would be safer to do the job himself, thus awarding the necessary level of legitimacy to the chosen heir.

The attempt to launch a satellite in April 2009 and the second nuclear test in May 2009 are quite understandable in precisely this context—namely, the decision to start the succession process. Notwithstanding the international outcry, in the absence of any significant economic successes, taking advantage of the only lucky chance provided by a relatively better harvest in 2008, Kim Jong Il resorted to the "sputnik" launch and the nuclear test as the only means available to unite and inspire both his own elite and the people, garnering support once again for the hereditary power transfer. No doubt he also wanted to demonstrate that his military-first policy had borne fruit and that the regime and his heir had a deterrent powerful enough to prevent any attempts at regime change from outside the country. Observers now know from a documentary run by North Korean television on January 8, 2012 (Kim Jong Un's birthday), that on the day of the launch in 2009, he visited the space center to supervise the action and even reportedly gave an order to counter by force any attempt by "outside forces" to interfere with the process.

Certainly, both steps were designed to send a number of strong signals to the international community. The first was an unequivocal message to the Obama administration: take North Korea seriously, and move faster to address its concerns. Second, potential customers of missile and nuclear technologies, plus those willing to put their satellites into orbit from the DPRK's launching pads, should be also encouraged. South Korea, which had planned to launch its own satellite by end of July 2009 using a Russian-made rocket, was to be outpaced in both time and prestige; South Korea, "dependent" on outside forces, contrasted sharply with North Korea, which made its launch independently, on the long-cherished principle of self-reliance.

Strengthening the family's position within top policy-making bodies was another major direction of Kim Jong Il's actions to ensure the smooth transfer of power. At the WPK conference, convened after a forty-four-year break on September 28, 2010, Kim Jong Un was elected to the key position of vice chair of the WPK Central Military Commission (CMC).[4] Two more Kim family members were also promoted: Kim Jong Il's sister Kim Kyung Hee, gained membership in the Politburo of the WPK Central Committee, and her husband, Chang Song Taek, was elected the Politburo's alternate member.[5] Just one day before the conference, Kim Jong Un and Kim Kyung Hee were given the military rank of four-star general, along with Choe Ryong Hae, another party official, son of a comrade in arms of Kim Il Sung, and the former defense minister.[6] Earlier, in April 2009, Chang Song Taek had been promoted to membership in the powerful National Defense Commission (NDC), and in June 2010 he became the vice chair of the NDC. He reached full membership in Politburo at the fourth WPK conference, held April 11, 2012. Meanwhile, at the same conference his wife, Kim Kyung Hee, was elected to the very important position of WPK Central Committee secretary.[7]

Their rise was very similar to what happened in 1993: just a year before his death, Kim Il Sung returned his younger brother, Kim Yong Ju, to the WPK Central Committee Politburo after an eighteen-year absence from public life and appointed him to the post of the DPRK vice president. As with Kim Yong Ju in 1993, Kim Kyung Hee's and Chang Song Taek's elevation to high party and state posts was designed to strengthen the Kim clan's position in the top policy-making bodies and to provide a young, inexperienced heir with a close aids and, when necessary, seasoned teachers.

At the WPK Central Committee Politburo meeting held on December 30, 2011—the day after official funeral events finished and just two weeks after Kim Jong Il's death—his third son and heir was "courteously proclaimed" the supreme commander of the Korean People's Army (KPA) "according to the behest" of Kim Jong Il of October 8, 2011. Kim Jong Un was also named "the only center of unity, cohesion and leadership of the WPK."[8]

Just one hundred days later (the initial mourning period of the same length following Kim Il Sung's death in 1994 comes to mind), at the fourth WPK conference on April 11 and at the Supreme People's Assembly (SPA; North Korea's parliament) session of April 13, 2012, Kim Jong Un was awarded top party and government positions, though under slightly different titles—he was made the first secretary of the WPK (instead of secretary-general) and the first chair of the NDC (instead of chairman). The original titles were "forever" assigned to Kim Jong Il, as had happened with Kim Il Sung, who was given the title "eternal president." The relevant changes were made in the WPK chapter and the country's constitution.[9]

All the events of April 2012 in North Korea were devoted to the one hundredth anniversary of Kim Il Sung's birthday. The only event that spoiled the "greatest national holiday" happened to be an unsuccessful attempt to launch a satellite, apparently to celebrate the advent of Kim Jong Un's era. The North Koreans, who had invited several hundred foreign journalists to cover the show, went out of their way to demonstrate that they did not care too much, rejected the United Nations (UN) Security Council presidential statement condemning the act as a ballistic missile launch, and promised to continue a "peaceful exploration of outer space."[10]

The April holiday drew a line under the succession process and led most experts to accept that the system of hereditary power transfer built by Kim Il Sung and Kim Jong Il during a period of almost half a century proved quite instrumental for fulfilling the task.

KIM JONG UN'S SYSTEM: AN OUTLINE

The promotions in April 2012 and earlier reshuffles led to the appointment of seasoned and experienced functionaries to every sphere of party and government activity. It is expected that Kim Jong Un can rely on them; they were placed in the top party and state decision-making bodies because first, they were expected to give good advice to the young leader, and second, they assumed the daily management of the particular spheres of party and state activities until he acquired enough experience.

In foreign policy, these top individuals are likely to include the following: the nominal head of state, member of the presidium of the Politburo of the WPK Central Committee, and president of the presidium of the SPA Kim Yong Nam; Politburo member and deputy prime minister Kang Seok Ju (both he and Kim Yong Nam made their careers in the WPK Central Committee International Department and the DPRK Foreign Ministry); Politburo member, secretary of the WPK Central Committee, and chair of the SPA Choe Tae Bok; and alternate Politburo member, secretary of the WPK Central Committee, and director of the WPK Central Committee International Department Kim Yong Il. In military affairs, Kim Jong Un is likely to receive advice from the "gang of four" vice marshals, recently promoted by him. They are chief of the KPA Main Political Department (MPD) Choe Ryong Hae; minister of the People's Armed Forces Kim Jong Gak; first deputy minister of the People's Armed Forces Hyon Chol Hae; and chief of the KPA general staff Hyon Yong Chol, who is a newcomer among the top brass. The first three were also elected to the Politburo of the WPK Central Committee at the April 2012 party conference. In general, such a system of leadership during the transition period is almost identical to the one that was used in North Korea during initial period after Kim Il Sung's death.

So far Kim Jong Un serves as a symbol, the regime's "face." However, in the future, he is unlikely to share the top power with anyone else. The North Korean political system was founded and developed for one-man rule and would not tolerate or function under any dualism. Therefore, Kim Jong Un—like his father after Kim Il Sung's death—will eventually rule alone. His power base is the circle of those people who were selected by him or chosen earlier by Kim Jong Il.

A number of signs, especially the numerous personnel changes during 2009–2011, indicate that the diseased leader tried to align carefully the balance of power among top officials, as well as among the top party and government bodies. However, the swift removal of two key military figures - chief of the KPA general staff Ri Yong Ho (in July) and the minister of People's Armed Forces Kim Jong Gak (in November), especially in view of the fact that the latter was appointed just 7 months ago, demonstrated that nobody's place is permanent.[11]

The event leads one once again to dwell on the extent of the military's real influence among the country's elite. Certainly, a group of top military commanders occupies a special place in the country's leadership. Since the advent of the military-first policy in the 1990s, some analysts, noting that these military commanders were almost always present in

Kim Jong Il's entourage and occupied top places in the leadership line-up, even suggested that Kim Jong Il may have become their hostage and could not rule without their consent. In contrast, there is no doubt that the former leader did a great deal to win the top brass over to his side —the highest military ranks and awards, as well as various privileges, rained on them as if from the horn of plenty.

However, in assessing the real extent of power and influence enjoyed by any particular individual among North Korea's highest officials, including the military ones, it is important to bear in mind that every high-ranking official, including the top brass, personally remained voiceless and unprotected from the leader's self-will. DPRK history provides many examples of the most brilliant careers ruined, of party members and state leaders who suddenly disappeared from the political arena and were later spotted, at best, in managerial positions in county-level bodies. One of the most striking examples of this is the fate of Ri Yong Ho's two predecessors. The first, Choe Kwan, chief of the KPA general staff and WPK Central Committee political committee's alternate member, after being criticized by Kim Il Sung for his links with a "military-bureaucratic group" at the end of the 1960s, suddenly disappeared from public view and later reappeared as director of a county automobile company in South Hwanhae Province.

His successor in the position, O Kuk Ryol, a four-star general and Politburo member, was overtaken by a similar fate in 1988. But he had a better landing and found himself in a position in the WPK Central Committee department dealing with South Korea. The irony was that by that time, Choe Kwan, Kim Il Sung's old comrade, had been forgiven, had returned to Pyongyang to serve in North Korea's cabinet as a vice premier in charge of fishery, and—do not be surprised—had immediately returned to the chief of general staff's seat, which happened to become vacant. As for O Kuk Ryol, during recent reshuffles he became an NDC member, then was promoted to become vice chair of the body, and finally, in April 2012 was elected to the Politburo as an alternate (not full) member of the

WPK's top decision-making organ, at the age of eighty-three.[12] Ri Yong Ho—whose father was also a comrade in arms of Kim Il Sung, and who himself is now only seventy years old—may also experience new twists of fate.

Almost all the members of North Korea's incumbent leadership at various stages of their careers have been punished, purged, sent to receive revolutionary reeducation (many of them more than once), and even removed from political life—Kim Yong Ju, Kim Il Sung's younger brother, was banned for almost two decades. But Kim Il Sung, the founder of the clan and its patriarch, usually did not resort to extreme measures against his clan's members and close friends from the "partisan" period, and most often eventually returned the guilty ones to his entourage. Kim Jong Il, in general, followed this line, too. Even Chang Song Taek —the seemingly almighty husband of Kim Jong Il's sister, who was in fact Kim Jong Il's deputy for party affairs, suddenly disappeared in 2004. He reemerged two years later, in January 2006, and was entrusted with running one of the key WPK Central Committee's divisions, the Department of Administrative Organs, reportedly established especially for him.

Such methods have enhanced, to some extent, the effectiveness of the state machinery, providing it with new vigor and very often shifting responsibility for the Great Leader's wrong decisions to low-level officials. At the same time, such arbitrary practices, which entail the loss of face and public humiliation of rather respectable people who themselves, as a rule, are heads of their own clans, could hardly contribute to broadening the ranks of genuine supporters of the Kim clan. Most of those who were purged have already died, but their children know well their fathers' life stories and may be waiting for the time to take revenge.

In this context some experts' claims that Chang Song Taek is allegedly a regent for the new leader seems unconvincing. Also unlikely is the emergence of a duumvirate or tandem rule with Chang Song Taek. In North Korea there is an absolute leader around whom power is concentrated. And other members of the leadership (usually referred to as "relevant employees") will compete only for the opportunity to have the leader's ear more frequently than others. Certainly, family members (as scholars know from the history of other countries) are often placed closer to the ruler, and they may therefore enjoy greater confidence. So Chang Song Taek's and his wife's influence, especially in matters of domestic policy and the selection of personnel, may well be among the weightiest.

When assessing the likelihood of personnel changes in the future, it is important to bear in mind that, as the experience of the DPRK has shown, a formal position held by a person in the North Korean official hierarchy often does not reflect his or her real political weight. After Kim Il Sung's death, as representatives of the old guard were leaving the political arena because of their physical conditions, Kim Jong Il rather quickly picked up as his closest aids the officials who did not belong to the highest ranks —they were neither the elderly members of the Politburo nor ministers but rather the younger and more capable first deputy directors of the most important departments of the WPK Central Committee. Chang Song Taek has emerged from exactly this level of party functionaries. Moreover, considering the age of most members of North Korea's top leadership (among the Politburo's thirty-three members and alternate members, eleven people are over eighty, twelve over seventy, and only one under sixty years old), the repetition of this scenario of leadership change during the next two or three years looks quite possible. Thus, if Kim Jong Un manages to stay in power for the next several years, he has every chance of surrounding himself with much younger aids, whom he would choose himself.

Of course, internally Kim's clan is not a monolithic one. It consists of several groups that, allegedly, will compete for influence over Kim Jong Un and to enjoy more benefits. Recently, the structure of the clan has become even more complex because new miniclans have emerged around Kim Jong Il's other wives and children (at least three sons and one daughter are known) and their relatives. There are also the family clans of those top members of the leadership structure whose founders happened to be Kim Il Sung's old-time comrades and were lucky to survive numerous purges in the 1950s and 1960s. But for the time being the Kim clan's unity is stipulated by its common interest in preserving power and perhaps to no lesser extent—after the well-known events in Eastern Europe, the Balkans, Iraq, and Libya—by a fear of retribution for past deeds. The situation in the upper echelons of the ruling elite may change in the future under the impact of both domestic and external factors unfavorable for Kim's family, or even as a result of certain contradictions within the clan itself.

Therefore, an official inauguration of Kim Jong Un as Kim Jong Il's successor would not have provided a full guarantee that he is to retain his position. The heir's performance in safeguarding the ruling elite's power and in pulling the country out of the current dangerous situation without making too many concessions to "imperialists" will be a key factor in determining his future.

Factors of Stability and Looming Challenges

In spite of chronic economic problems and drastically complicated international environment, the North Korean leaders have managed to retain their positions, ensuring political and social stability and sustainable control over the situation in the country. Control over the country and social stability were once again confirmed by the smooth succession process after Kim Jong Il's death, and even earlier by the successful coping with the aftermath of the 2009 currency reform and the convocation during a period of just eighteen months of two WPK conferences to promote Kim Jong Un as successor and to renovate the party's top governing bodies. There have been no signs of any open mass display of discontent with Kim Jong Un's takeover, nor has organized opposition in any form emerged.

At the top echelons, the North Korean leadership still appears united. The regime's law-enforcement apparatus, with its all-embracing network of informers is still strong and effective enough to prevent at an early stage the emergence of any organized opposition group or conspiracy against the system. Therefore, even according to Lenin's teaching on the two absolute necessities for revolution—namely, that members of the lower stratum, or people, do not want to live like they did before, and that the upper stratum (the ruling elite) cannot rule as it did before—conditions have not yet ripened in North Korea.

At the grassroots level persistent, all-embracing brainwashing through official propaganda and the almost total isolation of the majority of the population from a real picture of the outside world constitute main factors of stability. There is little doubt that as a result of several decades of brainwashing, a sizable part of North Korea's population still believes in sharing "the same idea, the same wishes, the same future and the same destiny" with the present regime. For comparison, even after several decades have revealed Stalin's crimes in the Soviet Union, recent polls conducted in Russia have shown that up to one-third of the country's population still believes that he was "the greatest leader" and even an "efficient manager." Only since the mid-1990s in North Korea have there been more signs of social deviation than ever before, signs that manifest themselves in the drastically increasing outflow of defectors, the emergence of a "grey economy" and so-called home-style capitalism, and widespread corruption and other crimes.

A number of factors that could have become potential sources of destabilization of the regime—and on which some circles abroad had pinned so much hope—clearly did not. The infighting between conservatives (ideologists) and technocrats (pragmatics) that many politicians and experts in the West expected to escalate after Kim Jong Il's demise is apparently without extremes, if it is actually taking place. The North Korean ideologists have repeatedly shown that they can, if necessary, become successful pragmatics; with virtually no major trump cards in hand, they made major world powers enter into direct talks with North Korea regarding its nuclear program. And pragmatics have enough brains to understand that the factional infighting and drastic shifts in policy can trigger processes that could eventually lead to their being ousted from power along with conservatives.

Likewise, the so-called contradictory interests of the DPRK Foreign Ministry officials and the North Korean military that from time to time reportedly surfaced during the talks with the United States perhaps threaten stability less than one might think. Though it is true that the military's profile in the DPRK is now higher than during Kim Il Sung's era and that its stance is now more rigid in dealing with the United States, it would be misleading to overestimate military influence or imagine that its core interests differ from those of the regime. Both civil and military branches of the ruling elite are interested first of all in ensuring the regime's survival.

Certainly, awareness of being in the same boat does not preclude the existence of different opinions on some policy issues or even of disputes between conservatives and supporters of change, including those in economic policy. Such discussions are taking place and are sometimes even made public. Some publications in the WPK news outlets have contained, inter alia, criticism of unnamed supporters of a nontraditional industrial structure for the country, with its emphasis on heavy industry, and have rejected the views of "some people" who allegedly argued for transition to the "export model" of development.[13]

As for the conflict of generations within the ruling elite, an earlier version of which may have taken place during Kim Jong Il's own succession process, it has ended for natural reasons: old partisan cadres are ever more quickly leaving this world.

So a repetition of the scenarios that occurred in Eastern Europe and in the former USSR is unlikely. A "peaceful revolution from below," as in Eastern Europe, appears to be impossible in North Korea because of an almost total absence of the elements of a civil society and the presence of tough control over the media. The probability of radical reforms from above, akin to Gorbachev's perestroika in the USSR, is almost equally unlikely in North Korea. First, Kim Jong Il and his clan were hardly inspired by perestroika, which led to the removal from power of the ruling Communist Party and its leader, Gorbachev, as well as to the country's disintegration. Second, with the exception of Kim Jong Il's 2001 appeal to *kanbu* to use "a new thinking," he never gave any signs of his possible retreat from the "principles of socialism."[14]

In his early works Kim Jong Il defended resolutely the WPK's monopoly on power and rejected accusations of totalitarianism: "The reality of our country proves that slander and attacks by imperialists ... that leadership of the party allegedly curb creative abilities of people are a counter-revolutionary trick aimed at fanning bourgeois liberalism and disorganizing socialism."[15] The gist of his important speech delivered before WPK Central Committee high-ranking officials on May 5, 1991, can be presented in the following points: (1) proletarian dictatorship must be strengthened in order to root out counterrevolutionary elements, (2) a multiparty system will not be allowed in North Korea because political parties other than the working-class party must not compete for power, (3) North Korea will maintain a planned economic system and will not permit any form of a private ownership system, (4) collectivism is the mainstay of North Korean politics and routine affairs, and finally, (5) the revolutionary task of the Great Leader must be inherited generation after generation, and the leadership of the party must be guaranteed permanently.[16] In a similar speech on January 3, 1992, he had concentrated on attributing the failure of socialism in a number of countries to the shortcomings in the communist parties' leadership and to their inability to correctly implement Marxist-Leninist theory.

Kim Jong Il also emphasized the need to keep the people from being "contaminated by foreign culture," saying that

> socialism and capitalism cannot coexist abreast with each other.... To let a multi-party political system exist in socialist society will eventually result in yielding the way to counter-revolutionaries for them to destroy the socialist foundation and thus to overthrow the people's government.... To prevent imperialist ideology and culture from infiltrating into our country remains the key to protecting our socialism and to guaranteeing the development of socialist culture.[17]

Every attempt to crack this monolithic unity from the outside has so far ended in failure, ultimately ensuring the survival of the DPRK. As long as Kim Jong Un remains at the helm of governance, he and his clan will be able to keep the ship afloat.

This said, North Korea's strident resistance to foreign influence does not preclude new attempts to reinvigorate the country's economy. One of the major implications of the current economic situation is that the regime will not be able to delay indefinitely the solution of urgent economic problems and continue its "hermit kingdom" policy based mainly on noneconomic coercion and ideological indoctrination that postpone economic reforms.

The experience of the Eastern European countries, especially Romania, demonstrated that self-isolation from the challenges a country is faced with is very dangerous and could result in the leadership's losing control of the situation, leading to a social explosion and the high probability that the ruling clan will be completely ousted from power and even exterminated. It seems that the DPRK's ruling elite now, more than ever before, is aware of the hard imperative that in order to survive while deflecting increased international pressure to give up its nuclear program, it is necessary to try new approaches to economic problems. Among the remarkable signs of departure from its formerly rigid stance are the state measures of July 2002; the decisions to go ahead with a number of steps promoting economic exchanges with South Korea and establishing special trade and industrial zones, including quite recently in the areas bordering China; the attempts to attract investors from other countries; and the creation of several governmental and quasi-governmental bodies to promote foreign investment in the country's economy. One can only hope that the removal of Ri Yong Ho, who was apparently a leading figure in the military branch of the ruling elite, is a first sign that Kim Jong Un and his inner circle not only understand the urgency of the current economic problems but also have the political will to do something about them. The new leader's recent calls for building a prosperous country and improving the economy's management also speak to this effect.[18] It is highly desirable to not waste the moment but to utilize every opportunity suitable for promoting various kinds of economic and related ties; this is the only available channel for engaging North Korea and promoting its integration into a world community.

Economic cooperation with the outside world will help develop the DPRK economy and do more to prepare North Koreans to live in a modern society. In other words, it will help lessen the existing gap between the two parts of the country and cut the cost of unification. The engagement process itself will help enlarge and strengthen in the North an ever-growing stratum of people interested in stable, cooperative relations with the outside world. It is worth emphasizing once more that there is no sustainable channel other than the economic one for realizing human, cultural, and informational exchanges between North Korea and the outside world—and for thus beginning the real integration of the DPRK into the globalized world.

One should keep in mind the inevitable movement to the fore of a younger part of the ruling elite, growing in both numbers and influence, and whose value orientation is close or similar to those in societies characterized by liberal democracy and market-economy systems. Those people could be compared, to a certain extent, to the so-called 386 generation in South Korea. This stratum includes managers of joint ventures, export-import and general trading companies, some military officers, technical specialists and students educated and trained abroad, and some prominent figures in arts and culture. Taking into consideration the experience of China, the former USSR, and the Eastern European countries, these younger actors are working on the consolidation of their political and economic base in the North and are preparing to negotiate with the South conditions acceptable for reunification. Yet one should not expect the members of Kim Jong Un's leadership to be much more democratic or more inclined toward any radical reforms or unification with South Korea. On the contrary, they may well be politically more conservative than not, highly pragmatic, and very tough in negotiating for a unification formula that will ensure that they retain "appropriate" social status and material well-being in the unified Korea—shielded from the fate of their Eastern European counterparts.

ENDNOTES

1. Kim Il Sung, pronouncements at the meeting with Yakov Ryabov, deputy chairman of the USSR Council of Ministers, March 22, 1986.
2. M. L. Titarenko, *Russia and East Asia: Problems of International and Inter-Civilizational Relations* (Moscow: Kuchkovo Pole, 1994), 22–28; Alexander Zhebin, *The DPRK Political System's Evolution under Conditions of Global Changes* (Moscow: Russian Panorama, 2006), 13–24.
3. *Rodong Sinmun*, July 1, 1998.
4. KCNA, "Central Military Commission Organized," September 28, 2010.
5. KCNA, "Members and Alternate Members of Political Bureau," September 28, 2010.
6. *Rodong Sinmun*, September 28, 2010.
7. KCNA, "Members of WPK Central Guidance Body Elected to Fill Vacancies, Elected and Appointed," April 11, 2012.
8. KCNA, "Report on Meeting of Political Bureau of C.C., WPK," December 31, 2011.
9. See KCNA dispatches on the fourth WPK conference from Pyongyang, April 11, 2012.
10. KCNA, "DPRK Rejects UNSC's Act to Violate DPRK's Legitimate Right to Launch Satellite," April 17, 2012.
11. KCNA, "Ri Yong Ho Relieved of All His Posts in DPRK," July 16, 2012.
12. KCNA, "Members of WPK Central Guidance Body Elected to Fill Vacancies, Elected and Appointed," April 11, 2012.
13. *Rodong Sinmun*, September 17, 1998.
14. *Rodong Sinmun*, January 4, 2001.
15. Kim Jong Il, *Socialism of Our Style Serving the Interests of Working Masses Will Be Victorious* (Pyongyang: Foreign Languages Publishing House, 1991).
16. Ibid.
17. Kim Jong Il, *Socialism Construction's Historical Lesson and Our Party's General Line* (Pyongyang: WPK Publishing House, 1992).
18. KCNA, "Kim Jong Un Sets Forth Tasks for Effecting Kim Jong Il's Patriotism," August 3, 2012.

LOOKING AHEAD

THE DAWN OF THE KIM JONG UN ERA

CHALLENGES AND OPPORTUNITIES FOR THE REST OF THE WORLD

Han S. Park

The Korean Peninsula is without doubt the most militarily fortified spot in the world, with over two million well-trained uniformed forces on either side of the demilitarized zone (DMZ), coupled with some 75,000 US ground forces stationed in South Korea and Japan. The level of hostility shown across the border was clearly evidenced by a number of incidents during the last two years in which North Korea tested nuclear bombs and launched numerous missiles despite international sanctions. Last year alone, two serious military incidents occurred in the disputed waters off the west coast that could have easily escalated into major wars. Another war in Korea would create devastation of an unprecedented scale. The death of Kim Jong Il from natural causes at the age of sixty nine at this unsettling historical junction has left the world shrouded in uncertainty regarding his successor—the Dear Leader's youngest son, Kim

Jong Un, age twenty-eight. As the youthful, inexperienced, and untested man takes control, the world anxiously awaits some indication of his direction for leadership. Yet if one knows the intricacies of North Korean politics and belief systems, little is mysterious and unpredictable. There are certain principles and imperatives to which Pyongyang must adhere, and there are established patterns of policy goals and strategies. These make a reasonably convincing analysis possible.

When it comes to foreign policy, one must understand that Pyongyang's foreign policy conduct has been and will continue to be determined by actions and policies taken by the surrounding governments toward it. Therefore, it is imperative to analyze Pyongyang's foreign policy behavior in the dynamic system of interactions among major players, including the United States, China, Europe, and other Asian and global systems, as well as the Seoul government. The present chapter analyzes the likely course of policy development in the Kim Jong Un era, both proactively by the new leadership and reactively to a series of hypothetical or likely policies of the neighboring governments toward the DPRK.

Three Generations of Leadership in the DPRK

Since the inception of the Democratic People's Republic of Korea (DPRK) in 1948, its founding leader, Kim Il Sung, established a clearly discernible system of characteristics for the state with the creation of *juche*, or self-reliance, ideology. *Juche*'s core value was national sovereignty, and its main policy goal was to establish a legitimate system of governance. The long period of the first generation (1948–1994) coincided with a period of "legitimacy war" between the two political systems across the border that both claimed the right to control the entire peninsula following the brutal, massively destructive war (1950–1953). As the South became grossly dependent on the United States and external assistance, Kim Il Sung aspired to and pursued a policy of *juche* that eventually isolated and alienated the North and often left it ridiculed by the US-dominated West. However, national solidarity and political integration (rather than divisiveness) resulted from the policies and politics of *juche*, which helped the political system muddle through at a time when the Soviet Union, along with all its satellite systems in Europe and elsewhere, went down the drain.

By the end of Kim Il Sung era, the world was awash with the tide of American supremacy. Under the doctrine of the Washington Consensus, America intervened in the domestic politics of many sovereign states with the intention of effecting regime change in line with liberalization and democratization. North Korea quickly became the target of the sole military superpower on the planet, which manipulated its traditional allied states, including South Korea and Japan, at will. The United States has also exerted substantial control over the world's financial system. At a time when Washington had become obsessed not only with denuclearizing North Korea but also with changing the regime's characteristics, Kim Il Sung passed away abruptly and unexpectedly in 1994. When he died, the world anticipated an imminent collapse of the DPRK.

Then came the second generation of leadership, with power and authority succeeded by the Dear Leader, Kim Jong Il (ruling 1994–2011). Despite his having been groomed to lead the country, the consensus emerged in the West that his government was not durable and would certainly collapse within months, not years. The new leader had to make sure that neither implosion nor aggression from outside could threaten the system. These challenges were formidable indeed. Several landmark events and developments demonstrated the external threat and hostility to the regime.

Washington planned surgical attacks against the North Korean nuclear site in Yongbyon on several occasions in 2003 and 2006, as it had done in 1994. Had there been no intervention by former US president Jimmy Carter, who visited Pyongyang and met with Kim Il Sung, the military operation in 1994 would likely have become a reality. As recently as 2006, the Pentagon stepped up planning for attacks targeting North Korea's nuclear program. In conjunction with these actions, in 2004 the US Congress adopted and President Bush signed into law the North Korea Human Rights Legislation, which encourages critics of North Korea, especially defectors, and their activities. The act provides the United States new tools to address the human rights situation in North Korea by focusing US efforts to help both those who flee the regime and those who are "trapped" inside the country. The act earmarked $124 million a year for such causes and made North Koreans eligible for political asylum in the United States.

Following Pyongyang's nuclear tests and missile launchings, a string of economic and financial sanctions by the United States, Western governments, and the United Nations ensued, exacerbating food shortages initially caused by severe flooding in successive years during the mid-1990s. In the process, Washington used the DPRK as the most fitting and convenient scapegoat for beefing up its defense industry, especially its missile defense system. The military industrialists and their collaborators have consistently and effectively portrayed North Korea as a military superpower with capacities far beyond the state's actual capabilities. The DPRK is also depicted as an evil system that is predisposed to launching a military assault against the United States. In fact, North Korea has been used almost exclusively to justify development of the costly missile defense system by the US government. Undoubtedly, many conservative circles would prefer that North Korea continue to be seen as a dangerous country capable of harming the United States.

As North Korea's regional and global support system of the communist bloc dissipated, the security alliance among the United States, South Korea, and Japan intensified—an ever-growing source of security concern for North Korea. This triad of allies has rationalized the US military presence in South Korea and Japan, totaling over 75,000 US troops, as well as the routine US–South Korea joint military exercises in the disputed territorial waters off the west coast, inviting occasional military skirmishes. These exercises were continued even under the Kim and Roh presidencies in the South.

Important measures of inter-Korean tension reduction under the Rise of the Sunshine Policy were initiated and implemented by the Kim Dae Jung and Roh Moo Hyung governments in the Republic of Korea (ROK). But even at the Sunshine Policy's apex, military tension along the DMZ was never eased at all. The Sunshine Policy receded in the face of a hostile South Korea under the Lee Myung Bak government (2008–2012). As major mass media outlets, particularly major newspapers and television networks, were effectively coopted by the economic establishment in South Korea, public opinion turned against the progressive politics and policies, paving the way for the election of Lee Myung Bak as president in 2007. From the outset of the new government, South Korea launched a series of policy measures extremely hostile toward the North and invariably insulting to thc Kim Jong Il government. The main policy objectives toward North Korea included the doctrine that "the North must denuclearize, reform and open its political system and governing structure, and then, and only then, the South will guide the North to achieve $3,000 GDP/PC." On the pretense of Pyongyang's provocation along the west coast at the time of joint military exercises, the Lee government cut off practically all interaction, economic or otherwise, with the North, paralyzing the operation of the Kaesong Industrial Complex and discontinuing tourism at Kumkang Mountain.

Finally, the reckless train of the Washington Consensus represented yet another challenge to the DPRK. At a time when the communist bloc was aching and gradually dying, the concept of the consensus was introduced in 1989 in Washington, DC, with the intent of injecting a heavy dose of economic liberalism and political democracy into the developing world, initially in Latin America, but eventually expanding to the former Soviet republics and Eastern European countries. As America emerged as the sole superpower, this doctrine was encouraged by misguided academics who advocated the inevitable "end of history" as a result of the victory of liberalist ideology of democracy. The steam of this train clouded and dismantled selected political systems in the Islamic world (Iraq and Libya), making Kim Jong Il's North Korea keenly wary about the true intention of American foreign policy. The phenomenon of the Arab Spring may be viewed in this light.

These facts posed a tremendous challenge to Kim Jong Il in key sectors of the country: security, national identity, and economy. The Western forces were designed to force the DPRK to relinquish its security guarantor (nuclear capability), compromise its national identity and sovereignty, and suffer economically to a point that the system itself could not be sustained.

How Did Kim Jong Il Respond?

To address the concern of external threats, the Kim Jong Il leadership advanced the development of nuclear weapons, culminating in underground tests of nuclear devices in October 2006 and in the development of long-range missiles. North Koreans believe (and it is not farfetched, by any means) that it was their nuclear weapons capability that deterred certain aggression from the United States. This belief has been reinforced by the US-led attacks on Iraq and the subsequent demise of Saddam Hussein and his regime. More directly, the violent collapse of Gaddafi's Libya can be attributed to his relinquishing the ambition to arm the country with nuclear weapons, a conclusion that surely provided yet another lesson to the Pyongyang leadership.

The United States, unwilling to conduct direct negotiations with the DPRK, persuaded China to host a series of multilateral talks for the purpose of denuclearizing North Korea. China welcomed this opportunity, which gave it the leading role in a multinational forum. Kim Jong Il went into the talks with the intention of abandoning the nuclear program if a stable security environment was created at the same time. The multilateral forum comprised the DPRK, the ROK, the United States, China,

Russia, and Japan, and its only aim was to find a peaceful solution to end the DPRK's nuclear program. The first round of talks started in August 2003; senior officials from the six countries gathered in Beijing. In 2005 the first joint statement was issued after the fourth round of talks. In this paper, the DPRK agreed to abandon all nuclear programs and promised to return to the Non-Proliferation Treaty as soon as possible. But this agreement was made with the full expectation of reciprocal actions by the United States. In the absence of any reciprocity, the United States spearheaded the imposition of bilateral and international sanctions. On April 5, 2009, the DPRK proceeded with its announced satellite launch despite international objections. Later the same month, the DPRK said it would never again take part in the six-party talks. However, the Kim Jong Il government agreed to rejoin the Beijing meeting, suggesting that Pyongyang was ready to proceed with talks at a time when the Lee government of the South was staying away from the forum for other reasons.

During his tenure, Kim Jong Il aggressively pursued reaching out to former Cold War adversaries, including the United States, Japan, and Europe, as well as South Korea. Despite repeated economic sanctions by the United States and US-backed international organizations, such as the United Nations, Pyongyang's efforts to directly engage in talks with Washington were persistent. In order to engage with Japan, Kim Jong Il even admitted to the abduction of Japanese citizens and apologized to the visiting Japanese prime minister, Koizumi, in 2005. This action suggests that Kim Jong Il was committed to improving relations with Japan. With respect to relations with the South, Kim Jong Il accommodated all the policy gestures of presidents Kim Dae Jung and Roh Moo Hyung, leading to the successful historic summits with both South Korean presidents in 2000 and 2006.

Although South Korea's Sunshine Policy was constrained by the domestic conditions in South Korea, the degree and speed of inter-Korea cooperation and collaboration on economic and social exchanges were remarkable, culminating in the development of the Kaesung Industrial Complex and the Kumkangsan Tourism project. The 6.15 Declaration of 2000 and the 10.4 Agreements were also adopted during Kim Jong Il's tenure. In addition, the Kim Jong Il era produced tangible results in terms of economic cooperation with European countries, especially the Nordic countries in the area of sustainable development.

Songun as the Trademark of Kim Jong Il

The ideology of *songun* ("military first") will undoubtedly be credited with establishing military preparedness to deter external threats to national security and thereby with the sustenance of the system itself. In addition, to address the domestic concerns about possible sources of instability and to ensure the well-being of the people, two distinct measures were advanced: *songun* politics and controlled economic reforms. Indeed, *songun* was the backbone of Kim Jong Il's leadership; Kim Jong Il himself was credited with its creation. It would be not only too simplistic but also wrong to understand this doctrine as a political strategy to put the military first in order to provide it with privileges and power. Rather, *songun* is a comprehensive system of values and norms designed to lay out a road map for politics and society.

This doctrine is predicated on the principle of the militarization of civilians and the civilianization of the military: the civilian is mandated to be combat ready at all times and the military is charged with the obligation and responsibility to be and to work for civilian society (noted in chapter 5 of this volume on the contemporary role of the military in North Korea). Thus, there is to be no distinction between the two sectors. Not only are the two sectors closely coordinated, but they are also often embodied in the same person. Without understanding this, outsiders will find it nonsensical that a military general is also simultaneously a member of the Central Committee of the Workers' Party of Korea and holds a position in the Supreme People's Assembly. With this doctrine pervasive in the society, the political system achieved and maintained a solid foundation of political integration and power solidification and was able to survive the external adversities already alluded to. As Smith pointed out in chapter 4 of this volume, in the economic arena, the Kim Jong Il era witnessed the implementation of the market mechanism, though this was limited. Kim Jong Il's North Korea did not undermine the incentive system for citizens and citizen groups.

Kim Jong Un Emerges in Particular Contexts

Before speculating about the nature and character of the man, one must understand the historical and political contexts that were presented to Kim Jong Un and his confidants. As one attempts to forecast the direction and orientations of policies in both the domestic and the international arena, one tends to pay almost exclusive attention to the person, and if what is being discussed about the post–Kim Jong Il era is any indication, North Korea is not an exception. As important as the leader himself is, the contextual characteristics within and surrounding the country are very important, and they hold a great deal of explanatory and predictive power. The domestic, inter-Korea, and international contexts may be observed as follows.

The domestic context is clearly one of economic shortcomings, with food shortages as the most pressing need. In this situation, the Kim Jong Un leadership is fully expected to build its policies on economic expansion by first continuing the same outreach policy strategies carried over from the Kim Jong Il era. In order to ensure national security from external hostility, Kim Jong Un will be left with few options apart from strong militarization, which includes nuclear preparedness. At the same time, in order to ensure political stability and national integration, Pyongyang is fully expected to maintain *songun* politics.

As for the context of inter-Korea relations, Kim Jong Un is faced with a South Korea that is undergoing a profound change in its political dynamics and public sentiment. A presidential election will take place in December 2012, preceded by a general election for the legislative body. If the election of nonpolitician Park Won Soon as mayor of Seoul in late 2011 and the swirling political wind surrounding the popularity of yet another nonpolitician, professor Ahn Chul Soo, is any indication, South Korean politics most likely faces a great change and profound transformation: politics as usual may not last very long.

The grassroots and youthful intellectuals increasingly reject aspects of politics as usual and suggest several things. First, the political maneuvering organized by established politicians and political parties that often involves secrecy and the illegal transactions of slush funds will only be counterproductive; second, the conservative agenda of protecting and promoting the interests of the wealthy and established through the control of the conventional media outlets (newspapers and televisions) will be effectively challenged by the myriad of today's information technologies that facilitate alternative means of mass communication. These new media will continue to be utilized by the younger segments of the population. Third, the "ideological color card" will not work any longer. For decades now, the incumbent leadership has frequently used this card as a tactic whereby political opponents are framed as North Korea sympathizers in order to influence public opinion about certain politicians. Fourth, the public will not accept any policy toward the North that could bring about a military clash with North Korea, as evidenced by the regional elections held in 2010. Public sentiment in South Korea is shifting away from accepting the status quo and toward rejecting the current stalemate and costly tension in inter-Korea relations.

In dealing with inter-Korea relations, one must not forget that the Kaesong Industrial Complex is still open and running. This was a remarkable achievement by president Kim Dae Jung and continued by president Roh Moo Hyung. It was so grand and visionary that even the Lee Myung Bak government could not completely shut it down. The

Kumkangsan Tourism project is yet another joint venture that is closed at this time but will most likely be reactivated.

The international and global context that the Kim Jong Un leadership will confront is also fluid and changing. Following the implosion of the Soviet Union and demise of the "second world," the United States emerged as the only superpower and has been the center of hegemonic power in the post–Cold War world order for the last two decades. But American hegemony has faced a fateful limitation, for the world became an interdependent global village in which no one state is allowed to maintain hegemonic status. The world is an integral and complete system of mutual interdependence. This interdependence spans many sectors, including the global market system, communication and information technology and mechanisms, and the ecological and environmental system. Despite these areas of mutual interest and dependence, the world has seen increasingly volatile interactions characterized by ethno-national self-centeredness between diverse cultures and civilizations. Information technology advancements that penetrate all corners of the world give voice to the resentments and frustrations of people belonging to certain echelons of social and economic strata that have led to mass uprisings that toppled a string of governments in the Arab world (Tunisia, Egypt, Libya, possibly Syria). The Arab Spring was preceded by US and Western military intervention in Iraq and Afghanistan. The turmoil in the Arab world, especially in Iraq and Libya, led the North Koreans to strengthen their resolve to hang on to their nuclear capability, which Pyongyang believes has been the only deterrence against US-led military strikes in the last two decades. The mutually dependent world has helped China become a superpower that can undermine the supremacy of the United States. Yet because of mutual dependence, especially in the economic arena, China and the United States are not expected to come to a hostile confrontation. The rise of China has great implications for the DPRK.

KIM JONG UN'S PRIORITIES AND ANTICIPATED STRATEGIES

Historically, if the Kim Il Sung era is identified with *juche* and the Kim Jong Il era is seen in terms of the politics of *songun*, Kim Jong Un's era may be given its identity as a system for *kangsong daekuk* ("prosperity"). Now that the DPRK has achieved a solid basis of military capability, this doctrine of *kangsong daekuk* is to be realized in pursuing economic prosperity. The domestic context in which Kim Jong Un's leadership arrived is one of rather serious economic difficulties, especially food shortages. Yet contrary to fashionable speculation around the world, there is little room in the North for collective dissent from the grass roots, nor is there much likelihood of a power conflict within the leadership circles. Kim Jong Un is challenged with the unenviable task of achieving economic development without risking national security or regime stability. Will Kim Jong Un's North Korea be able to induce economic development while at the same time maintaining the military and security strategies that it has inherited from the previous two generations of leadership? What kind of economic development will this Kim pursue, and how will (or should) he pursue it?

One might say that as a very latecomer, North Korea has a long way to go to catch up with the Asian tigers, especially South Korea. I suppose that North Korea is not pursuing, nor should it pursue, the course of economic expansion that was employed by South Korea. Pyongyang has valued distributive justice by maintaining a socialist system, and it is expected not to deviate from it. In the last two decades or so, North Korea has placed an enormous emphasis on sustainable development, whereby it hopes to avoid the environmental pitfalls that the Asian tigers have created. By doing this, North Korea is trying to be different from, and not inferior to, the South in terms of economic achievement. To what extent will North Korea's development strategies be in the interest of sustainability? No one knows for sure, but I am certain that the country will continue to wage concerted efforts in this area.

The world is anxious to find clues that might indicate the direction and orientations of the Kim Jong Un leadership. Much of the answer to this question depends on how the neighboring governments and the international community treat the new leadership. A few scenarios may be crafted.

If the United States maintains the current policy in which Washington, demanding denuclearization and reforms toward more open and liberal policy measures as conditions of dialogue and negotiations, Kim Jong Un will have no choice but to stick to hard-line policies. If, however, Washington shows a willingness to include the issue of security threats to the DPRK in the dialogue agenda, the road to a peace treaty and diplomatic normalization might be a distinct possibility. With Obama's reelection, the chances for this development could be within sight. Washington's instinctive desire is to avoid yet another military tension when it is fighting two wars in the Middle East and is involved deeply in conflict situations around the world. As a young leader facing high expectations from the population and mounting suspicions from the external world, Kim Jong Un cannot afford to show any appearance of weakness, and this may force him to be more prone to risk taking. Thus, it is crucially important that Washington change its approach to Pyongyang from one of hostility and alienation to one of engagement and cooperation.

The Seoul government could also go either way. If it continues with president Lee Myung Bak's policy measures toward the North, the future of inter-Korea relations might become even darker than it is under the current Lee government. For instance, if the Lee administration demands an apology for the Cheonan boat incident and the Yeonpyeong incidents as a condition for any other topics of discussion, it will face nothing but deadlock. It is vital that South Korea's future leadership maintain a coherent and consistent policy toward the North, and that policy must be predicated on the premises of mutual development and noninterference in domestic affairs for both systems. It is clear that no political circles or individuals would opt for military confrontation as a method of reintegration; it must come through cooperation and collaboration grounded on mutual acceptance and respect. The two sides must first reaffirm the earlier agreements (6.15 and 10.4) made by their heads of the state and then move on to implementing them. The Kim Jong Un leadership should be amenable to this. It is already unfortunate that the Lee Myung Bak government decided not to allow even civilian individuals or groups, let alone government officials, to attend the funeral of Kim Jong Il.

Japan has a legitimate reason to be concerned about North Korea's nuclear capability. The very inception of the DPRK under the leadership of Kim Il Sung was based on widespread anti-Japanese sentiment. Japan has always been regarded by the North Koreans as the primary villain owing to its vicious colonial rule. To this date, North Korean public attitudes are pervasively negative toward Japan. That some old-guard military personnel kidnapped Japanese citizens in the 1970s was not entirely unrelated to collective Korean memory regarding Japan. Although those civilians apprehended by the North Korean soldiers were personally innocent, the reality is that the level of animosity in North Korea toward Japan is such that even kidnapping Japanese citizens may not cause an unbearable sense of guilt for some North Koreans. Japanese public sentiment today overwhelmingly rests and hinges on the abduction issue. Demands for a resolution to this matter as a precondition for any diplomatic improvement represent the single most crucial obstacle to rapprochement between the two countries. In fact, there is a huge discrepancy between the two governments regarding the number of abductees, and this issue must be dealt with through bilateral dialogues specifically on this issue, rather than as part of the six-party talks, which were exclusively designed to address the nuclear issue. It seems obvious that if Japan insists on addressing the abduction issue as a precondition for further bilateral dialogues, the prognosis is extremely bleak.

Then there is China. China's position bears huge implications for North Korea's new leadership. What does China want from North Korea? It wants a stable Kim Jong Un government, one capable of succeeding the legacies of the previous leaders. There are solid bases for compatibility between the two traditional allies. First of all, the DPRK has a communist system like that of China itself. The rest of the world is seemingly turning away from one-party systems, it is crucially important that China maintain a neighboring ideological ally.

Second, as dire as North Korea's economic situation may appear, China sees a great deal of economic benefit from cooperating with North Korea in the economic sector. For one thing, North Korea may have already decided to develop its economy through a strategy patterned after the Chinese model. For Pyongyang, it is comforting to know that "controlled" capitalism in the economic sector can accompany political communism with one party at the center. China has demonstrated that the odd marriage of economic capitalism and political communism can be sustained for a long period and in the process generate an extremely productive economy. Of course, specific conditions in the culture and the global economic system made China's rise possible. In this regard, North Korea seems to be endowed with the same cultural and exogenous economic system. In providing technical and economic assistance and through participating in selected facets of North Korea's development programs, China could benefit greatly. From the Kim Jong Un leadership's perspective, China does not pose any security or ideological threat.

Third, China's military or security interest in keeping the DPRK as an ally serves as a buffer against the United States and the West. This aspect is particularly important to China because North Korea is a formidable military power in the world. With these multifaceted interests in North Korea, China will continue to expand its economic and political presence in North Korea as the Kim Jong Un leadership commits to developing its economy. China will make attractive offers to explore economic opportunities in such areas as setting up special economic zones, developing infrastructure (including roads and airports), and developing human capital through exchange and training programs. There appear to be no major barriers to China's moving ahead with aggressive programs, and North Korea's level of dependence on China is likely to escalate in the months and years ahead.

As American superpower policies are weakened, European countries are likely to explore opportunities with North Korea with or without endorsement by Washington. One area in which a North Korea–Europe nexus is likely to expand is sustainable sources of energy. This is particularly the case with the Nordic countries of Denmark, Norway, Sweden, and Finland, as well as the Netherlands. The DPRK has shown a great interest and made tangible efforts in the last two decades in developing alternative and renewable energy sources by expanding interaction with selected European countries.

CONCLUSION

The Kim Jong Un era has dawned. There are abundant speculations regarding what will happen to the DPRK and how the rest of the world should respond. As an American scholar with a sustained interest in the country and who has worked to develop expertise with a scholarly conscience, I have witnessed the three generations of Kim leadership, the third one just dawning on the horizon. This chapter presents several thoughts on the nature and course of the Kim Jong Un leadership, and the discussion may be summarized as follows.

The leadership succession has been and will continue to be stable for convincing reasons. The policies pursued by the two preceding generations will continue to be pursued without interruption. *Juche* and *songun* will continue as the supreme principles of governance and policies. Pyongyang will conduct its foreign policy in such a way as to facilitate the continuation of the policy goals established by the first two generations, which include security, national identity and sovereignty, and economic and social prosperity—yet it will largely respond to other countries' actions toward itself.

Bibliography

Alford, C. Fred. *Think No Evil: Korean Values in the Age of Globalization.* Ithaca, NY: Cornell University Press, 1999.

Almond, Gabriel A., G. Bingham Powell, Kaare Strom, and Russell J. Dalton. *Comparative Politics Today: A World View.* Moscow: Aspect, 2002.

Auster, Bruce B., and Kevin Whitelaw. "Pentagon Plan 5030: A New Blueprint for Facing Down North Korea." *US News and World Report,* July 21, 2003, http://www.usnews.com/usnews/news/articles/030721/21korea.htm.

Becker, Jasper. *Rogue Regime: Kim Jong Il and the Looming Threat of North Korea.* New York: Oxford University Press, 2005.

Bell, Daniel A. *East Meets West: Human Rights and Democracy in East Asia.* Princeton, NJ: Princeton University Press, 2000.

Bleiker, R., and Emma Hutchison. "Fear No More: Emotions and World Politics." *Review of International Studies* 34 (2008): 115–135.

Central Bureau of Statistics (DPRK). *2004 Nutrition Assessment: Report of Survey Results.* Mimeograph. Pyongyang: Institute of Child Nutrition, 2005.

Chinoy, Mike. *Meltdown: The Inside Story of the North Korean Nuclear Crisis.* New York: St. Martin's, 2008.

Cho Myung-chul. *Kyŏngjegwalli kaesŏn choch'i hyŏnhwang p'yŏnggawa kwaje: Pukhan kyŏngje kaehyŏgŭi chŏnmang* [Prospects for North Korea's economic reform. A study on the economic administration adjustment and its performance]. Seoul: Korea Institute for International Economic Policy, 2003.

Chong Bong-uk, ed. *North Korea: Uneasy, Shaky Kim Jong-il Regime.* Seoul: Naewoe Press, 1997.

Clemons, Steven. "Why Bush Won't Attack Iran." *Salon.com*, September 19, 2007. www.salon.com/opinion/feature.

Crawford, Neta C. "The Passion of World Politics: Propositions on Emotion and Emotional Relationships." *International Security* 24, no. 4 (2000): 116–156.

Cumings, Bruce. *North Korea: Another Country*. New York: Free Press, 2004.

Dobriansky, Paula. "Principles of Good Governance." *Economic Perspectives* 8, no. 2 (March 2003), http://www.4uth.gov.ua/usa/english/trade/ijee0303/dobrians.htm.

Eberstadt, Nicholas. *The North Korean Economy: Between Crisis and Catastrophe*. New Brunswick: Transaction, 2007.

———. "Tear Down This Tyranny." *Weekly Standard* 10, no. 11 (November 29, 2004), http://weeklystandard.com/Content/Public/Articles/000/000/004/951szxxd.asp.

Fahy, Sandra. "Turning Points in the Experience of Famine: Survivor Testimony from the Democratic People's Republic of Korea." Unpublished manuscript, School of Oriental and African Studies, London, 2008.

Food and Agriculture Organization of the United Nations (FAO). *FAO/WFP Crop and Food Supply Assessment Mission to the Democratic People's Republic of Korea*. Rome: FAO, 2001.

———. *FAO/WFP Crop and Food Supply Assessment Mission to the Democratic People's Republic of Korea*. Rome: FAO, 2004.

Frank, Rudiger. "Can Economic Theory Demystify North Korea?" *Korea Review of International Studies* 9, no. 1 (2006): 3–26.

———. "Classical Socialism in North Korea and its Transformation: The Role and the Future of Agriculture." *Harvard Asia Quarterly* 10/2 (2006): 15–33.

———. "Economic Reforms in North Korea (1998–2004): Systemic Restrictions, Quantitative Analysis, Ideological Background." *Journal of the Asia Pacific Economy* 10, no. 3 (2005): 278–311.

———. *The GDR and North Korea: The Reconstruction of Hamhŭng, 1954–1962.* Aachen: Shaker, 1996.

———. "Money in Socialist Economies: The Case of North Korea." *Asia-Pacific Journal* (February 2010). http://japanfocus.org/-Ruediger-Frank/3307.

———. "The Political Economy of Sanctions against North Korea." *Asian Perspective* 30/3 (2006): 5–36. http://www.asianperspective.org/articles/v30n3-b.pdf.

———. "Socialist Neo-Conservatism in North Korea? A Return to Old Principles in the 2008 New Year Joint Editorial." *Napsnet Policy Forum Online* 08-032 (2008). http://www.nautilus.org.

Frank, Rudiger, and Sabine Burghart. *Driving Forces of Socialist Transformation: North Korea and the Experience of Europe and East Asia.* Vienna: Praesens, 2009.

General Accounting Office (GAO). *Foreign Assistance: North Korea Restricts Food Aid Monitoring.* Washington, DC: GAO, 1999. www.gao.gov.

Gordon, Joy. "Economic Sanctions, Just War Doctrine, and the 'Fearful Spectacle of the Civilian Dead.'" *Cross Currents* 49, no. 3 (Fall 1999). www.crosscurrents.org/gordon.htm.

Grindle, Merilee S. "Good Enough Governance: Poverty Reduction and Reform in Developing Countries." *Governance: An International Journal of Policy, Administration, and Institutions* 17, no. 4 (2004): 525–548.

———. "Good Enough Governance Revisited." *Development Policy Review* 25, no. 5 (2007): 199–221.

Haggard, Stephan, and Marcus Noland. *Famine in North Korea: Markets, Aid, and Reform.* New York: Columbia University Press, 2007.

———. "Famine in North Korea Redux?" East-West Center Working Papers, Economic Series No. 97, Honolulu, Hawaii, October 2008.

Harrison Lawrence E., and Samuel P. Huntington, eds. *Culture Matters: How Values Shape Human Progress.* New York: Basic Books, 2000.

Harrison, Selig. "Did North Korea Cheat?" *Foreign Affairs* 84, no. 1 (February 2005): 99–110.

Hecker, S. "A Return Trip to North Korea's Yongbyon Nuclear Complex." Center for International Security and Cooperation, Stanford University, November 20, 2010. http://iis-db.stanford.edu/pubs/23035/HeckerYongbyon.pdf.

———. "Can the North Korean Nuclear Crisis Be Resolved?" Paper presented at the conference Rethinking Nuclear Issues in Northeast Asia, organized by the Institute for Far Eastern Studies at Kyungnam University (IFES) and the Friedrich Naumann Foundation for Freedom (FNF), Seoul, Republic of Korea, March 21, 2012.

Helgesen, Geir. *Democracy and Authority in Korea: The Cultural Dimension in Korean Politics.* New York: St. Martin's, 1998.

Helgesen, Geir, and S. R. Thomsen, eds. *Politics, Culture, and Self: East Asian and North European Attitudes.* Copenhagen: NIAS Press, 2006.

Huntington, Samuel P. *The Clash of Civilizations and the Remaking of World Order.* New York: Simon & Schuster, 1996.

Inglehart, Ronald. *Modernization and Postmodernization: Cultural, Economic, and Political Change in Forty-three Societies.* Princeton, NJ: Princeton University Press, 1997.

Inglehart Ronald, and Wayne E. Baker. "Modernization, Cultural Change, and the Persistence of Traditional Values." *American Sociological Review* 65 (2000): 19–51.

Institute of Far Eastern Studies (IFES). *Transfer of Management Rights to Chinese Investment Companies within North Korea.* Seoul: Institute for Far Eastern Studies, 2011.

Ireson, Randall: *Food Security in North Korea: Designing Realistic Possibilities.* Stanford, CA: Shorenstein APARC, 2006. http://iis-db.stanford.edu/pubs/21046/Ireson_FoodSecurity_2006.pdf.

Jervis, Robert. *Perception and Misperception in International Politics* (Princeton, NJ: Princeton University Press, 1976).

Jorganson, John. "Tan'gun and the Legitimization of a Threatened Dynasty: North Korea's Rediscovery of Tan'gun." *Korea Observer* 27 (1996): 273–306.

Kang Chol-hwan and Pierre Rigoulet. *The Aquariums of Pyongyang: Ten Years in a North Korean Gulag*. Translated by Yair Reiner. Boulder, CO: Perseus, 2001.

Kim Jong Il. *The Guiding Principles of the Juche Idea*. 1982. http://www3.cnet-ta.ne.jp/j/juche/pdf/e-works4.pdf, 19–51.

———. *Inminkundaeui kanhwahamy kunsaryl chunsihanun sahwejok kiphunyl seuldae tahayo* [On strengthening the People's Army and creating the *songun* atmosphere in society]. Talk with responsible officials of the WPK Central Committee, February 4, 1992. Pyongyang: WPK Publishing House, 1999.

———. "Konhvagukyn pulphy vireky chinin juche y sahvechuy kukaida" [The republic: A socialist state of *juche* possessing invincible force]. KCNA, October 10, 2008.

———. *On Preserving the Juche Character and National Character of the Revolution and Construction*. 1997. http://www.korea-dpr.com/library/111.pdf, 41–75.

———. *On the History of Juche: Treatise Sent to the National Seminar on the Juche Idea Held to Mark the 70th Birthday of the Great Leader Comrade Kim Il Sung, March 31, 1982*. http://www3.cnet-ta.ne.jp/j/juche/pdf/e-works1.pdf, 19–51.

———. *Socialism of Our Style Serving the Interests of Working Masses Will Be Victorious*. Pyongyang: Foreign Languages Publishing House, 1991.

———. "*Songun* Revolution Line Is Our Epoch's Great Revolutionary Line, Our Revolution's All-Winning Banner." Talk with responsible officials of the WPK Central Committee, January 29, 2003. Pyongyang: Foreign Languages Publishing House, 2011.

———. "21seginŭn kŏch'anghan chŏnbyŏnŭi segi, ch'angjoŭi segiida" [The twenty-first century is a century of great change and creation]. *Rodong Sinmun*, January 4, 2001, 2.

Korea Economic Institute. *North Korea's Economy*. Washington, DC: Korea Economic Institute, 2008.

Korea Trade and Investment Promotion Agency (KOTRA). *2009 Pukhanŭi taewoemuyŏk tonghyang* [Trends in North Korean trade, 2009]. KOTRA Paper 10-038. Seoul: KOTRA, 2010.

———. *2011 Pukhanŭi taewoemuyŏk tonghyang* [Trends in North Korean trade, 2011]. KOTRA Paper 12-018. Seoul: KOTRA, 2012.

Kornai, Janos. *The Socialist System: The Political Economy of Communism*. Princeton, NJ: Princeton University Press, 1992.

Larmour, P. "State, Society, and Governance in Melanesia: Making Sense of Good Governance." Discussion paper, Research School of Pacific and Asian Studies, the Australian National University, Canberra, Australia, 1998.

Lautensach, Hermann. *Korea: A Geography Based on the Author's Travel and Literature*. Berlin: Springer Verlag, 1945/1988.

Lautze, Sue. *The Famine in North Korea: Humanitarian Responses in Communist Nations*. Somerville, MA: Feinstein International Famine Center, Tufts University, 1997. http://repository.forcedmigration.org/show_metadata.jsp?pid = fmo:1744.

Lee, Karin, and Julia Choi. *North Korea: Unilateral and Multilateral Economic Sanctions and U.S. Department of Treasury Actions, 1955–April 2009*. Washington, DC: National Committee on North Korea, 2009.

Manyin, Mark, and Mary Beth Nikitin. *Foreign Assistance to North Korea*. Washington, DC: Congressional Research Service, 2011.

McDermott, R. "The Feeling of Rationality: The Meaning of Neuroscientific Advances for Political Science." *Perspectives on Politics* 2, no. 4 (2004): 691–706.

Mercer, J. "Rationality and Psychology in International Politics." *International Organization* 59 (Winter 2005): 77–106.

Michell, Anthony. "The Current North Korean Economy." In *Economic Integration of the Korean Peninsula*, edited by Marcus Noland, 137–163. Washington, DC: Institute for International Economics, 1998.

Moïsi, D. "The Clash of Emotions." *Foreign Affairs* 86, no. 1 (2007): 8–12.

Myers, Brian R. "The Watershed that Wasn't: Re-Evaluating Kim Il Sung's 'Juche Speech' of 1955." *Acta Koreana* 9/1 (January 2006): 89–115.

Nikitin, Mary Beth, Emma Chanlett-Avery, Mark Manyin, Dick K. Nanto, Dianne Rennack, and MiAe Taylor. *Implementation of UN Security Council Resolution 1874.* Special report, November 11, 2010. Washington, DC: Congressional Research Service, 2010.

Nisbett, Richard E. *The Geography of Thought: How Asians and Westerners Think Differently... and Why.* New York: Free Press, 2003.

Noland, Marcus. *Avoiding the Apocalypse: The Future of the Two Koreas.* Washington, DC: Institute for International Economics, 2000.

Norenzayan, A., I. Choi, and Richard E. Nisbett. "Cultural Similarities and Differences in Social Inference: Evidence From Behavioral Predictions and Lay Theories of Behavior." *Personality and Social Psychology Bulletin* 28, no. 1 (2002): 109–120.

Paik, Haksoon. "North Korea Today: Politics Overloaded and Secularized." In *North Korea: 2005 and Beyond,* edited by Philip W. Yun and Gi-Wook Shin, 37–54. Stanford, CA: Walter H. Shorenstein Asia-Pacific Research Center, 2006.

———. *Pukhan kwŏllyŏgŭi yŏksa: Sasang, chŏngch'esŏng, kujo* [The history of power in North Korea: Ideas, identities, and structures]. Seoul: Hanul Academy, 2010.

Panin, A., and W. Altov. *Severnaya Koreya: Epocha Kim chen ira na zakate* [North Korea: The Kim Jong Il epoch heading south]. Moscow: Olma Press, 2004.

Paqué, Karl-Heinz. *Die Bilanz: Eine wirtschaftliche Analyse der Deutschen Einheit* [German unification: An economic analysis]. München: Hanser Verlag, 2009.

Park, Han S. "Human Needs, Human Rights, and Regime Legitimacy: The North Korean Anomaly." In *Understanding Regime Dynamics in North Korea,* edited by Chung-in Moon, 221–235. Seoul: Yonsei University Press, 1998.

———. *North Korea: Ideology, Politics, Economy.* Englewood Cliffs, NJ: Prentice-Hall, 1996.

———. *North Korea: The Politics of Unconventional Wisdom.* Boulder, CO: Lynne Rienner, 2002.

———. "Succession in North Korea." *Global Asia* 4, no. 2 (Summer 2009).

Park, Kyung-Ae, ed. *New Challenges of North Korean Foreign Policy.* New York: Palgrave Macmillan, 2010.

Pinkston, Daniel A., and Philip C. Saunders. "Seeing North Korea Clearly." *Survival* 45, no. 3 (2003): 79–102.

Pye, Lucian W. *Asian Power and Politics: The Cultural Dimensions of Authority.* Cambridge, MA: Belknap Press of Harvard University Press, 1985.

Pyongyang Chamber of Commerce. *Country Report.* Mimeograph. Pyongyang: Chamber of Commerce, 2001.

Ritter, Gerhard A. *Der Preis der Deutschen Einheit: Die Wiedervereinigung und die Krise des Sozialstaates* [The price of unity: Unification and the crisis of the welfare state]. München: C. H. Beck, 2007.

Rosati, Jerel A. "A Cognitive Approach to the Study of Foreign Policy." In *Foreign Policy Analysis: Continuity and Change in Its Second Generation,* edited by Laura Neack, Jeanne A. K. Hey, and Patrick Jude Haney, 49–70. Englewood Cliffs, NJ: Prentice Hall Humanities/Social Science, 1995.

Rosati, Jerel A. *The Power of Human Cognition in the Study of World Politics.* Malden, MA: Blackwell, 2001.

Rosegrant, Susan. "Carrots, Sticks, and Question Marks: Negotiating the North Korean Nuclear Crisis." With Michael D. Watkins. Unpublished paper, John F. Kennedy School of Government, Harvard University, 1995.

Savada, Andrea Matles, ed. *North Korea: A Country Study.* Washington, DC: GPO for the Library of Congress, 1993. http://countrystudies.us/north-korea.

Servan-Schreiber, David. *Behandling af Stress, Angst og Depression uden medicin eller terapi* [Treating stress, anxiety, and depressions without medicine or therapy]. Copenhagen: Gyldendal, 2004.

Sing, K. *Aid and Good Governance: A Discussion Paper for the Reality of Aid*. Delhi, India: Public Interest Research Group, 2003.

Smith, Hazel. "Crime and Economic Instability: The Real Security Threat from North Korea and What to Do about It." *International Relations of the Asia Pacific* 5, no. 2 (2005): 235–249.

———. "Food Security: The Case for Multisectoral and Multilateral Cooperation." In *Reconstituting Korean Security*, edited by Hazel Smith, 82–102. Tokyo: United Nations Press, 2007.

———. *Hungry for Peace: International Security, Humanitarian Assistance, and Social Change in North Korea*. Washington, DC: United States Institute of Peace Press, 2005.

———. "La corée du nord vers l'économie de marché: Faux et vrais dilemmas." *Critique Internationale* (April 2002): 6–14.

———. "North Korea: Market Opportunity, Poverty, and the Provinces." *New Political Economy* 14, no. 3 (June 2009): 231–256.

Socialist Constitution of the Democratic People's Republic of Korea. Pyongyang: Foreign Languages Publishing House, 1998.

Statistics Korea. *Pukhanŭi chuyo t'onggye chip'yo* [Main statistical indicators of North Korea]. Taejŏn: Korea National Statistics Office, 2011.

Suh Jae Jean. *The Lee Myung-bak Government's North Korea Policy: A Study on its Historical and Theoretical Foundation*. Seoul: Korea Institute of National Unification, 2009.

Sung Chull Kim. *North Korea Under Kim Jong Il: From Consolidation to Systemic Dissonance*. Albany: State University of New York Press, 2006.

Thieme, H. Jörg. "Wirtschaftssysteme." In *Vahlens Kompendium der Wirtschaftstheorie und Wirtschaftspolitik*, Band 1, edited by D. Bender, 1–17. München: Franz Vahlen, 1992.

Thiessen, Friedrich, ed. *Die Wessis: Westdeutsche Führungskräfte beim Aufbau Ost* [The westerners: West German executives in the reconstruction of the east]. Cologne: Boehlau, 2009.

Thompson, Drew. *Silent Partners: Chinese Joint Ventures in North Korea.* Washington, DC: US–Korea Institute, 2011.

Titarenko, M. L. *Russia and East Asia: Problems of International and Inter-Civilizational Relations.* Moscow: Kuchkovo Pole, 1994.

Toloraya, Georgy. *The Economic Future of North Korea: Will the Market Rule?* Academic Paper Series on North Korea, vol. 1. Washington, DC: Korea Economic Institute, 2008. http://www.keia.org/Publications/OnKorea/2008/08Toloraya.pdf.

Totten, George, and Zhou Shulian, eds. *China's Economic Reform: Administering the Introduction of the Market Mechanism.* Boulder, CO: Westview Press, 1992.

"2002 Nyŏn kukka yesan chiphaengŭi kyŏlsan'gwa 2003 nyŏn kukga yesane taehan pogo" [Report summing up the execution of the 2002 state budget and on the 2003 state budget]. *Rodong Sinmun*, March 26, 2003. http://www.kcna.co.jp/calendar/2003/03/03-27/2003-03-27-002.html.

United Nations Children's Fund (UNICEF). *An analysis of the Situation of Children and Women in the Democratic People's Republic of Korea 2000.* Pyongyang: UNICEF, 1999.

United Nations Development Programme (UNDP). *Second Country Cooperation Framework for the DPRK, 2001–2003.* New York: UNDP, 2001.

United Nations Office of the Coordination of Humanitarian Assistance (UNOCHA). *Consolidated Inter-Agency Appeal for the DPRK, 2001.* Geneva: UNOCHA, 2000.

United States Geological Survey (USGS). *2007 Minerals Yearbook: North Korea.* Advance release. Washington, DC: US Department of the Interior, USGS, 2008. http://www.nkeconwatch.com/nk-uploads/usgs-dprk.pdf.

Weiss, T. G. "Governance, Good Governance, and Global Governance: Conceptual and Actual Challenges." *Third World Quarterly* 21, no. 5 (2000): 795–814.

Williamson, Oliver E. "The New Institutional Economics: Taking Stock, Looking Ahead." *Journal of Economic Literature* 38, no. 3 (2000): 595–613.

Woo, Jung-en. *Race to the Swift: State and Finance in Korean Industrialization.* New York: Columbia University Press, 1991.

Yoon, Edward. *Status and Future of the North Korean Minerals Sector.* San Francisco: Nautilus Institute, 2011.

Zhebin, Alexander. *The DPRK Political System's Evolution under Conditions of Global Changes.* Moscow: Russian Panorama, 2006.

Index

About the Contributors

Bruce Cumings is the Gustavus F. and Ann M. Swift Distinguished Service Professor and Chair of the Department of History at the University of Chicago. His research and teaching focus is on modern Korean history, 20th-century international history, U.S.–East Asian relations, East Asian political economy, and American foreign relations. He is the editor of the modern volume of *The Cambridge History of Korea* (forthcoming) and is a frequent contributor to *The London Review of Books*, *The Nation*, *Current History*, the *Bulletin of the Atomic Scientists*, and *Le Monde Diplomatique*. A member of the American Academy of Arts and Sciences, Cumings was also the principal historical consultant for the Thames Television/PBS six-hour documentary, *Korea: The Unknown War*. In 2007, he won the Kim Dae Jung Prize for Scholarly Contributions to Democracy, Human Rights and Peace. He has just completed *Dominion From Sea to Sea: Pacific Ascendancy and American Power* and is currently working on a synoptic single-volume study of the origins of the Korean War, as well as a book on the Northeast Asian political economy.

Regan Damron is a consultant in the Washington, DC, area providing methodology development and analytical support to U.S. government clients. Prior to this position, he worked for the U.S. Department of Defense on national security matters. He holds a PhD in political science from the University of Georgia.

Rüdiger Frank is Professor of East Asian Economy and Society at the University of Vienna and the Acting Director of the Vienna School of Governance. He is also an adjunct professor at Korea University and at the University of North Korean Studies in Seoul, as well as a research affiliate of the Modern East Asia Research Centre in Leiden, Netherlands. He holds an MA in Korean studies, economics, and international relations as well as a PhD in economics. He spent one semester as a language student at Kim Il-sung University in Pyongyang (1991–1992) and has been following North Korea ever since. His research focuses on the transformation of state socialist systems in East Asia, governance in East Asia, and regionalism in East Asia, with a strong emphasis on the Korean peninsula. He also held positions at Humboldt–University Berlin, Columbia University and Korea University. He is a coeditor of the yearly volume Korea: Politics, Economy and Society and of the book series Brill's Korean Studies Library. He has authored or coauthored seven books and over 80 articles on Korea and East Asia and was a consultant to European and Asian governments on Korean affairs, including a testimony before the European Parliament in Brussels and a report on North Korea for the French government. At the University of Vienna, he is responsible for coordinating social sciencebased research on contemporary East Asia. In June 2011, Professor Frank was invited to join the World Economic Forum, Global Agenda Council on Korea.

Geir Helgesen is Director of the Nordic Institute of Asian Studies in Copenhagen, Denmark and leading coordinator of the Eurasia Political Culture Research Network (EPCReN). He is also a senior advisor to the Danish Ministry of Foreign Affairs on Korean matters, as well as a frequent guest lecturer and a widelyused commentator in public media on Korean issues. Dr. Helgesen holds both MA and PhD degrees in Cultural Sociology from Copenhagen University in Denmark. His previous academic appointments include Senior Research Fellow at the Center for Pacific Asia Studies (CPAS) at Stockholm University and a Guest Researcher at the Institute of Comparative Politics, of Bergen University in Norway. In addition, Dr. Helgesen is a consultant to Nordic companies with activities in Korea, as well as a course instructor for the Federation of Danish Industries (DI) concerning Korea and cross-cultural business matters. He is the author of several journal articles and four books, including *Good Government: Nordic and East Asian Perspectives*, which is coauthored with Uichol Kim; and the forthcoming *Poli-*

tics, Culture and Self: East Asian and North European Attitudes, with S.R. Thomsen.

Han S. Park is University Professor of Public and International Affairs and the founding Director (in 1995) of the Center for the Study of Global Issues (Globis) at the University of Georgia. Dr. Park's areas of specialty include political development, globalization, and comparative politics, with an emphasis on East Asian studies. Among his numerous publications are *North Korea: The Politics of Unconventional Wisdom* and *Human Needs and Political Development*. He has been deeply involved in a number of peacemaking initiatives with North Korea. Under his leadership, Globis has hosted several Track II seminars with participants from North Korea, South Korea, and the United States, most recently in October 2011. Dr. Park was also instrumental in realizing former president Jimmy Carter's trips to Pyongyang in 1994 and 2010, which may well have averted a possible military confrontation between the United States and the DPRK. He has been relentless in his efforts to alleviate the nuclear tension on the Korean peninsula, making more than 50 trips to North Korea since 1990. His work has been widely praised, and in 2010 Dr. Park received the Gandhi, King, Ikeda Community Builders Award in recognition of his "extraordinary global leadership through nonviolence and reconciliation." Past recipients of this award have included former South African President Nelson Mandela, Archbishop Desmond Tutu, and former Israeli Prime Minister Yitzak Rabin.

Jonathan Polk is a PhD candidate in the Department of International Affairs at the University of Georgia, and a research associate at the Center for the Study of Global Issues. He holds an MA from the University of Georgia, and a BA from St. John's College. He has published in several journals such as *Comparative Political Studies* and *European Union Politics*.

Hazel Smith is Professor of Resilience and Security and Director of the Resilience Centre at Cranfield University in the United Kingdom. Her most recent monograph is *Hungry for Peace: International Security,*

Humanitarian Assistance and Social Change in North Korea. She recently directed three research projects that have each resulted in edited publications (2007). These are *Humanitarian Diplomacy: Practitioners and Their Craft*, edited with Larry Minear of Tufts University; *Diasporas in Conflict: PeaceMakers or PeaceWreckers?*, edited with Paul Stares of the Council on Foreign Relations, New York; and *Reconstituting Korean Security: A Policy Primer*. Dr. Smith has undertaken extensive field work in the DPRK, Nepal, China, and Nicaragua--carrying out scholarly research and working for various intergovernmental and nongovernmental organizations. She commentates for the international media on the DPRK, East Asian security, the United Nations, and humanitarian assistance. She is regularly interviewed on AsiaPacific security, North Korea, and international affairs by the BBC and global media outlets, including CNN, Voice of America, and Radio Free Asia, and she was recently a panelist for Forum at PressTV, hosted by Andrew Gilligan.

Alexander Zhebin is Director of the Center for Korean Studies (CKS) of the Institute of Far Eastern Studies (IFES) of the Russian Academy of Sciences in Moscow. He worked for 17 years as a journalist at the TASS News Agency. He served as TASS correspondent in Pyongyang, then TASS Bureau Chief in Pyongyang until 1990. He joined the IFES in 1992. In 1998 he served as First Secretary and Counselor of the Embassy of the Russian Federation in the DPRK till 2001. He is author of *Pyongyang, Seoul, then Moscow* (1991, in Korean) and *Luster and Misery of the Kim's Empire* (1992, in Japanese). Dr. Zhebin has also authored numerous articles on political developments in the DPRK, Russia–North Korea relations, and security of the Korean peninsula.